Milwaukee
City by the Waters

Contents

Introduction 7
Bob Uecker captures the essence of Milwaukee as he reflects on the qualities that make his city great.

Photo-Essay 22
Milwaukee's finest photographers contribute their most captivating images to create an enduring portrait of the city.

Profiles in Excellence 274
Profiles of the organizations that have made this book possible weave an informal history of the local business community.

Photographers 444

Index of Profiles 446

City by the Waters

◆ © STEVE BAKER / HIGHLIGHT PHOTOGRAPHY

By Bob Uecker

I can't begin to say how fortunate I am. My baseball career has certainly been a dream for me. I have had the privilege not only of playing professionally, but also of broadcasting this great game. I'm sure it would please anyone to say that.

But I feel fortunate because I was able to play and to broadcast for my hometown—Milwaukee. That's more than anyone could ask.

To be born and raised in Milwaukee, to play baseball and to broadcast games here . . . what a thrill! At the same time, it was embarrassing to play in front of friends and family. It felt strange playing in a ballpark where I once sat and watched my childhood heroes, many of them Hall of Famers.

I lived at 47th and Galena, across from the old Milwaukee Zoo. It was literally five minutes from County Stadium. I used to be at the ballpark all the time. We would wait until the fifth or sixth inning, back then, so we wouldn't have to pay to get into the game.

I never, ever thought of leaving here. I had opportunities to leave and work in other cities, but I never entertained that thought seriously. This is home. It's as good as any in the country.

Sure, this isn't Chicago. It's not New York. It's not Los Angeles. But Milwaukee is a great place to raise a family. It has an excellent school system. This city has much to offer.

For instance: I travel a lot. Yet, everywhere I go, people talk about the great restaurants in Milwaukee. I have my favorites, but I'll be honest, there are so many other wonderful spots in the city that people often can't believe how good the food is across town. I truly believe visitors to Milwaukee will be satisfied more often than not with our selection of restaurants. ▶

© TROY FREUND

Milwaukee means "gathering place by the water," and it truly is. I love to fish. I love the water. And, in Lake Michigan, we have one of the greatest resources. It's one of the most beautiful lakes in the country. I don't know what I'd do without the lake because I spend so much time out there fishing. As a recreational venue, Lake Michigan is one of the best.

Milwaukee is one of the leading ports in the country, linked to the Great Lakes chain, the St. Lawrence Seaway, and beyond. The port is magnificent. It's a means of transportation that has thrived, and it has helped maintain Milwaukee as a world leader for exporting and importing everything from grain to heavy machinery. With 33 shipping lines entering the port, approximately 2.5 million tons are moved every year. Cement, coal, plywood, motor vehicles, steel, salt, twine, limestone, and petroleum are among the inbound commodities. Heavy machinery, leather, lumber, and iron are outbound.

In addition, with Lake Michigan as a gateway to the city, huge tourist boats include Milwaukee as a port of call. That tells you something about this city and what cruise people think about it. ▶

▶ © DICK BLAU

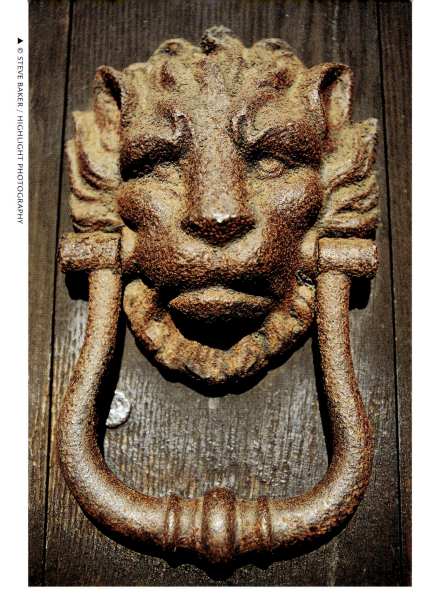

What attracts visitors to the city are the beautiful, 19th-century cream brick buildings in the downtown area. A number of the buildings were designed by world-famous architects, including Frank Lloyd Wright, whose last completed work is the Greek Orthodox Church of the Annunciation. The Milwaukee Art Museum, housed in the Milwaukee County War Memorial Center, was designed by Eero Saarinen. An area on the city's east side, the Historic Third Ward, is on the National Register of Historic Places.

Milwaukee brims with activities, too. Not just a slogan, the City of Festivals aptly describes the place. Beginning with the Lakefront Festival of Arts in June, practically every weekend in the summer will find the city's rich and diverse cultural heritage being celebrated. Milwaukee is a melting pot of ethnic flavors and traditions, and its cultures are distinguished in its festivals—the Italian, the Polish, the German, the Irish, the Mexican, the African-American—all of which are alluring annual attractions. People come from all over to participate in these special festivals. There's no place like it, anywhere.

The granddaddy of all these wonderful galas is Milwaukee's Summerfest, which is world renowned. Other cities have tried to duplicate it, but they pale in comparison. Summerfest has been one of the largest summer festivals in the United States for more than 30 years. For two fun-filled weeks, top performers—the biggest music acts and the biggest names in show business, whether comedy or dance—make Milwaukee the mecca of entertainment.

City by the Waters

The Wisconsin State Fair is held right here, too. For 10 days in August, folks from around Wisconsin and northern Illinois converge on Milwaukee for what is recognized as one of the nicest fairs in the country.

Where else but here has the Great Circus Parade made its home? It has become so well received that the event is televised nationwide. The parade winds through the city's downtown streets with its historic wagons—it truly is a sight to see. Hundreds of thousands of visitors come to town for these summer activities, making Milwaukee a fun place to be.

As a kid growing up, there was never a shortage of facilities for recreation. With more than 140 parks in the Milwaukee area, families can enjoy picnicking during the summer; and ice skating and sledding during the winter. The county parks' special attractions include the picturesque, 90-mile Oak Leaf Trail; the colorful Wehr Nature Center; and the Boerner Botanical Gardens.

One of my favorite area attractions is the Mitchell Park Horticultural Conservatory. With its three domes—tropical and arid, as well as the Floral Show Dome that has thematic displays—the conservatory features exquisite sights year-round.

Considered one of the largest animal collections in the country, the Milwaukee County Zoo is made up of a system of moats that allows visitors to view approximately 3,000 animals—predator and prey alike, in close proximity—in environments that resemble their native habitats. ▶

© MARY JO WALICKI / MILWAUKEE JOURNAL

In the winter, the Pettit National Ice Center takes center stage with Olympic-caliber athletes training and competing in Milwaukee. Several of the world's greatest skaters have called Milwaukee home: Olympians Eric Heiden, Dan Jansen, and Bonnie Blair trained at the Pettit Center when it was still an outdoor skating facility at the fairgrounds. Their success and reputation paved the way for the beautiful new facility.

If you are a sports fan, no city the size of Milwaukee can boast having as full a complement of professional sports. I have broadcast Major League Baseball games for the Milwaukee Brewers for the past 30 years and have thoroughly enjoyed myself. Aside from the Brewers, County Stadium had been home to the Milwaukee Braves, whom I've had the privilege to play for during my career. Hall of Famers Henry Aaron and Robin Yount have given baseball fans plenty to cheer about over the years. The National Football League Green Bay Packers also played at County Stadium for more than 40 years with the likes of Bart Starr, Willie Davis, and Paul Hourning, all coached by the legendary Vince Lombardi. Contemporaries like Reggie White and Brett Favre have kept up the rich Packer tradition. Today, the team plays in memorable Lambeau Field in Green Bay, a scenic, two-hour drive north of the city. The National Basketball Association Milwaukee Bucks, who've delighted fans with Hall of Famers Kareem Abdul-Jabbar and Oscar Robertson, have a modern facility in the Bradley Center, found right in the heart of the downtown district.

Three other professional teams play in the Bradley Center—the Milwaukee Admirals of the International Hockey League, the Milwaukee Wave of the National Professional Soccer League, and the Milwaukee Mustangs of the Arena Football League.

Auto racing fills the Milwaukee Mile grandstands to the rafters when NASCAR and Indy cars come to town each summer. Another annual event is the Greater Milwaukee Open, which features all the top professional golfers. ▶

I don't think many people are aware of how rich the cultural life of Milwaukee is. The plays, operas, musicals, and ballets at the Marcus Center of the Performing Arts, Florentine Opera, Milwaukee Repertory Theater, and Milwaukee Ballet Company are excellent. Other venues are the Riverside, Pabst, and Landmark theaters, all of which are historical treasures. The talent and professionalism of the Milwaukee Symphony Orchestra (MSO) are as good as any in large metropolitan markets; recently, the MSO became the first major U.S. orchestra to be invited to perform in Cuba in 37 years.

Higher education is well respected in Milwaukee. I've had the opportunity to broadcast both basketball and football for the University of Wisconsin-Milwaukee (UWM). Its campus is as large as any urban university in the country, with more than 20,000 students in attendance, thanks largely to the reputation of its schools of nursing and architecture.

Perhaps better recognized is Marquette University, with its law school and dentistry program. Located in the downtown area of Milwaukee, Marquette has had a tremendous sports tradition, particularly in basketball. Founded in 1881 and achieving university status in 1907, it features a 15th-century, stone chapel that was brought to the United States in 1927 from France and dedicated to St. Joan of Arc.

Among the other dozen or so colleges and universities of note in the area are the nationally recognized Milwaukee School of Engineering, Wisconsin Conservatory of Music, and Milwaukee Area Technical College.

City by the Waters

© JONATHAN POSTAL / TOWERY PUBLISHING, INC.

Milwaukee is a very blue-collar city. I watched my father and relatives work in the community. The city's leading industry is the manufacture of machinery. It is one of the largest consumers of steel in the United States. Nicknamed "the machine shop of America," the city produces equipment for generating, transmitting, and distributing electric power. Other heavy manufacturers are industrial cranes, monorails and controls, mining machinery, hoists, speed chargers, drives, and gears. Milwaukee also excels in the manufacture of computers, aircraft components, medical instruments, water desalination systems, electrical circuit boards, and industrial robots.

Today, one of the leading industries in the city—recognized worldwide—will soon celebrate its centennial. All you have to say is Harley-Davidson and people from around the world know immediately what you're talking about. Well, the Harley's made right here, and every five years, thousands of HOG lovers converge on Milwaukee to show their support and love for the motorcycle that's become something of an institution. ▶

© SCOTT BOEHM

Another major player in this city's great success is Miller Brewing Company. What Miller has done for Milwaukee and other communities is second to none. Miller is proud to be part of Milwaukee's landscape. It has civic responsibilities. It contributes to many organizations and is an active partner in the city's civic life. Miller makes money here. It employs people here. It makes its product here. Because of this, Miller gives back to the community in many ways—some very public (by helping finance the Milwaukee Brewers' new ballpark, Miller Park, for instance) and many more not so public. It's a wonderful organization that really cares about Milwaukee.

There are many other organizations like Miller—too many to mention—that are helping Milwaukee move quickly into the 21st century with a gusto that's the envy of cities around the world. New hotels, modern living facilities, and, of course, the Midwest Express Center have all given Milwaukee a lift. The Midwest Express Center is a beautiful facility showcasing Milwaukee's commitment to growth. And the additions to the Milwaukee Art Museum and the Milwaukee County War Memorial Center, along with the renovations to the lakefront, all point to the future.

Milwaukee is right up there with other major cities in the United States. The city recognizes its potential and resources. It has a big-city mentality with a small-town heart. The people make Milwaukee genuine. Frankly, it's a great place on a great lake. I feel fortunate indeed to call it my home.

P ICTURE THIS: LOCATED ON the shores of Lake Michigan, the Milwaukee region boasts a population exceeding 900,000 people, making it the 17th-largest metropolitan area in the country. A bustling community with active sports, arts, and civic scenes, the city offers nearly 15,000 acres of parkland and a calendar overflowing with festivals and celebrations.

City by the Waters • **23** •

RAISE YOUR HAND IF YOU want to go for a wild ride. Thrill-seeking Milwaukeeans will find many such opportunities at the Wisconsin State Fair, held each August. Attracting nearly 1 million visitors each year, the event features livestock and horse shows in addition to its midway excitement.

MILWAUKEE AND ITS SUR-rounds offer a variety of activities in many spheres of interest, from fun on the playground to sightseeing on the road. The Lake Michigan leg of the Great Lakes Circle Tour leads drivers along Wisconsin's scenic eastern coast and through its historic towns.

City by the Waters

LIFE STARTS OUT ON THE right foot in kid-friendly Milwaukee. Some 17 area hopsitals offer prenatal and birthing services to help ensure each child has a good beginning.

MILWAUKEE IS BLESSED with an abundance of houses of worship, including the Cathedral of St. John the Evangelist (OPPOSITE) on North Jackson Street. Almost 80 years after its construction in 1847, a fire destroyed the building, leaving only the tower standing. Through the dedication of its clergy and the devotion of its congregation, the cathedral was rebuilt in 1942.

COMPLETED IN 1967 AT A cost of $4.5 million, the Mitchell Park Horticultural Conservatory—better known as the Domes—took shape over several years, one glass beehive at a time. Architect Donald Grieb created a facility that netted some 15,000 square feet of growing space, spread among three climatically distinct buildings.

City by the Waters

• 33 •

Cultivating curiosity in all its visitors, the Domes hosts permanent exhibits in its Arid and Tropical buildings. In its third unit, the conservatory sponsors numerous seasonal displays, including *Tracks Across Wisconsin* (OPPOSITE), an exhibit of miniature railroads. Not only is the facility a popular place for family outings, but it also serves as a fitting showcase for the area's many natural wonders (PAGES 36-39).

City by the Waters

• 35 •

One of the area's most prominent cultural organizations, the Milwaukee Ballet has raised the barre for performing arts soloist Yumelia Garcia (OPPOSITE), the group stages about 45 performances—including 26 shows of *The Nutcracker*—for some 80,000

THE RENOWNED MILWAUKEE Art Museum, under the leadership of Director Russell Bowman (ABOVE), has enjoyed near-constant expansion of both its campus and its collection, culminating in the opening of a new wing in May 2001. Showing in galleries and museums across the country, the surreal, often humorous images painted by Milwaukee native Fred Stonehouse (OPPOSITE) have garnered a national audience.

MILWAUKEE HAS ITS SHARE of tough guys, and whether they work on fuel valves or on right hooks, many of them perform important roles in the community. At The Shop, ace mechanic Tim Schneider (ABOVE) and crew make sure the city's classic motorcycles run properly. Boxing coach Fidel Medina (OPPOSITE) trains fighters like heavyweight "Mighty" Mike Word (PAGE 46) to knock out the competition. And in the arts community, the Florentine Opera Company gives local actors like Matt Jaeger (PAGE 47) a chance to play the heavy.

City by the Waters

· 45 ·

CLASSIC ARCHITECTURE mirrors classic drama in a city steeped in history and culture. A class act in its own right, the Florentine Opera Company (OPPOSITE), one of the state's oldest arts organizations, stages some of the best arias in the area.

MILWAUKEE'S STORIED history can be read in the intricate architectural flourishes that enliven structures like the Blatz Brewing Company building (TOP) and the Pabst Theater (OPPOSITE). Built in 1931, the Milwaukee County Courthouse (PAGE 53)—designed by New York-based architect Albert Ross—stands as an imposing landmark, while other local buildings celebrate life's many small pleasures, from Milwaukee's fine cuisine to its trademark brews (PAGES 54 AND 55).

City by the Waters

City by the Waters

Statuary of every type—from playful cherubs to serious politicians—abounds in downtown Milwaukee. Representing a proud local history, the numerous monuments comprising the Court of Honor (OPPOSITE) point out to new generations the accomplishments and sacrifices of those who preceded them.

In downtown Milwaukee, ornate, historic buildings stand side by side with modern corporate edifices, reflecting the city's sense of architectural grandeur and style.

CAPTAIN FREDERICK PABST, president of one of the most successful breweries in Milwaukee, built his opulent mansion (ABOVE) in 1890, and it remains one of the city's finest examples of residential splendor. Designed by local architect George Ferry of Ferry & Clas, the house features the ornate Pabst Pavilion (OPPOSITE), which was originally constructed to showcase Pabst Brewing Company products at the 1893 Colombian Exposition in Chicago. When the fair ended, the structure was disassembled and moved to Milwaukee, where it served as the family's sun room.

Milwaukee

RISING ABOVE WATER STREET, the Mitchell Building stands as a monument to its namesake and first owner, banker and businessman Alexander Mitchell. Besides representing the region in the U.S. Congress for four years, Mitchell also controlled much of the banking and insurance industries in the city.

City by the Waters

IN DOWNTOWN MILWAUKEE, ornate, historic buildings stand side by side with modern corporate edifices, reflecting the city's sense of architectural grandeur and style.

FORGOTTEN

Time and progress have made landmarks of some buildings, while leaving other historic structures empty and abandoned. But current restoration efforts—in combination with the city's undying appreciation of its past—strive to make sure no corner of history is ever forgotten.

City by the Waters

Milwaukee's Civil War monument commemorates Wisconsin's role in American history, as well as the many sacrifices of its citizens. Dedicated in 1898 during the city's Carnival festival—which celebrated 50 years of statehood—the sculpture stands in the Court of Honor.

Milwaukee

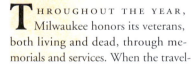

Throughout the year, Milwaukee honors its veterans, both living and dead, through memorials and services. When the traveling Wall That Heals (ABOVE) stopped in nearby Port Washington in May 1998, thousands visited the site to pay their respects.

City by the Waters · 69 ·

Milwaukee

A POIGNANT PAINTING BY several local artists graces the wall of the Milwaukee American Legion Hall (ABOVE). The mural joins with numerous military cemeteries in the area in patriotic salutes to the high price of freedom.

City by the Waters

In a stunning series of 1988 portraits, Manitowoc-based J. Shimon & J. Lindemann Photographers captured the faces of veterans confined to the Clement J. Zablocki Veterans Affairs Medical Center. Among those featured were Joe Starr (ABOVE) and Oscar D'Hooge (OPPOSITE), both of whom served their country during World War I. The medical facility is named after the region's longtime U.S. representative, who died in 1983.

NOWHERE IS THE GREAT outdoors greater than in Wisconsin, where more than 80 state parks and almost 90 national forests showcase countless breathtaking vistas (PAGES 74-77).

A Wisconsinite not out casting a reel is like a fish out of water. Each midwestern March, schools of locals wade into the Milwaukee River at Kletsch Park, hoping to catch the elusive rainbow trout, which migrates upstream every year to spawn.

MILWAUKEEANS HAVE A reputation for going against the flow. And while they often end up reaching their destinations, they do occasionally find themselves out on a limb.

City by the Waters

© DARRYL R. BEERS

LAKE MICHIGAN PLAYS A profound role in day-to-day life in Milwaukee (PAGES 82-85). From its heyday as a trade route that brought ships to local ports, to its present-day status as a center of maritime recreation, the lake has even influenced local architecture, such as the Edmund M. Gustorf Boat House (BOTTOM), a local fixture since 1924.

City by the Waters

· 85 ·

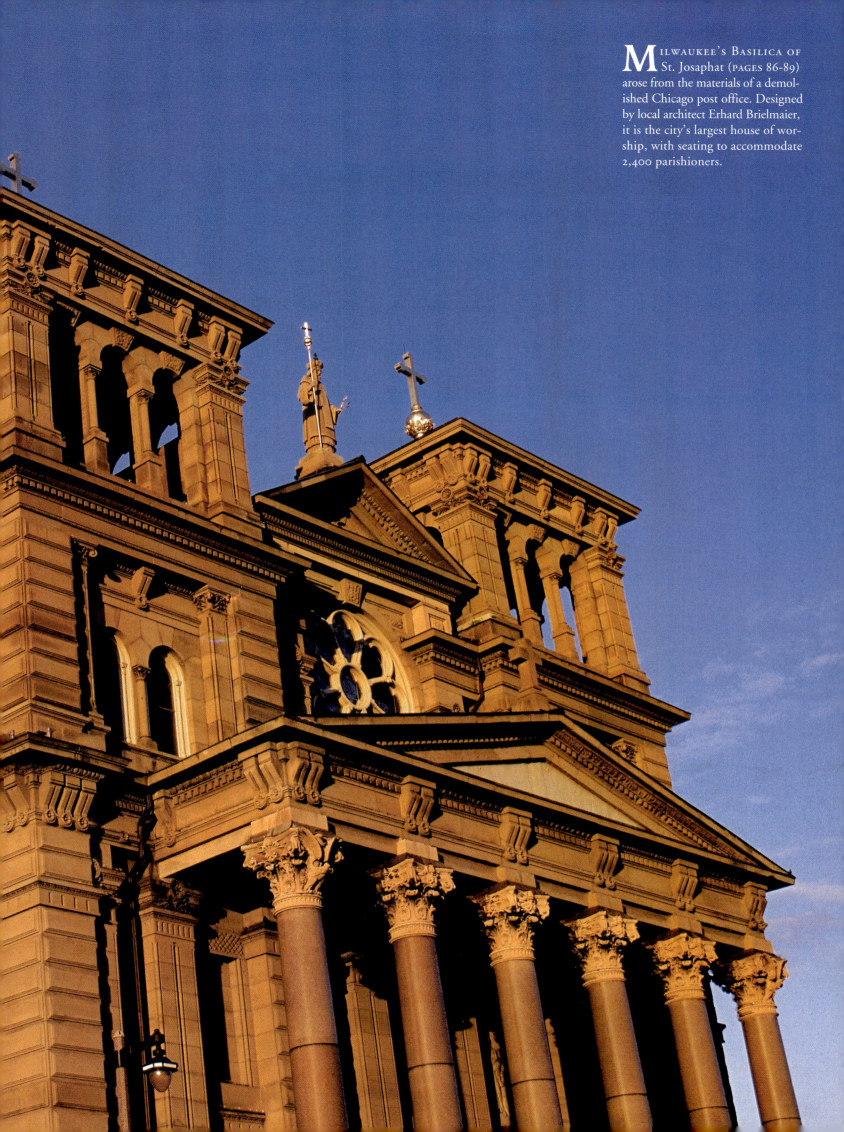

MILWAUKEE'S BASILICA OF St. Josaphat (PAGES 86-89) arose from the materials of a demolished Chicago post office. Designed by local architect Erhard Brielmaier, it is the city's largest house of worship, with seating to accommodate 2,400 parishioners.

METAL OF HONOR: IRON men of every shape and size have contributed to the development of Milwaukee. In the mid-1800s, workers bolted together components forged in New York City to make one of the country's only cast-iron structures—the Iron Block Building (RIGHT) on Wisconsin Avenue. And after a hard day's work, tapping an ice-cold aluminum keg from one of the city's many fine breweries might be just what the doctor ordered.

City by the Waters

Founded in 1855, Miller Brewing Company has a lot on tap in its hometown city. The local facility produces several million barrels of beer each year, and the international popularity of its famous brands—including such favorites as Miller Lite and Icehouse—has made it the second-largest brewer in the country.

City by the Waters

Long known as the beer capital of the world, the city of Milwaukee resonates with names from the past. While many of these historic companies have either closed or moved headquarters, their castle-like buildings stand as reminders of the industry's legacy.

City by the Waters

In 1996, Milwaukee celebrated its sesquicentennial anniversary by showcasing one of its most beloved and familiar attractions, City Hall—which had celebrated its own centennial the year before. Designed by local architect H.C. Koch, the building is topped with a 350-foot tower containing an 11-ton bell that is rung three times a day.

City by the Waters

In fall 1996, Milwaukee broke ground on the state-of-the-art Miller Park, which replaces historic County Stadium (OPPOSITE) as the home for Brewers baseball. Built in the original stadium's centerfield parking lot, the 43,000-seat Miller Park—which opened in spring 2001—features the country's only fan-shaped retractable roof, which weighs approximately 12,000 tons and allows for a natural grass playing field.

City by the Waters

· 99 ·

The only Major League Baseball team to play in both the American and the National leagues, the Milwaukee Brewers have drawn increasingly large crowds to their home games. This trend culminated in September 2000, with the team's highest attendance ever—more than 50,000 fans—for the final ball game in County Stadium.

City by the Waters

JUMPING AT THE CHANCE TO participate, Milwaukeeans play sports with a very competitive spirit. The city's A-League soccer franchise, the Milwaukee Rampage (OPPOSITE) attracts thousands of fans to games at Uihlein Soccer Park.

City by the Waters

Milwaukee

EVEN MORE THAN THE CHILLY weather or cold winters, the Pettit National Ice Center is what makes ice skating a favorite spectator sport in Milwaukee. The facility hosts a number of events throughout the year, including the speed-skating world championships. During the competition in 2000, the Netherlands' Gianni Romme (LEFT) and German Claudia Pechstein (OPPOSITE) took top honors in their respective categories.

City by the Waters

IT'S ALL DOWNHILL FROM HERE: Children and adults alike brave the icy hills of Milwaukee on sleds and homemade gliders, steering clear of trees and ditches to reach the bottom safely. For those less inclined to take risks, viewing the region's seasonal beauty can yield some jaw-dropping discoveries (PAGES 108 AND 109).

IN WISCONSIN, EACH SEASON reveals its own colorful identity, from winter's white blankets of snow, to autumn's fading light and changing leaves, to the intense, refreshed hues of spring and summer (PAGES 110-117).

City by the Waters

City by the Waters

Known as the City of Festivals, Milwaukee experiences no shortage of reasons to have fun. Dressed in reds and greens, members of the city's Mexican population take to the streets in celebration of Cinco de Mayo and Fiesta Mexicana.

City by the Waters · 119 ·

The largest gathering of its kind in the country, the Indian Summer Festival showcases southern Wisconsin's Native American history and tribal cultures, including those of the Woodland Nations and the Plains Indians. Featuring music, food, and crafts, the event also sponsors a competitive powwow, giving locals an opportunity to perform traditional dances in full colorful costume.

E ACH YEAR, MORE THAN 100,000 attendees get a real kick out of Milwaukee's annual Irish Fest, where troupes like Ceoltoiti An Anoigh, which features steppers of all ages, employ dance to interpret traditional Irish stories and myths.

City by the Waters

ONCE HE ADMITTED TO HIM-self that he was powerless to curb his addiction to the official music of Wisconsin, Don Hedaker (ABOVE, ON RIGHT) formed the Polkaholics and proclaimed himself the Clown Prince of Polka. Playing polka with a punk rock attitude since 1997, he and his fellow addicts have garnered many local fans, who attend concerts to go through the 12 steps to recovery—dance steps, that is.

City by the Waters

PERHAPS THE FESTIVAL TO end all festivals, Milwaukee's Rainbow Summer Fest presents a summerlong concert series of all types of music, from country and gospel to jazz and rock.

City by the Waters

DURING THE AFRICAN WORLD Festival each August, Milwaukee's African-American population celebrates its heritage with displays of brilliant color, as well as with family and community togetherness.

MILWAUKEE—WHERE THE beer is cold, but the hospitality's always warm. From the people in neighborhood establishments to the reflections of everyday life, the city has much to offer (PAGES 130-135).

Fueled by the growth of local industries during the late 1800s, Milwaukee experienced an economic boom that resulted in the building of many lavish residences. Jason Downer, a prominent attorney, built his home (ABOVE, ON RIGHT) in 1874. George P. Miller received his mansion (ABOVE, ON LEFT) as a gift from his father-in-law, the founder and owner of local department store T.A. Chapman Co. Still, as some area buildings reveal, all men are created equal—even if their houses aren't (PAGES 138 AND 139).

City by the Waters

CHECK IT OUT: Each day, hundreds of students, researchers, and readers peruse some of the nearly 3 million books, videos, periodicals, and documents at the Milwaukee Central Public Library. Since 1898, the facility—listed on the National Register of Historic Places—has stood as a reminder of the premium the community places on knowledge and learning.

City by the Waters

· 141 ·

Standing in stark contrast to their surrounds, many Milwaukee monuments mark a storied past. Seven governors, 27 mayors, and three beer barons are among the many prominent Milwaukeeans buried at historic Forest Home Cemetery (LEFT). Built in 1873, the 175-foot North Point Water Tower (OPPOSITE) prevented the freezing of water pumped from Lake Michigan; today, that process is performed by more high-tech methods.

City by the Waters

· 143 ·

Viewed through a glass darkly or observed in the time-weathered surfaces of prominent statuary, relics of religious life abound throughout Milwaukee, reminders of lifetimes of faith and remembrances.

Milwaukee

During Festa Italiana in summer 2000, hundreds of faithful Catholics greeted the arrival of Our Lady of the New Millennium, a 33-foot, stainless-steel likeness of the Virgin Mary that travels to churches throughout the region. Chicago native Carl Demma commissioned the statue in 1999, selling his liquor store to fund the project; he died shortly before it arrived on local shores.

City by the Waters

LIFE IMITATES ART: Local alternative band Violent Femmes had a hit with a song called "I Held Her in My Arms," perhaps inspired by sights around town.

City by the Waters

THE FRIGID TEMPERATURES of winter send many a Milwaukeean scurrying for cover and protection from the winds. But even when it's frozen stiff, the area displays a certain snowy charm (PAGES 152-155).

City by the Waters

© FREDERICK "THE SHOOTIST" KILBEY

Milwaukee

IF A TREE FALLS IN MILWAUKEE and no one is around, does it still make a sound? In Wisconsin, weather can profoundly change the landscape—bringing down once-sturdy trees or coating the city in several layers of ice (PAGES 156-159).

City by the Waters

· 157 ·

© JOHN J. BACIK III

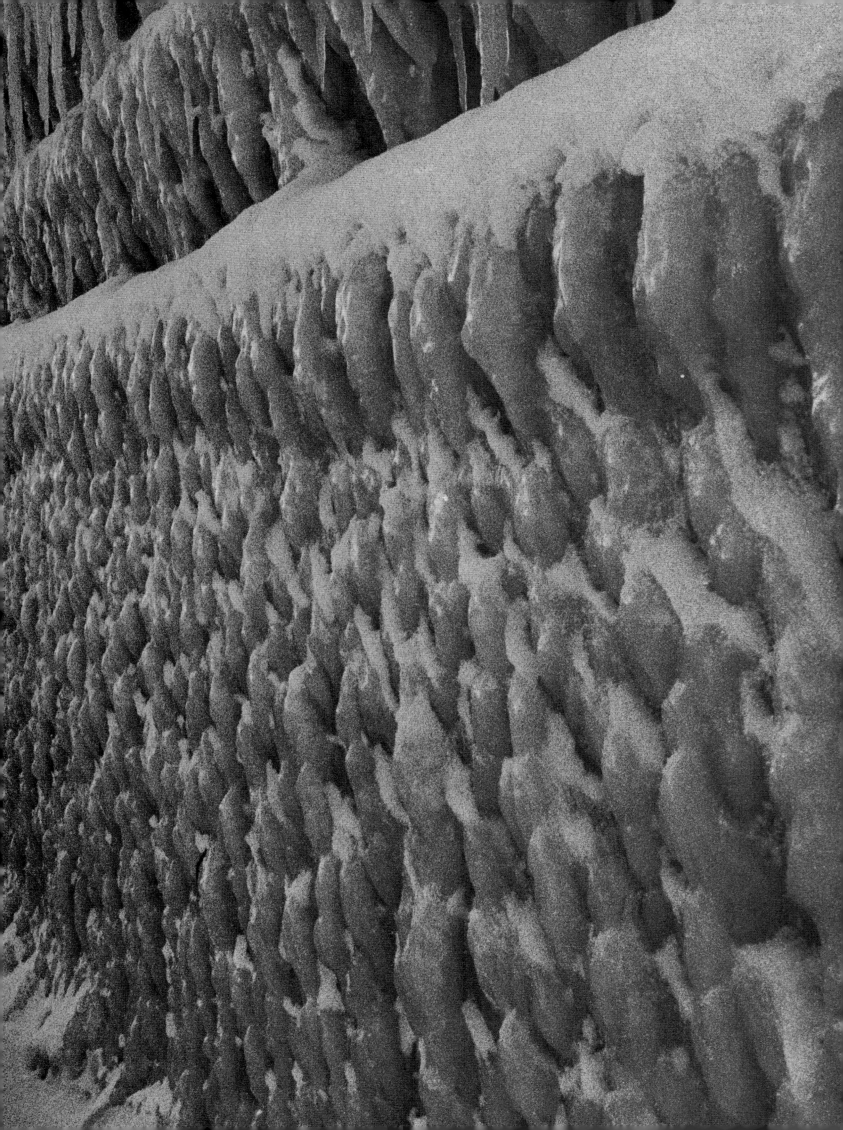

LEAN INTO IT: Whether riding tall in the saddle or getting on board, Milwaukeeans kick up a lot of excitement as they jockey for position at the top of their game.

City by the Waters

During the 1998-1999 season—his first as head coach of the Milwaukee Bucks—George Karl (ABOVE) led the team to its first play-off season in more than seven years. Today, the team remains a strong contender in the NBA's Central Division and, with top scorers like Ray Allen and Glenn "Big Dog" Robinson (OPPOSITE), attracts thousands of fans to its home games at the Bradley Center.

City by the Waters

RACING FANS TURN OUT in droves for events at the Milwaukee Mile, located on the Wisconsin State Fair grounds. One of the oldest major tracks in the world, it held its first competition in 1903, and today sponsors a full roster of fast-paced races, including the Miller Lite 225 (ABOVE).

© DONALD MIRALLE / ALLSPORT USA

City by the Waters

· 165 ·

· 166 ·

Milwaukee

When local racing fans root for the home team, they're usually cheering for the Miller Racing crew, which boasts an enviable record in the sport. Racing legend Bobby Rahal (OPPOSITE RIGHT) drove to fame when he won four victories and the CART series title in 1992. Driving for Miller during the 1980s, Danny Sullivan (OPPOSITE LEFT) took the championship flag at the Indy 500 in 1985.

City by the Waters

KNOCK 'EM DOWN: WHETHER aiming for pins or for opponents, Milwaukeeans face off in their favorite sports with energy and excitement to spare. One of several boxers training in local gyms, Luis Velez (OPPOSITE) challenges other fighters in rings around town. At Falcon Bowl (PAGES 169-171), one of the oldest bowling alleys in the country, Riverwest residents still gather for leisurely games and beers—not to mention victory-dance-inducing strikes. For more competitive players, the neighborhood tavern also sponsors numerous leagues that play regularly.

City by the Waters

• 169 •

City by the Waters

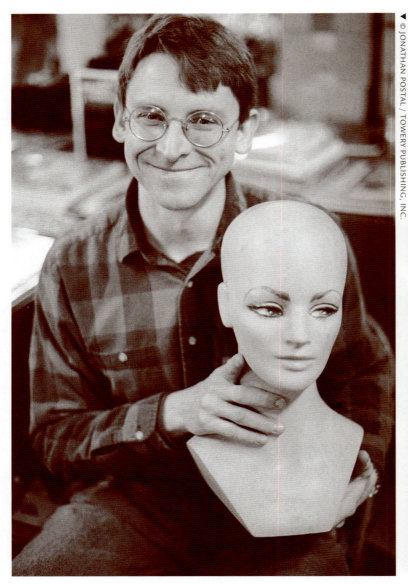 

From amazing bargains at the monthly Rummage-O-Rama (ABOVE LEFT) to the Milwaukee Ballet's costumes (ABOVE RIGHT), local attire and accessories come in a vast assortment of colors, sizes, and styles (PAGES 173 AND 174). A vintage clothing store in the Third Ward, Marlene's Touch of Class (PAGE 175) makes sure customers don't wig out when they want to play dress up.

· 172 ·

Milwaukee

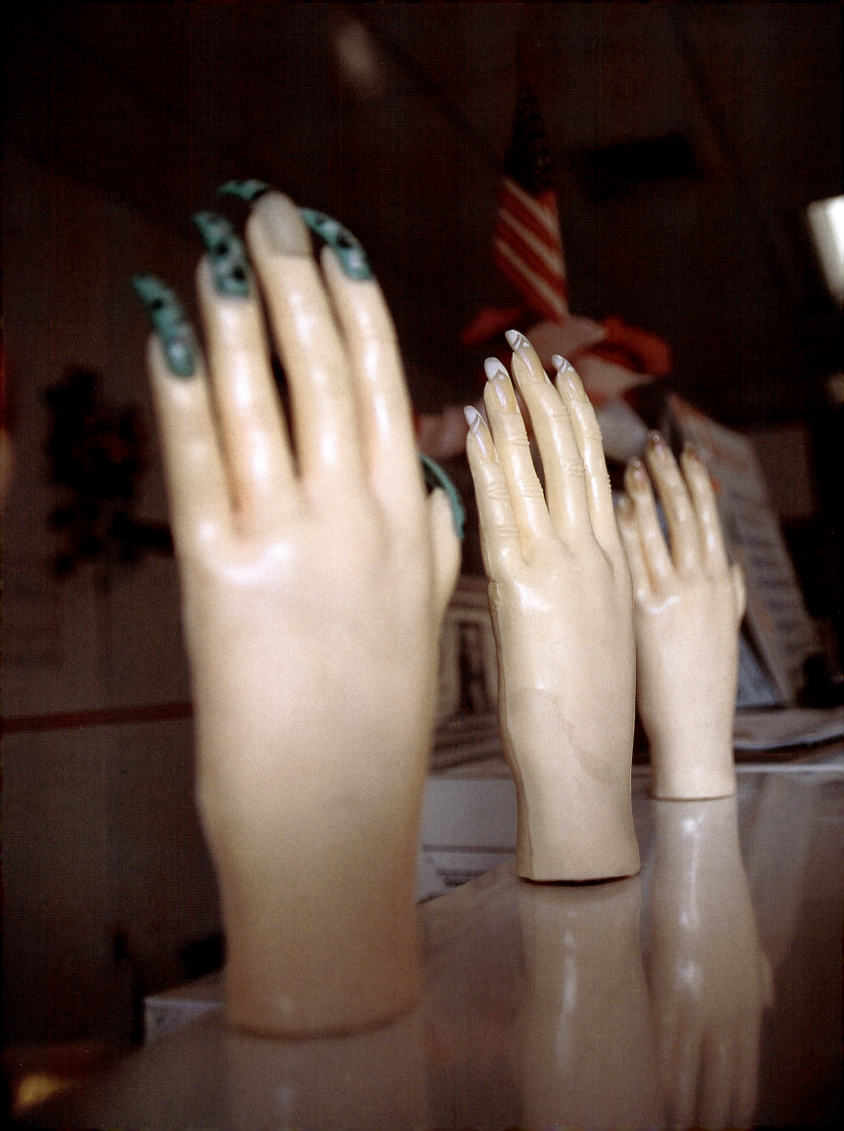

MILWAUKEE IN MINIATURE: Playful figurines often resemble the city's human residents, who make a point to get dolled up when they go out—whether that's out on the town, out on stage, or simply out to work.

City by the Waters

Milwaukee's bustling music scene leans on a firm foundation of stringed instruments, from telecasters to banjos to mandolins. A local guitar player with a soulful voice, Paul Cebar (OPPOSITE) fronts the highly popular Milwaukeeans, local veterans who have released three albums—including *The Get-Go* in 1999—to critical acclaim. When he's not on stage, Cebar is often in the studio at WMSE radio, where he has hosted *Way Back Home* since 1982.

City by the Waters

· 179 ·

According to many Milwaukeeans, you can only get good home-cooking at two places: at home and at Mr. Perkins' Family Restaurant. Operated today by Willie Perkins Jr. and his wife, Cherry (ABOVE), the restaurant serves some of the area's best catfish, greens, candied yams, and hot coffee—among many other dishes—in a cozy, neighborly environment.

City by the Waters

· 181 ·

R AILROAD TRACKS RUN through much of Milwaukee's history as a shipping and trading center. Today, fewer trains ride the rails, but repair shops in nearby Cudahy—along with local businesses like Northern Rail Car Corporation, which fixes and refurbishes old cars, locomotives, and cabooses—help the industry stay on track.

City by the Waters

· 183 ·

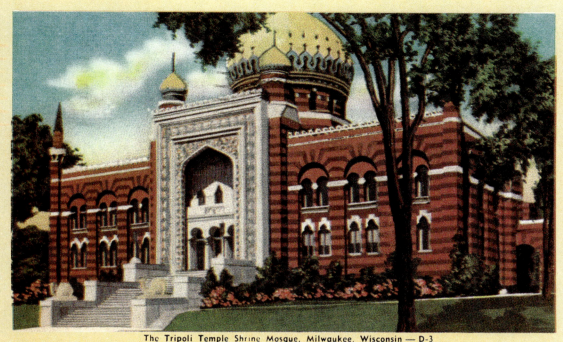

The Tripoli Temple Shrine Mosque, Milwaukee, Wisconsin — D-3

HOME TO THE TRIPOLI Shrine Temple fraternal order, the Tripoli Mosque stands as Milwaukee's own version of the Taj Mahal. Built in 1928 and financed by Shrine members, the building features intricate architectural flourishes both inside and out. Rising some 100 feet into the air, the main dome—long a dominant feature in the city's skyline—spans more than 30 feet in diameter and features Saracenic artwork. Today, the mosque attracts thousands of visitors each year and houses the offices of the Shrine potentate and the service and administration staffs.

City by the Waters

REDEFINING ANIMAL MAGnetism, the Milwaukee County Zoo attracts thousands of children and adults alike each year. The 200-acre zoo, which was founded in 1892, features a menagerie of more than 2,500 animals representing some 300 species.

PROVING THAT THE REAL polar bear club isn't at the zoo, dozens of fearless Milwaukeeans ring in the new year with their annual plunge in Lake Michigan, whose midwinter waters are just above freezing. Hundreds of spectators, opting not to take a dip, gather on the shore to watch the event.

W HETHER THEY LIVE AT the Milwaukee County Zoo, out in the forests of rural Wisconsin, or even among the stacked likenesses on an intricately carved totem pole, animals get a frosty change of scenery when winter snows hit.

City by the Waters

· 191 ·

FEELING A LITTLE SHEEPISH about the cold weather? Locals can take shelter on the benches in front of the Midwest Express Center. Curving over occupants to shield them from the wind, the benches' distinct shape was created by world-renowned artist Vito Acconci.

TO AND 'FRO: HOLDING basketball very deer, fans of the Milwaukee Bucks are a shade apart from those of other NBA teams. Marked by their unbridled enthusiasm and purple-and-green fashions, they loyally cheer on their favorite team—and its mascot Bango (OPPOSITE BOTTOM)—throughout the season.

· 194 ·

Milwaukee

City by the Waters

A T THE MILWAUKEE MILE, there's always a big event coming out of the turn. In July 1998, the track hosted the NASCAR Busch Series Grand National Diehard 250, where racing favorite Dale Earnhardt Jr. (OPPOSITE TOP) took the checkered flag.

City by the Waters

MILWAUKEE TOASTS THOSE who preserve their German ancestry through food and drink. At Karl Ratzsch's, a local culinary institution, John Poulos (LEFT) serves up a full menu of old-world dishes, from Wiener schnitzel to potato dumplings to sauerbraten. Randal Sprecher (OPPOSITE) founded Sprecher Brewing Company—the first microbrewery in the state—in 1985, and continues to use traditional methods to create an array of award-winning beers.

Standing on East Wisconsin Avenue since 1893, the stately Pfister Hotel is known as much for its attentive service and luxurious comfort—exemplified by its unmatched 80-piece art collection and top-notch restaurants like the Café Rouge and Blu—as for its architectural splendor. Discreetly and efficiently handling requests from guests, Chief Concierge Peter Mortensen also serves as the hotel's historian, leading tours every Sunday afternoon.

A PROFESSOR OF PHILOSOPHY at University of Wisconsin-Milwaukee, John Koethe has penned several volumes of poetry—including *The Last Wisconsin Spring* in 1984 and the award-winning *Falling Water* in 1996—that wrestle with questions of identity and existence. Collecting works by area writers, the Milwaukee Central Public Library (OPPOSITE) honors many of them, including Laura Ingalls Wilder, Thornton Wilder, and Carl Sandburg, on its Wisconsin Writers Wall of Fame.

City by the Waters

· 203 ·

EVIDENCE OF MILWAUKEE'S emphasis on grandeur and style can be found in the vaulted ceilings and tiled fountains of the city's public buildings, as well as in their history-worn towers (PAGES 204-207). Drawing thousands of visitors to the city each year for meetings, shows, and conventions, Midwest Express Center (LEFT) contains more than $1 million in art projects—ensuring the space is as comfortable and appealing as it is technologically advanced.

City by the Waters

© SAMUEL CASTRO

Stare case: Many Milwaukeeans dress up for a night out, viewing the occasion as an opportunity to see and be seen. During the day, though, others go shirtless, not only to beat the heat, but also to show off their skin-deep fashion sense.

WORKING IN A MULTI-tude of media, artists of every stripe call Milwaukee home. BJ Daniels (LEFT), the city's most popular "gender illusionist," uses his/her body as a canvas. Daniels retired from the stage in 1995, but continues to emcee local revues. Sally Kolf (OPPOSITE) painted a series of celebrity portraits on fake fur, and has recently turned her creative attentions to crocheting.

City by the Waters

· 211 ·

THE PABST THEATER, located next to City Hall on East Wells Street, features an intricately detailed, sandstone and orange-brick facade that adds drama to Milwaukee's skyline.

O NCE SLATED FOR DEMOLI- tion in the early 1970s, the 1,400-seat Pabst Theater today lives on as one of the city's foremost cultural institutions. It underwent a refurbishing in 1976, as well as a major renovation during the late 1990s, to maintain its opulent decor.

ALL MILWAUKEE'S A STAGE: The Pabst Theater presents about 200 events a year, including plays, musicals, concerts, dance performances, and the Milwaukee Repertory Theater's annual production of *A Christmas Carol*.

STRIKING A STIFF POSE, Milwaukee's storefront models display some startling fashions—from elegant evening gowns to retro beach wear—complete with new or vintage accessories.

City by the Waters

Each summer, Milwaukee becomes hog heaven for some 11,000 Harley Owners Group (HOG) members attending the Milwaukee Home Run. Commemorating the iconic American motorcycle, the event features tours of the Harley-Davidson factory and a Harley Expo—along with the friendly camaraderie of fellow bikers.

As the motorcycle capital of America, Milwaukee attracts a number of famous enthusiasts, including *Tonight Show* host Jay Leno (ABOVE). Peter Fonda (OPPOSITE) starred as Captain America, a rebel idealist who rides a Harley cross-country, in the 1960s counterculture film *Easy Rider*, which helped to revive the two-wheeler's popularity.

Born to be hog wild: Black leather and the trademark Harley-Davidson logo—along with more whimsical accessories—abound throughout the city, as participants in the annual Milwaukee Home Run take to the streets.

City by the Waters

As Milwaukee's couples rev up for romance, many of them celebrate their love—as well as their Harley lifestyle—by HOG-tying the knot.

TILL DEATH DO US PART holds true as much today as it did a century ago. Each year, some 30,000 Wisconsin couples take their wedding vows—many of them all the way to the grave.

City by the Waters

SINCE THE 1800S, THE MILwaukee Fire Department has fought diligently to keep the city's neighborhoods safe from the threat of flames (PAGES 230-233). In front of the main firehouse on West Wells Street, the Fallen Fire Fighter Memorial (OPPOSITE)—designed by retired St. Louis firefighter Robert Daus—stands in honor of the 106 Milwaukeans who died in the line of duty.

City by the Waters

· 233 ·

To the rescue: Dedicated firefighters from around the region train in simulated settings to prepare for real emergencies, when courage and quick thinking can make the difference between life and death (PAGES 234-237).

Milwaukee

NEITHER SNOW NOR RAIN nor gloom of night will stay Milwaukee's couriers from the swift completion of their appointed rounds. The city is the birthplace of the National Association of Letter Carriers, which was founded in 1889 with only 60 members. Today, the union's national membership exceeds 315,000.

City by the Waters

· 239 ·

The Milwaukee Police Department's horse patrol—reinstated in 1997 after a 50-year absence—monitors downtown and numerous residential neighborhoods in an effort to rein in crime and increase police visibility. Working to decrease drug activity in the city, the patrol teaches kids to just say neigh.

WHICH CAME FIRST, THE rabbit or the egg? Not the main course, but still the focal point of many holiday celebrations throughout Milwaukee, thousands of eggs are hard-boiled, hand-painted, hidden, and hunted by children and parents alike on Easter Sunday.

Milwaukee

· 244 ·

Milwaukee

THROUGHOUT MILWAUKEE, stone statues and stained-glass windows echo the population's deep-seated religious beliefs, illuminating the virtues of prayer, sacrifice, and selflessness.

City by the Waters

• 245 •

 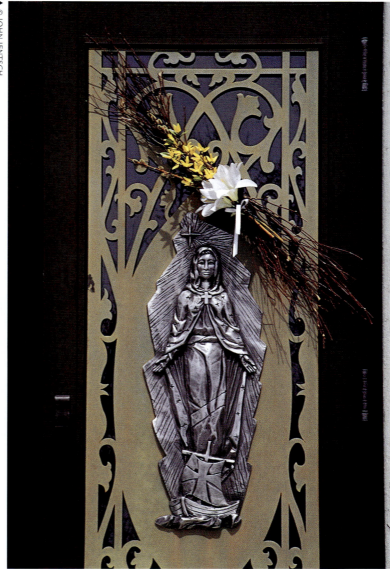

EVER SINCE THE FIRST SETtlers arrived in the area, southern Wisconsin's history has been closely intertwined with the spiritual life of the region's population. Opening their doors to all Milwaukeeans, local houses of worship—including St. Mary's Church—stand as reminders of the community's strong sense of faith and unity.

OFFERING MORE THAN JUST food and fun, Festa Italiana gives many locals an opportunity to explore their religious roots. Each year, thousands of Catholics from around the region follow the procession that carries the Virgin Mary's shrine to the Marcus Amphitheater, where the festival's Sunday mass is held.

City by the Waters

• 249 •

The road to you-know-where may be paved with good intentions, but those seeking images of underworldly critters need look no further than the canvases of local artist Fred Stonehouse, whose quirky paintings (OPPOSITE) are often haunted by demons and specters.

City by the Waters

MANY LOCAL BUILDINGS serve as backdrops for an array of urban artwork. Designs spray-painted on downtown walls prompt the question, Is graffiti vandalism or legitimate art? The Centre Building's massive trompe l'oeil mural (OPPOSITE) has passersby doing double takes as it appears—at first glance—to reflect a city skyline.

City by the Waters

BLONDES MAY HAVE MORE fun, but in Milwaukee, redheads and brunettes also sit on top of the world. For years, larger-than-life portraits of women have advertised the city's best bars and beers, but more recently, they have hawked a wider variety of alcohols, including La Perla's famous margaritas.

WHILE SOME LOCALS tower over their miniature collectibles, visitors to the Betty Brinn Children's Museum are reduced to Lilliputian scale by a recumbent statue of Jonathan Swift's Gulliver.

WHETHER CRAWLING around downtown or alighting in a park, insects of immense scale don't bug most Milwaukeeans. In fact, three gigantic ladybugs—part of a public art installation by local real estate developer John Burke Jr.—have even found a home on the side of an office building on North Water Street, much to the delight of area residents.

City by the Waters

EACH JULY, THOUSANDS OF residents and visitors line the streets to watch one of Milwaukee's most beloved and spectacular sights: the Circus Parade. Named one of the country's top events by the American Bus Association in 2000, the two-hour procession—first held in 1975—features around 60 antique circus wagons and animals galore.

Milwaukee

An ark's worth of wild animals and several carloads of colorful clowns march through downtown as part of the Circus Parade. Also walking the route are more than 700 horses, who—along with their carousel counterparts (PAGES 264 AND 265)—inspire lots of excitement among young spectators.

City by the Waters

· 263 ·

© DICK BLAU

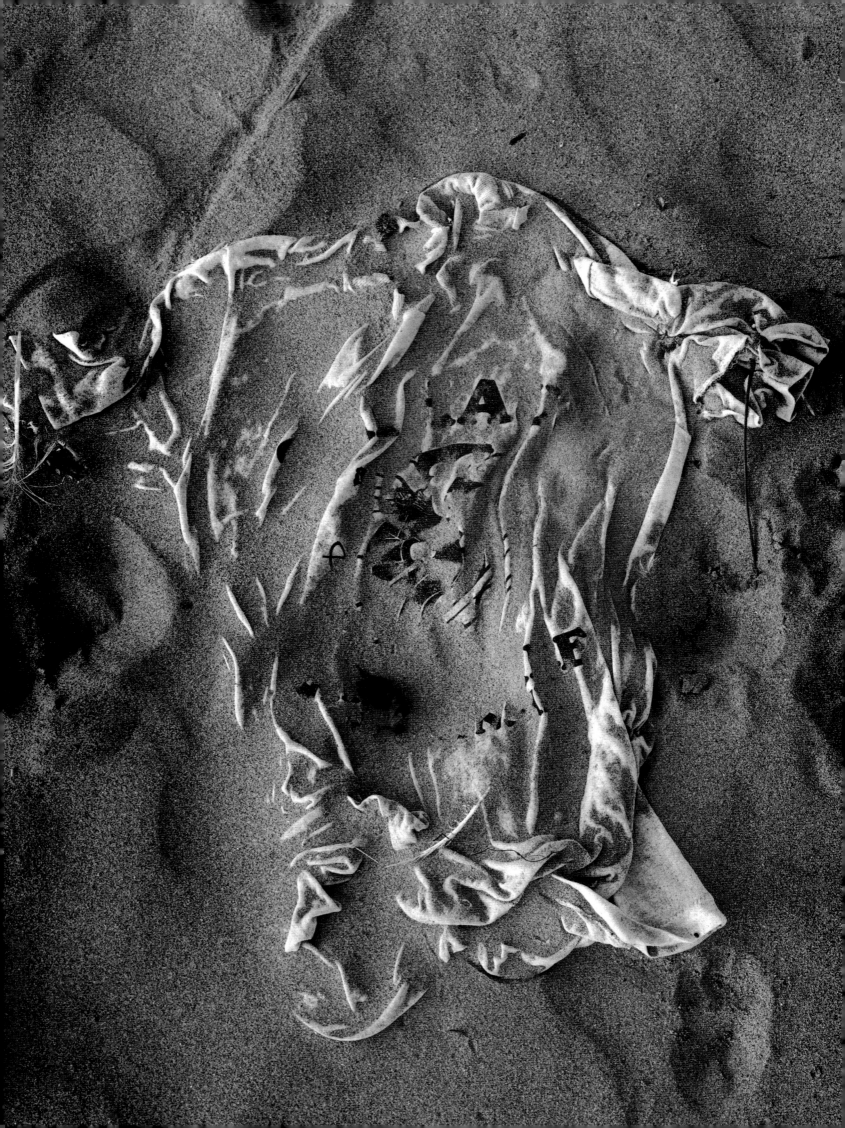

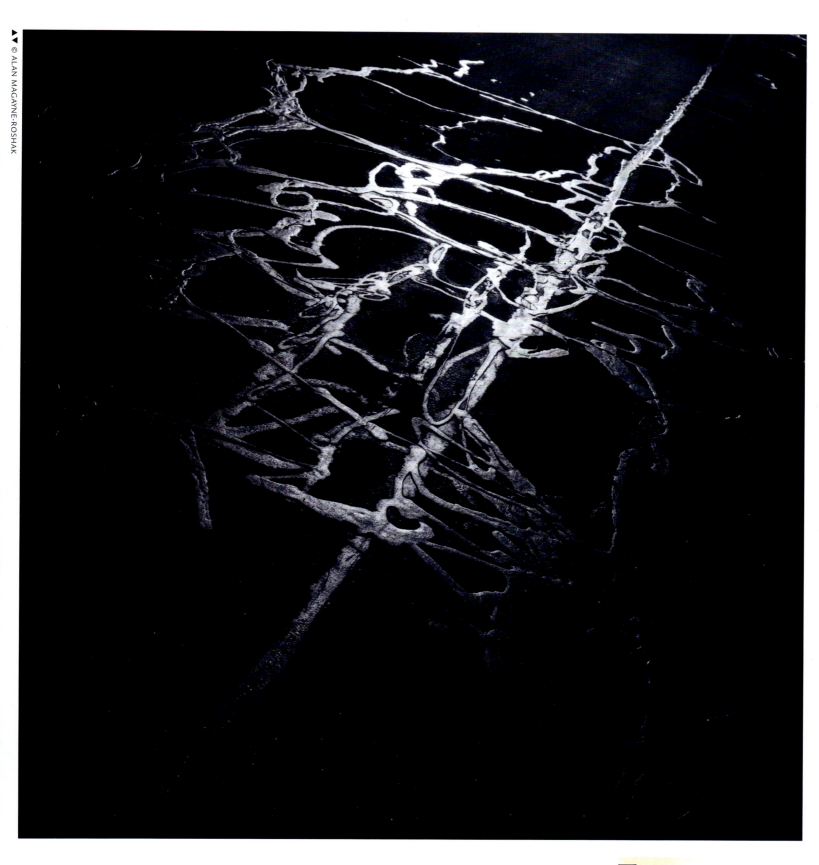

From the beach to the boulevard, from the State Fair to Lake Michigan, Milwaukee traces its lines in bold, broad strokes (PAGES 266-269).

City by the Waters

© RAY F. HILLSTROM

As the sun sets on Lake Michigan, reflections of its changing light provide moments of serene grandeur for this city by the waters (PAGES 270-273).

Profiles in Excellence

A look at the corporations, businesses, professional groups, and community service organizations that have made this book possible. Their stories—offering an informal chronicle of the local business community—are arranged according to the date they were established in the Milwaukee area.

A.N. Ansay & Associates, Inc.
ABB Automation Inc.
ABB Flexible Automation
Andrus, Sceales, Starke & Sawall, LLP
The Archdiocese of Milwaukee
Big Brothers Big Sisters, Inc.
The Bradley Foundation
Brady Corporation
The Business Journal
Catholic Family Life Insurance
CDI Information Technology Services, Inc.
Children's Hospital of Wisconsin
Columbia-St. Mary's, Inc.
Corrigan Properties, Inc./Bayshore Mall
Coventry Homes, Ltd.
Danfoss Graham
DeRosa Corporation
Earth Tech
Emmpak Foods, Inc.

The F. Dohmen Co.
FABCO Equipment Inc.
Fortis Health
Froedtert Memorial Lutheran Hospital
GE Medical Systems
Grede Foundries, Inc.
Grubb & Ellis | Boerke Company
Heartland Advisors, Inc.
Helwig Carbon Products Inc.
Heritage Relocation Services
High Gear, Inc.
Human Resource Services, Inc.
HUSCO International, Inc.
Kaerek Builders Inc.
Kalmbach Publishing Co.
Klement Sausage Co., Inc.
Lakeland Supply, Inc.
Lincoln State Bank
Manpower Inc.

© JOHN J. BACIK III

Midwest Express Airlines
Miller Brewing Company
Milwaukee Brewers Baseball Club
Milwaukee Journal Sentinel
Milwaukee Neurological Institute
Milwaukee Radio Group
Milwaukee School of Engineering
Multi Media Catalog Corporation
New England Financial/The Marris Group
North American Clutch Corporation
P&H Mining Equipment
Pereles Brothers, Inc.
Plunkett Raysich Architects
Potawatomi Bingo Casino
The Revere Group
Rockwell Automation
Shoreline Company, Inc.
Stratagem, Inc.
STS Consultants, Ltd.

TEC
TexPar Energy, Inc.
Thomas A. Mason Co., Inc.
Time Warner Cable-Milwaukee Division
Ultra Tool & Manufacturing, Inc.
Verizon Wireless
Vilter Manufacturing Corporation
Voss Jorgensen Schueler Co., Inc.
Waukesha Engine
Western Industries, Inc.
Western States Envelope Company
Wisconsin Energy Corporation
WTMJ-TV
WTMJ and WKTI Radio
Yale Equipment & Services, Inc.
YMCA of Metropolitan Milwaukee

1837-1855

1837
Milwaukee Journal Sentinel

1837
WTMJ TV

1837
WTMJ and WKTI Radio

1843
The Archdiocese of Milwaukee

1846
New England Financial/
The Marris Group

1848
Columbia-St. Mary's, Inc.

1855
Miller Brewing

Milwaukee Journal Sentinel

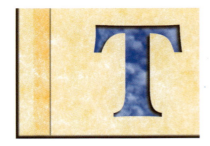

THE *Milwaukee Journal Sentinel* HAS UNDERGONE A transformation from the days when editors in green eyeshades made seat-of-the-pants news judgments, and newsboys on street corners hawked "Extra!" editions containing late-breaking news. ■ Today, the Internet has transformed this downtown Milwaukee news operation into a deadline-a-minute, news-gathering engine, where stories and photographs are instantly transmitted to millions of users by a staff of 300 journalists equipped with laptop computers, digital cameras, and wireless modems, and where readers regularly log on to chat with reporters about news stories.

Despite changes, the written word has always provided the weave and fabric of Milwaukee culture. As the city's flagship newspaper and the largest of only a handful of employee-owned newspapers in the country, the *Milwaukee Journal Sentinel* has a history of civic responsibility and leadership.

The newspaper's predecessors are the *Milwaukee Sentinel*, founded by Milwaukee's first mayor, Solomon Juneau in 1837, and *The Milwaukee Journal*, which began publishing in 1882 under the leadership of Lucius Nieman. The *Milwaukee Journal Sentinel*'s current workforce of some 2,850 is representative of the diverse communities the newspaper serves. The company consistently receives awards for its commitment to diversity in reporting and its minority hiring records, which are above the industry average.

The Journal Sentinel Inc. is the largest company within Journal Communications—a diversified media company and the oldest continual employee-owned company in the United States.

Reporting Tomorrow's History Today

Guided by such principles as a commitment to accuracy, fairness, and ethical behavior, the *Journal Sentinel* was created in 1995 when the two powerful papers already owned by Journal Communications merged the best of their resources. The *Journal Sentinel* is Wisconsin's largest and most influential newspaper, with the second-strongest readership numbers in the country.

The newspaper's mission—to be the indispensable source of news and information in its chosen markets, connecting people and helping them manage and enrich their lives—is supported by industry statistics. With an 81 percent cumulative readership of the Sunday and daily papers, the *Journal Sentinel* is read by four out of every five people in metropolitan Milwaukee.

As the *Journal Sentinel* maintains news bureaus in Waukesha, Racine, Madison, and Port Washington, as well as in Washington, D.C., no other local news medium can offer the same depth of coverage. Editors seek to discover trends, strive for insight into complex issues, and explore ways to connect their findings to reader concerns and interests.

Staying connected to customers and connecting them to one another are functions of the state's top paper. Advertisers like to place their ads in carefully read newspapers—and, by presenting a tapestry of viewpoints and ideas, as well as by offering

JS ONLINE FEATURES BEST-OF-THE-WEB COVERAGE ON MILWAUKEE AND WISCONSIN, DELIVERING COMPLETE, CONCISE NEWS AND INFORMATION AS IT HAPPENS.

AT THE *MILWAUKEE JOURNAL SENTINEL*'S DOWNTOWN HEADQUARTERS, FOUR EDITIONS OF THE NEWSPAPER—BASED ON GEOGRAPHIC ZONES—ARE PRODUCED EACH DAY, THEN LOADED ONTO A FLEET OF SOME 28 TRUCKS AND DELIVERED STATEWIDE BY MORE THAN 2,500 ADULT CARRIERS.

valued goods and services, the *Journal Sentinel* keeps Milwaukee's melting pot bubbling. An advertiser base of some 8,000 businesses, plus thousands of individuals who place classified ads, comprises more than half of each edition's content.

Print and Integrated Media

Two of the company's operating principles are to do whatever it takes to understand and meet client expectations, and to develop businesses, products, and services that meet the needs of present and future customers.

The company is investing $106.6 million in a new production facility and three new printing presses. "Never has there been a more exciting time in the newspaper publishing business," says Keith Spore, president and publisher. "We are committed to producing the best possible newspaper. This investment will equip us to do so."

Construction of the new, 435,000-square-foot plant in West Milwaukee, scheduled to begin printing and packaging the newspaper in 2002, began in June 2000. The state-of-the-art facility will contain a 350-foot-long press line comprised of the largest installation of offset printing presses in the country.

Journal Interactive, the Internet division of Journal Sentinel Inc., produces several award-winning Web sites. Chief among them is JS Online (www.jsonline.com), the most heavily trafficked news and information Web site based in Wisconsin. This multimedia news product exceeds the repurposed wire copy and ticker scripts found on many "news" sites, according to Patrick Stiegman, Journal Interactive editor.

Groundbreaking, award-winning sports coverage, particularly via Packer Plus Online and Badger Plus Online, is a hallmark of JS Online's Web presence. "Packer Plus epitomizes the ultimate team site," says Stiegman. "Fans can read articles, review team statistics, and discuss the Packers with fellow Cheeseheads. RealAudio interviews complete the package."

In 2000, JS Online launched an all-emcompassing, total-access portal site, OnWisconsin (www.onwisconsin.com). As both a destination and a gateway, OnWisconsin is a confluence of the three traditional media—print, audio, and video—with the added fourth dimension of interactivity.

Leading Citizen

Journal Sentinel Inc. strives to have an impact on the community by creating a paper that informs the public and guides citizens to intelligent decisions. In addition, the *Journal Sentinel* participates in more than 100 community events every year, from the Wisconsin State Fair to Waukesha's RiverFest, and contributes to dozens of charities—including Books for Kids, Camp for Kids, Golf Foundation of Wisconsin, and Heartwalk. The Newspaper in Education program promotes literacy in hundreds of classrooms across the state.

In the metro Milwaukee area, most people cling to some basic habits, like cream puffs at the state fair, opening day for the Brewers, and reading the *Journal Sentinel* for the latest news. "Wisconsin is full of color and life," Spore says. "We believe its flagship newspaper should be, too."

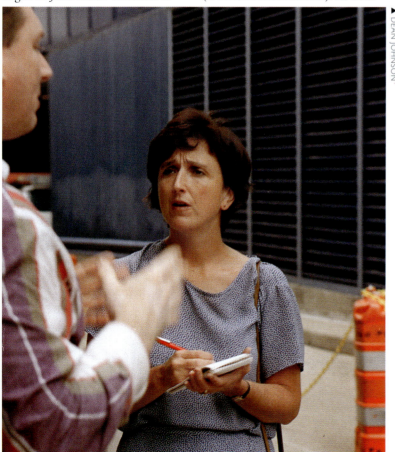

THE *JOURNAL SENTINEL*'S AWARD-WINNING REPORTERS SHINE A LIGHT ON CURRENT SOCIAL PROBLEMS AND DIG DEEPER TO INFORM READERS ABOUT UNDERCOVERED SUBJECTS (LEFT).

THE *JOURNAL SENTINEL*'S PRESSROOM CONDUCTS ONE LAST CHECK TO ENSURE THE QUALITY OF THE MORNING'S PAPER (RIGHT).

WTMJ TV

Throughout television history in the Milwaukee market, TODAY'S TMJ4 has been a pioneer leading the way in technology, news gathering, diversity, and community service. Along with the other Journal Broadcast Group Milwaukee operations properties—Newsradio 620 WTMJ and 94.5 WKTI—TODAY'S TMJ4 is one of only a handful of employee-owned television stations nationwide. The station's some 225 employees embrace a built-to-grow philosophy, along with the station's stated mission: "To provide growing audiences with excellent, relevant and targeted programming."

A Station of Firsts

Television became a part of everyday life in Milwaukee on Wednesday, December 3, 1947, when WTMJ TV's first broadcast went on the air at 8 p.m. Thousands of Milwaukeeans saw and heard the two-and-a-half-hour program over receiving sets in the lobby of the public museum and public library buildings, as well as in restaurants, bars, and private homes throughout the area. WTMJ TV was officially the 11th commercial television station in the United States and the first in the Milwaukee market.

The following year, WTMJ TV signed on as an affiliate of the NBC Television Network, and the station's first broadcast of a color television program came in 1953. Another first in the Milwaukee market occurred on July 1, 1985, when WTMJ TV began transmission of stereo sound. The current brand became part of southeastern Wisconsin's lexicon in 1992, when viewers were urged to Touch TODAY'S TMJ4.

Commitment to News

The history of WTMJ TV is steeped in a long tradition of news excellence. From its earliest years, the station set the bar for high journalistic standards and ethics. In 1948, the candidates for mayor of Milwaukee participated in a forum broadcast on WTMJ TV, a practice that continues today. In 2000, TMJ4 was the only television station in the market to broadcast a debate between the Milwaukee mayoral candidates, in a special edition of its *Sunday Night* program. The most experienced news team in Milwaukee regularly brings home to viewers the local perspective on major stories, including the Democratic and Republican national conventions and the Olympic Games.

Viewers have come to expect high-quality, diverse programming from TODAY'S TMJ4. Research indicates that TMJ4 is the station people in Milwaukee trust for coverage of major news events. From election results to severe weather to breaking news, viewers consistently tune in to TMJ4 as their primary local, national, and international news source.

As technology advances and viewers have more information resources available than ever, TMJ4 has adapted its coverage. A comprehensive Web site, www.touchtmj4.com, gives viewers complete, up-to-the-minute news and information, without having to wait for the next newscast. The Web site has proven to be a powerful tool, recording thousands of hits for special events such as election results and scores of high school sports events.

When severe weather happens, the number one place Milwaukeeans turn to is Storm Team 4, TODAY'S TMJ4's team of meteorologists. While the station's Web site is a valuable tool for alerting viewers to school and business closings that often occur during severe weather, the weather radar is the most frequently visited page on the site.

The rich news tradition of TMJ4 is rooted in its staff of dedicated journalists. TMJ4 is the news

TMJ4's Susan Kim and Mike Jacobs.

TMJ4's Mike Gousha and Carole Meekins.

· 280 ·

Milwaukee

leader in the Milwaukee market, with numerous honors to its credit, including awards from the Wisconsin Broadcasters Association, regional Emmys, and the prestigious Peabody award in 1986 for a series of Investigation 4 reports on checkered driving records of school bus drivers.

Commitment to Community

Local employee ownership has created a unique bond between TODAY'S TMJ4 and the community it serves. The station has long-standing commitments to a number of important public service campaigns. Thousands of dollars are raised each year through special programming for the Midwest Athletes Against Childhood Cancer (MACC Fund), and volunteers flock to the Wisconsin Special Olympics games in the spring through TMJ's recruitment efforts.

TMJ4's Give Us 4 campaign urges viewers to donate four hours of volunteer time during the year, while the annual Miller Lite Ride 4 the Arts helps raise funds in support of local arts groups. Groundbreaking efforts such as Stop Hunger Day and Harvest 4 the Hungry help raise food donations for people in need. TMJ4's Children's Fest is a fun-filled day of free entertainment for thousands of kids and their families each year during Milwaukee's Summerfest celebration.

As the future slowly becomes the present, TODAY'S TMJ4 is poised to continue its tradition of being the leader for southeastern Wisconsin viewers. As television entered the digital age, TMJ4 was the first commercial station in the market to broadcast digital television on Friday, November 3, 2000. Among the programs broadcast that night was *The Tonight Show with Jay Leno* at 10:35 p.m. While technology will continue to change, viewers can rely on the consistent quality, innovation, and diversity of TODAY'S TMJ4 for years into the future.

CLOCKWISE FROM TOP LEFT: TMJ4 DAYBREAK TEAM (FROM LEFT) AMY TAYLOR, MIKE MILLER, AND JIM OTT.

TMJ4 POSITIVELY MILWAUKEE REPORTER BILL TAYLOR.

4 ON YOUR SIDE CONSUMER REPORTER LYNISE WEEKS.

TMJ4 METEOROLOGISTS (FROM LEFT) PAUL JOSEPH, JIM OTT, JOHN MALAN, AND PAUL ZANDT.

TMJ4 WEEKEND REPORT COANCHORS SCOTT FRIEDMAN AND CONTESSA BREWER.

THE TMJ4 SPORTS TEAM (FROM LEFT) KEVIN HUNT, JESSIE GARCIA, DENNIS KRAUSE, AND LANCE ALLAN.

City by the Waters

WTMJ and WKTI Radio

Newsradio 620 WTMJ and 94.5 WKTI differ not only in location on the dial, but in audience and outlook. However, as parts of the Journal Broadcast Group and after years on top of the ratings, the two stations share a heritage that dwarfs the rest of the local Milwaukee radio market. Remaining true to their audience and their community has been the key to the stations' success.

Coupled with high-caliber on-air personalities at both stations, the stations' consistent quality has been rewarded with high ratings and distinguished awards. Both stations are institutions in the market, yet they are constantly evolving with their listeners.

Together, WTMJ and WKTI have more than 100 employees. The two stations share facilities with another Journal Broadcast Group institution, Channel 4, WTMJ-TV. The Journal Broadcast Group—whose parent is employee-owned Journal Communications, Inc., which also owns the *Milwaukee Journal Sentinel*—purchased nearly 35 radio stations across the country between 1997 and 2000. The Journal Broadcast Group continues to invest millions of dollars to make all of its holdings, including WTMJ and WKTI, market leaders that are committed to their community through both talk and action.

Newsradio 620 WTMJ

Newsradio 620 WTMJ dates to 1927 and the 50,000-watt powerhouse has a rich tradition as a pioneer in radio programming and technology. Its coverage area includes more than half of Wisconsin and extends from the Upper Peninsula of Michigan to south of Chicago. With few exceptions over the last 20 some years, WTMJ has consistently been the most listened-to radio station in the Milwaukee market. It has been widely recognized as the leading news/talk radio station in the area for decades, and in 2000 was honored with radio's most distinguished award, the Marconi, for the best news/talk/sports station in the country. In addition, as the flagship station for the Green Bay Packers, Milwaukee Bucks, Milwaukee Brewers, and Wisconsin Badgers, WTMJ is the longtime sports connection to Milwaukee's favorite teams.

"Compared to other local AM stations, WTMJ is more local and more diverse in what it offers—whether it's talk, news, or sports," says Jon Schweitzer, senior vice president and general manager of WTMJ and WKTI. "We offer a huge variety in forms of information and entertainment, and that's not happening anywhere else in Milwaukee."

Not only does WTMJ aim to provide a more interesting brand of talk radio, it provides an important forum for public discussion of issues vital to the community. The station's name recognition, reputation, and long-standing relationship with the community command a sense of authority and dependability. As a result, WTMJ's credibility in the marketplace may be unmatched.

Early mornings, *Wisconsin's Morning News* sets the agenda with the stories people will be talking about all day. It is the only local, live morning news program in southeastern Wisconsin. Jonathan Green's lively show, *The Green House*, is broadcast from 3 to 6 weekday

Clockwise from top:
The Newsradio 620 WTMJ Green House Gang (from left), Tom Carr, Phil Cianciola, Jonathan Green, Paul Joseph, and Len Kasper.

The Newsradio 620 WTMJ/General Motors Road Show at Lambeau Field in Green Bay.

Bob Reitman (left) and Gene Mueller comprise WKTI's morning team.

· 282 ·

Milwaukee

afternoons. And Gordon Hinkley—Wisconsin's only Hall of Fame broadcaster—is on the air Saturday mornings.

WTMJ is affiliated with the ABC Radio Information Network and the CBS Sports Radio Network. The station has a 24-hour news operation, a full staff of meteorologists, and the largest radio sports department in the state.

94.5 WKTI

The coverage area for 94.5 WKTI extends roughly from Sheboygan to south of the state line and west to Dane County. With its hot adult contemporary format, WKTI has been one of the area's most successful music stations over the last 20 some years, even winning Billboard magazine's Station of the Year award. More important, WKTI's popular personalities and promotions, including contests and money giveaways, always make it fun and entertaining for listeners to tune in every day. Personalities like Lips LaBelle, Danny Clayton, and the popular morning tag team of Bob Reitman and Gene Mueller are institutions at WKTI and in Milwaukee.

Without changing format, the station has followed its target audience, adults aged 25 to 49, by appealing to the same audience with different recording artists. Where WKTI once played Michael Jackson at the height of his popularity, now it plays current artists mixed with classic pop.

WKTI is number one in the marketplace in reaching women aged 25 to 54, and number one for all FM listeners aged 18 and up. As its original audience has grown, WKTI has likewise grown as a radio station. The result is tremendous listener loyalty: For many listeners, it's WKTI or no music radio.

But there's more than music in WKTI's special programming, from movie reviews with Gino Salomone to *Reporters Notebook* with Mueller and WTMJ-TV's Mike Jacobs. "WKTI remains intensely local," Schweitzer notes. "We don't offer a lot of programming provided by national syndicates unless there's a particular need not being met locally."

Like its sister station WTMJ, WKTI keeps its listeners entertained and informed so they can keep current on what's happening in Milwaukee. Both stations strive to always project a Milwaukee feel and attitude.

CLOCKWISE FROM TOP LEFT: JOURNAL BROADCAST GROUP HEADQUARTERS ON EAST CAPITOL DRIVE IN MILWAUKEE.

94.5 WKTI'S DANNY CLAYTON.

94.5 WKTI'S STREET STUDIO AT MILWAUKEE'S ANNUAL DINOSAUR DASH.

NEWSRADIO 620 WTMJ'S CHARLES SYKES.

City by the Waters

· 283 ·

The Archdiocese of Milwaukee

Founded in 1843 by Pope Gregory XVI, the Archdiocese of Milwaukee has continued to grow in spirit and faith for some 160 years. When a burgeoning of Catholics in Wisconsin led the bishops of the Fifth Provincial Council of Baltimore to petition the Holy See to establish a new diocese, Father Martin Kundig arranged for a tremendous showing of Catholics at Milwaukee's St. Patrick's Day parade in 1843. This showing boosted recognition of the city's rapid growth, and helped to convince decision makers that the seat of the diocese should be in Milwaukee rather than in an older, but dwindling, settlement such as Green Bay or Prairie du Chien.

A diocese is a regional church uniting local Catholic parishes under the spiritual leadership of the bishop. An archdiocese is the main diocese in a given territory. As the 21st century begins, the Most Reverend Rembert G. Weakland, O.S.B., is the archbishop of Milwaukee, and the Most Reverend Richard J. Sklba serves as the auxiliary bishop.

The Archdiocese of Milwaukee has more than 230 parishes, serving nearly 700,000 Catholics, in its 10 counties of southeastern Wisconsin. The Catholic population mirrors the rich diversity of ethnic backgrounds found in the area.

The people of the Archdiocese of Milwaukee live the gospel of Jesus Christ through word, worship, and service. An active and vibrant church, the Archdiocese of Milwaukee is known for its work in outreach ministries, social justice issues, education, and liturgy.

Religious education is a strength of the Milwaukee archdiocese. The archdiocese has 140 Catholic elementary schools and 13 Catholic high schools, serving more than 40,000 students. In addition, more than 50,000 children attend organized religious education programs throughout the archdiocese.

The bishops are the primary teachers of the faith in the archdiocese. Their teaching is reflected in their writings, homilies, and talks. In their pastoral letter titled *Eucharist without Walls: A Vision of the Church for the Year 2000*, the bishops outlined the essential message of the Catholic faith—that the Catholic Church is a eucharistic church.

The archbishop celebrates Mass each Sunday at the Cathedral of Saint John the Evangelist, and that Mass is broadcast live on radio throughout the archdiocese.

The Cathedral of Saint John the Evangelist

A cathedral symbolizes the mission of the church, and Milwaukee's Cathedral of Saint John the Evangelist serves as the mother church in the Milwaukee archdiocese, housing the archbishop's official chair, the cathedra. A place of Christian hospitality, the cathedral welcomes all and reaches out to those in need in the surrounding community.

The cathedral, more than any other parish within the archdiocese, is called to be a visible witness to the secular society of the church's compassion, concern, and advocacy for all people. It is a living image of the holiness to which the local church is called, as well as a symbol of the church's teaching ministry and moral and pastoral leadership. In these roles, the Cathedral of Saint John the Evangelist works for the poor, the homeless, the elderly, the lonely, the mentally and physically ill, students, and those overwhelmed with problems that destroy the city.

Though the cornerstone for the cathedral was laid in 1847, due to languishing funds, the building took six years to complete. The Reverend John Martine Henni, then bishop, even begged for funds in Cuba and

CLOCKWISE FROM TOP:
THE MOST REVEREND REMBERT G. WEAKLAND, O.S.B., WAS NAMED THE NINTH ARCHBISHOP OF MILWAUKEE IN 1977.

WHEN THE SANCTUARY OF THE CATHEDRAL OF SAINT JOHN THE EVANGELIST WAS DESTROYED BY FIRE IN 1935, SERVICES WERE MOVED TO THE ADJACENT HIGH SCHOOL.

MILWAUKEE'S CATHEDRAL OF SAINT JOHN THE EVANGELIST SERVES AS THE MOTHER CHURCH OF THE ARCHDIOCESE OF MILWAUKEE.

Milwaukee

Mexico. The beauty of the cathedral and the great care given to its design and upkeep over time have provided an aesthetic and prayerful environment for the people of the archdiocese.

When the cathedral's sanctuary was destroyed by fire in 1935, services were moved to the adjacent high school, bringing into clear focus the privilege of celebrating Mass in the cathedral. Catholics throughout the archdiocese responded to Archbishop Samuel Stritch's 1936 appeal for cathedral restoration funds. When the Reverend Moses E. Kiley became the new archbishop in 1940, he established a fund to complete the project by the 1943 centennial celebration of the archdiocese. Christmas Eve 1942 brought the congregation back together in the new cathedral to celebrate midnight Mass.

The Cathedral Project

The Cathedral of Saint John the Evangelist is located in downtown Milwaukee and the cathedral property covers an entire city block. In August 2000, the Archdiocese of Milwaukee announced plans to renovate the entire block and update the cathedral's interior. Some of the property and the buildings had fallen into disrepair. The Cathedral Project's goal is to restore the cathedral church and surrounding property, transforming the site into a model of prayer, worship, teaching, and social ministry for the entire community.

Planned interior renovations to the cathedral include increasing the congregation seating capacity; having barrier-free access to all parts of the cathedral complex; and installing new heating and cooling systems, as well as new sound and lighting systems. The project will restore the interior paint scheme; add a weekday chapel for daily Mass; and create space for the cathedral archive, museum, and reliquary. New liturgical furnishings will be installed, such as the altar, ambo, and baptismal font, which will all be placed in a more central location.

The project will also reshape the entire block, creating a cloistered green space to serve as a buffer zone between the sacred interior of the cathedral and the surrounding neighborhood, and a glass atrium, to be used as a gathering space.

The Archdiocese of Milwaukee's revitalized Cathedral of Saint John the Evangelist is sure to be a center of worship, culture, art, and beauty well into the 21st century.

THE ARCHDIOCESE OF MILWAUKEE HAS MORE THAN 230 PARISHES, SERVING NEARLY 700,000 CATHOLICS, IN ITS 10 COUNTIES OF SOUTHEASTERN WISCONSIN.

THE ARCHDIOCESE OF MILWAUKEE HAS A STRONG TRADITION OF CATHOLIC EDUCATION. MORE THAN 90,000 CHILDREN ATTEND CATHOLIC SCHOOLS OR RELIGIOUS EDUCATION PROGRAMS.

City by the Waters

NEW ENGLAND FINANCIAL/THE MARRIS GROUP

When William C. Marris, chartered life underwriter (CLU), joined New England Financial's franchise in Milwaukee as general agent in 1984, he found morale to be extremely low. The firm was ranked 87th out of 88 offices across the country, and the company was planning to close the office and use its Chicago agency to serve the area.

Despite this office's atrophy, the president of New England Financial at the time, John Fibiger, was a native of southeastern Wisconsin and wanted to give the Milwaukee office another chance.

Marris, a naval reserve officer, stepped up to lead the Milwaukee office and subsequently adopted a nautical theme for the company—apparent in office decor and company printed materials. It only seemed natural, as New England Financial used the historic naval vessel Old Ironsides as its emblem. In just two years, the Marris Group won the company's President's Trophy as Agency of the Year, having increased sales volume eight times in that period of time.

Diverse Products, Focused Leadership

New England Financial is one of the oldest financial services firms under continuous management in Milwaukee. The Marris Group has a franchise agreement with New England Financial, which was founded in 1835 as the nation's first chartered mutual life insurance company. Its first Wisconsin policy was sold to a Mineral Point landowner in 1844. The first Milwaukee office was founded in 1846 by Josiah Noonan, postmaster and head of the local Democratic Party.

Milwaukee native William Marris is the 10th general agent and managing partner in the line. His Marris Group now has some 125 employees and 10 offices, including Madison, Wausau, Stevens Point, and the Fox River Valley. Approximately 60 employees work in the Milwaukee area. The company is the oldest insurance agency in Wisconsin and one of the state's largest in life insurance sales. The firm also offers disability insurance, group and individual health insurance, retirement planning, security products, and long-term care insurance.

Out of approximately 80 New England offices, the Marris Group ranks number one in retirement plan sales, including pension and 401(k) plans, and ranks number three in annuities. While the Marris Group is a New England franchise, it represents the insurance and investment products of more than 300 companies. By offering diverse products from a variety of providers, plus a solid New England Financial base of products, the firm has a keen competitive advantage.

"New England Financial allows its franchises the latitude to offer products from other companies, to the benefit of our clients and sales force," Marris notes. "The Marris Group has 75 registered sales representatives who sell only our insurance and investment products. The average annual income of our agents is $110,000. Last year, we paid nearly $5 million in commissions."

New England Financial/The Marris Group has served the Milwaukee area since 1846.

Milwaukee

OUT OF APPROXIMATELY 80 NEW ENGLAND OFFICES, THE MARRIS GROUP RANKS NUMBER ONE IN RETIREMENT PLAN SALES, INCLUDING PENSION AND 401(K) PLANS, AND RANKS NUMBER THREE IN ANNUITIES.

Client-Focused Approach

Marris agents approach clients as consultants first, carefully matching solutions after ascertaining client needs. Because they offer many product lines from many providers, agents can more easily provide a custom solution rather than a one-size-fits-all approach. It is not unusual for an agent to conduct three interviews with a client before asking for a sale. By then, he or she has a clear idea of what product will be of greatest benefit.

"Our agents comprise a very professional group," Marris says. "Most have attained advanced professional designations from the industry. Our approach is long-term, building client relationships for the future. A customer purchases a product once, but a client purchases for a lifetime."

Backing up the company's sales representatives is a staff of product specialists. They typically specialize in a particular product area to develop exclusive expertise, often achieving a specific professional designation after a course of study. In this way, product specialists remain current and can provide agents with up-to-date product information.

In addition to selling its insurance and investment products, the Marris Group provides back-office support and processing, and augments the sales staffs of third-party affiliates. Twenty percent of the group's business comes from these seamlessly integrated business partnerships. For example, a large company may need assistance in distributing and maintaining its employee pension or disability benefits. The Marris Group can step in and provide a turnkey solution.

Valued Relationships

A golden age has followed the mid-1990s merger of Metropolitan Life with New England Financial. But in the early 1990s, New England Financial went through some difficulties, losing many agents around the country. However, the Marris Group lost virtually no one. Marris attributes that, in part, to the positive corporate culture at the firm's Wisconsin offices. Employee turnover remains very low, and the company added 30 percent more office space in 2000. The firm continues to expand operations throughout the state, largely by increasing business with existing clients by solving multiple needs.

"I'm a hands-off manager," Marris says. "I believe in forming a strong team and allowing members to succeed. I view my position almost as the mayor of a small town that includes not just employees, but their families as well. On any given day, there will be life-changing events as in a small town—a birth, a death, an illness. They affect all of us to some degree. Relationships with our employees, as well as with our clients, are extremely important to us."

With a strong focus on long-term relationships—both with valued clients and within its team of company professionals—the Marris Group has positioned itself for future growth within the Milwaukee area and beyond.

City by the Waters

· 287 ·

Columbia-St. Mary's, Inc.

THE 1995 JOINT AGREEMENT BETWEEN COLUMBIA HOSPITAL and St. Mary's Hospital joined two renowned Milwaukee health care institutions with a combined total of more than 350 years of providing quality health care services to the community. Today, Columbia-St. Mary's, Inc. is a comprehensive health care network committed to serving the needs of individuals and families in Milwaukee and Ozaukee counties.

Columbia-St. Mary's programs and services are readily accessible, at a reasonable cost, to all those who seek them, and equal attention is focused on the physical, spiritual, and emotional dimensions of health and wellness. Each year, the company serves more than 140,000 individuals through clinic and outpatient visits, as well as community outreach and education programs; approximately 35,000 patients are seen during hospital inpatient visits.

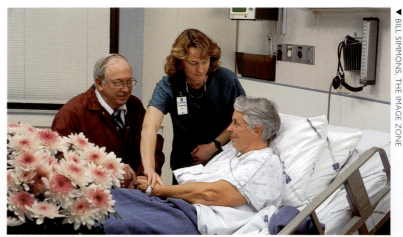

A Combined History of Service

Columbia-St. Mary's, which also includes Sacred Heart Rehabilitation Institute and St. Mary's Hospital Ozaukee, represents a joint effort of some of the finest medical institutions in the Greater Milwaukee area.

St. Mary's Hospital of Milwaukee, the state's first private hospital, celebrated its 150th anniversary in 1998. Bishop John Martin Henni contacted the Sisters of Charity in Maryland in 1848, asking them to come to Milwaukee, where they founded St. Mary's Hospital. The new facility filled a great need in the fledgling community. When it opened in 1959, St. Mary's Regional Burn Center was one of the first in the country, and today, the center is still the only one of its kind in the eastern half of the state; its physicians and staff continue to be pioneers in the care and treatment of patients with burn injuries.

In 1909, a small group of physicians and community leaders founded Columbia Hospital to provide additional patient care, and to encourage medical research and education. Columbia Hospital's Department of Orthopedics is one of the outstanding specialties that grew out of that forward-thinking tradition of medical excellence. Services and facilities offered by the four-campus Columbia Musculoskeletal Institute include spine treatments, rehabilitation services, an arthritis center, a pain management center, a sports medicine program, and a work fitness center to prevent and treat work-related injuries.

Mother Alexia of the School Sisters of St. Francis founded Sacred Heart Rehabilitation Institute in 1893 as an 18-bed sanitarium for patients with chronic and noninfectious diseases. Today, Sacred Heart physicians and staff offer comprehensive specialty programs for the rehabilitation of patients with brain injuries, coma, stroke, neuromuscular disorders, spinal cord and orthopedic injuries, and pediatric disorders and injuries.

St. Mary's Hospital Ozaukee was rebuilt in Mequon in 1994 to better serve the Ozaukee County community. The hospital provides patients and their families with a wide range of community-oriented inpatient and outpatient services, as well as emergency medical care services. Programs include a birthing center, a cancer center, and behavioral medicine services. St. Mary's Hospital Ozaukee, like all of the members of Columbia-St. Mary's, also supports the community through a variety of outreach efforts and programs aimed at caring for those in greatest need, while encouraging volunteerism among physicians and employees.

All told, Columbia-St. Mary's has about 4,500 employees and a medical staff of almost 1,000 physicians.

NURSES AT COLUMBIA-ST. MARY'S, INC. ENJOY A WELL-EARNED REPUTATION FOR EXCELLENCE AND COMPASSION (TOP).

THE PHYSICIANS AND STAFF OF COLUMBIA-ST. MARY'S DELIVER APPROXIMATELY 4,500 BABIES EACH YEAR, AND HAVE PROVIDED OBSTETRICS CARE LONGER THAN ANY OTHER HOSPITAL IN WISCONSIN (BOTTOM).

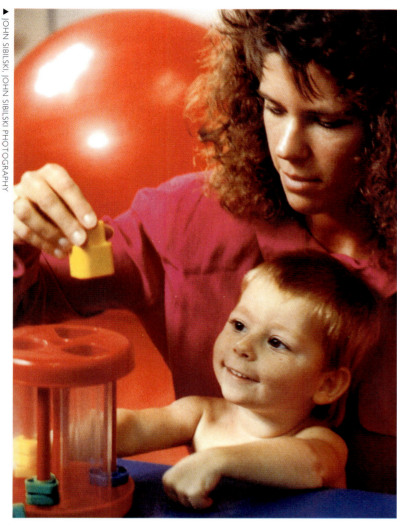

"Together, we are working to maintain our focus on quality patient care and medical innovation as we grow to meet the future needs of the community," says John F. Schuler, president and CEO. "With our mission and our core values guiding our efforts, our vision is to become the leading health care provider in southeast Wisconsin."

Charitable financial support for Columbia-St. Mary's is provided through the efforts of St. Mary's Foundation Milwaukee, Columbia Foundation, and St. Mary's Foundation Ozaukee. Columbia Health System and Ascension Health continue as the parent sponsoring organizations of Columbia-St. Mary's.

Additional Columbia-St. Mary's Services

Columbia-St. Mary's consists of more than hospitals and clinics. Columbia-St. Mary's Community Physicians, the largest primary care physician group in metro Milwaukee, includes 24 local community clinics and offices throughout Milwaukee and Ozaukee counties. Ninety percent of the 100 physicians specialize in primary care.

Mequon Care Center, established in 1970, is a Medicare-certified, 154-bed facility for short- and long-term care. Rehabilitation services include comprehensive physical, occupational, speech, and respiratory therapy programs, all geared to meet the individual needs of residents and their families.

Columbia College of Nursing dates back to 1901 and has been affiliated with Columbia Hospital since 1909. The college is currently affiliated with more than 50 clinical sites as well. In 1983, Columbia College of Nursing and Carroll College joined faculties and facilities to offer an intercollegiate baccalaureate degree program. Approximately 60 nurses graduate from the college annually.

Columbia-St. Mary's also supports two family practice residency programs, an obstetrics residency program, and a wide variety of major specialty medical programs, including cardiology, cardiac surgery, orthopedics, oncology, obstetrics, inpatient and outpatient surgery, pulmonary medicine, behavioral medicine, and treatment programs for patients with arthritis and diabetes.

Bringing It All Together

Columbia-St. Mary's continues to redefine its role in serving the community by focusing on the needs of its patients. "We will continue to spend our time, efforts, and resources to be sure that our patients and prospective patients see us as a superior health care choice," Schuler says. "As our mission states, we are here, first and always, to 'make a positive difference in the health status and lives of our community with special concern for those who are vulnerable.'"

PEDIATRIC REHABILITATION IS ONE SUBSPECIALTY OF COLUMBIA-ST. MARY'S COMPREHENSIVE REHABILITATION PROGRAM, WHICH ALSO INCLUDES THE CARE OF PATIENTS WITH STROKE, BRAIN INJURY, NEUROMUSCULAR DISORDERS, NEUROSPINAL DISORDERS AND INJURIES, AND ORTHOPEDIC CONDITIONS.

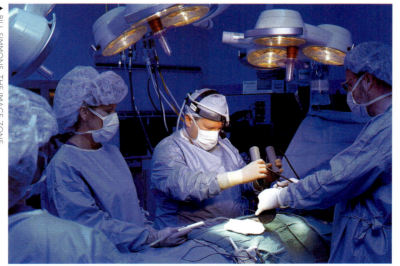

SURGEONS AT COLUMBIA-ST. MARY'S EXCEL IN MANY AREAS, INCLUDING CARDIOTHORACIC, MINIMALLY INVASIVE, GYNECOLOGICAL, ORTHOPEDIC, BURN, AND GENERAL SURGERY. SUPPORT STAFF, HIGHLY SKILLED IN A WIDE VARIETY OF SPECIALTIES, COMPLETE THE SURGICAL CARE TEAMS.

City by the Waters

Miller Brewing Company

WHILE HE MIGHT NOT HAVE BEEN DESCRIBED IN SUCH TERMS in the mid-1800s, history makes it clear that Frederick J. Miller, who founded Miller Brewing Company in 1855, was indeed a visionary. ■ Miller's vision took him far from his homeland in Germany, where he had learned to brew beer under the tutelage of European masters. It has been speculated that after Miller arrived in Milwaukee by way of New York, he made his decision to stay in this burgeoning Great Lakes city in large part because of its outstanding water supply and the abundance of locally grown grain—two key ingredients in brewing beer.

Miller was a strong-minded, no-nonsense man who believed in sound principles and lived by them. The unofficial motto of the Miller Brewing Company—Quality, Uncompromising and Unchanging—may well have its roots in Miller's attitude, because he carried that philosophy into every aspect of his business. His distaste for wastefulness and his willingness to reuse supplies marked him as an environmentalist long before the term became a household word.

Miller's interest in civic activity and his desire to make a difference in his adopted community of Milwaukee set Miller Brewing Company on a course from which it has not wavered in nearly 150 years.

From a simple 1850s wooden building on the western ridge of the city of Milwaukee, Miller Brewing Company has grown to become the second-largest brewer in the United States, and sixth largest in the world. The Milwaukee brewery is the oldest continuously operating brewery of its size in the nation. Miller produces more than 40 million barrels

IN 1855, GERMAN IMMIGRANT FREDERICK J. MILLER BOUGHT THE PLANK ROAD BREWERY IN THE MENOMONEE VALLEY, WEST OF THE CITY OF MILWAUKEE. IN HIS FIRST YEAR OF OPERATION, HE PRODUCED 300 BARRELS OF BEER. MILLER'S FRIENDS AND FAMILY WERE THE FIRST EMPLOYEES OF MILLER BREWING COMPANY.

WHEN THIS PHOTO WAS TAKEN IN ABOUT 1875, MILLER'S WORKFORCE HAD GROWN AND HIS BEER HAD BECOME ONE OF MILWAUKEE'S BEST-KNOWN BREWS. MILLER (FIRST ROW, FOURTH FROM THE LEFT), PROVIDED AN ENVIRONMENT WHERE WORKERS WERE NOT ONLY PAID, BUT OFTEN HOUSED AND FED. BY 1887, THE BREWERY WAS KNOWN AS THE FREDERICK MILLER BREWING COMPANY, A NAME IT WAS CALLED UNTIL 1927.

Milwaukee

MILLER'S KEY PARTNERS IN THE SALE OF ITS PRODUCTS ARE ITS DISTRIBUTORS. WORKING CLOSELY WITH A NETWORK OF NEARLY 500 DISTRIBUTORS, MILLER PROVIDES HIGH-QUALITY PRODUCTS TO CONSUMERS NATIONWIDE.

of beer annually, and more than one of every five beers consumed in the domestic market bears a Miller brand name.

While Miller now operates seven breweries in seven states and has a presence in more than 100 countries throughout the world, the Miller story begins and continues because of Milwaukee. The two are bound together in a relationship that has weathered crises, celebrated victories, survived two world wars and the Depression, made it through Prohibition, and endured other setbacks that may have dimmed, but have never shut out, the bright light generated by this city and the company that calls this city home.

Miller made its worldwide name on the strength of its great products. But locally, the company has become well known not only for making beer, but also for making a difference in the place where its employees live and work. Miller's history is rich in community involvement—still another legacy it inherited from its founder and chose to build upon.

No matter where you look in the city today, there is a good chance you will see the mark Miller has made on the Milwaukee community. From the company's multimillion-dollar investment in the Miller Park™ baseball stadium; to the annual Miller Lite Ride for the Arts™ in support of the United Performing Arts Fund™; to its sponsorship of sports teams and events, Summerfest™, the Wisconsin State Fair, and local programs to promote responsible drinking, combat domestic violence, encourage literacy, and fight hunger, it is clear that Miller puts its money—and its time—where its heart is: right here at home.

MILLER'S FAMILY OF BRANDS HAS BEEN DEVELOPED TO APPEAL TO THE TASTES AND PREFERENCES OF A WIDE RANGE OF LEGAL-AGE CONSUMERS. CORE BRANDS ARE MILLER LITE, MILLER GENUINE DRAFT, AND MILLER HIGH LIFE. IN ADDITION, MILLER ACQUIRED ITS PARTNER BREWERY, THE JACOB LEINENKUGEL BREWING CO. OF CHIPPEWA FALLS, WISCONSIN, IN 1988. MILLER ALSO HOLDS THE AMERICAN DISTRIBUTION RIGHTS TO FOSTER'S LAGER, AN AUSTRALIAN BEER.

Milwaukee . . . and the World

It has been said that when Frederick J. Miller arrived in Milwaukee, he had two things in his possession: cash in his pocket

City by the Waters · 291 ·

The Miller Lite Ride for the Arts™, held annually in early June, supports Milwaukee's United Performing Arts Fund™. The ride serves as the unofficial kickoff to a busy summer of festivals, fairs, and outdoor music events. Support for the arts is one of Miller's signature initiatives.

Miller displays its commitment to higher education through its support of the Thurgood Marshall Scholarship Fund, which provides merit-based scholarships to students attending the nation's historically black public colleges and universities. Miller President and CEO John Bowlin (left) and Executive Vice President Virgis Colbert (right) present a contribution to Dwayne Ashley, executive director of the fund.

and a burning ambition. He knew how to brew excellent beer and was willing to do anything to make that happen.

Miller purchased a fledgling operation, the Plank Road Brewery —a name Miller retains to this day—and was soon turning out beer for a very obliging population. Within a few decades, his brewery had gained wide-reaching acclaim and had expanded its operations beyond the city borders. Three generations of family members— and most prominently Frederick C. Miller, who died in a plane accident in 1954—put Miller Brewing Company on the national map.

In 1969 and 1970, Philip Morris acquired Miller. No stranger to success itself, Philip Morris was to add its renowned marketing muscle to the strong work ethic of Miller employees. Within 10 years, Miller Brewing Company had leaped from the eighth to the second-largest brewing company in the country. Innovative products such as Miller Lite, introduced in 1975, not only changed Miller, but fundamentally altered the industry in which the company competes. Today, the low-calorie beer segment, pioneered by Miller more than a quarter century ago, is the fastest-growing category in the beer industry. Other product innovations, such as the packaged draft category and the ice beer category, are the direct result of Miller product introductions.

Today, Miller's inventive marketing efforts have made the company a major player in the brewing business. The brewer has been able to leverage relationships with NFL football, Major League Baseball, NASCAR™, CART™ and NHRA™ auto racing, NBA™ basketball, and NHL™ hockey to give it a powerful presence in the world of professional sports, providing a direct entrance into a key consumer market. Miller has developed strategies that offer its retail partners the methods they can use to sell beer more profitably. Exciting consumer music promotions have been successful on local, national, and international levels. A recent packaging innovation–

Milwaukee

MILLER BEERS ARE PRODUCED WITH TOP-QUALITY INGREDIENTS AND SPECIAL ATTENTION TO DETAIL. QUALITY CHECKS BEGIN WITH SAMPLING AND ANALYZING EVERY SHIPMENT OF BARLEY, HOPS, AND OTHER INGREDIENTS THAT ARE USED IN MILLER BEERS. THROUGHOUT THE BREWING, FERMENTING, FILTERING, AND PACKAGING PROCESSES, THOUSANDS OF QUALITY CHECKS ENSURE THAT NOTHING BUT THE BEST PRODUCT REACHES THE CONSUMER.

the plastic beer bottle—was met with overwhelming consumer acceptance. Once again, Miller is on the forefront of change, and is ready for it.

Miller's worldwide presence has captured the imagination and interest of beer drinkers from Ireland to Brazil, and from Germany to Taiwan. Currently, Miller brands hold number one American import positions in Germany, Mexico, the Republic of Ireland, and South Korea. Partnerships with breweries in Europe, the Middle East, and the Pacific Rim have enabled Miller to bring the fresh taste of its brands to a whole new world of beer drinkers.

As a result, Miller has made an indelible imprint on the international brewing business, and has given new life and potential to the dream of a young brewmaster in 1855.

Taking a Stand

If Frederick J. Miller was anything, he was responsible. Personal responsibility was a trait he not only cultivated in himself, but encouraged in his employees as well. The idea of responsibility is a seed

well planted at Miller; today, the company approaches many issues with the notion that making sensible choices and living by them is essential.

Nowhere is that more evident than in Miller's corporate responsibility initiatives. The company's product is a beverage rich in history and tradition; it is used to celebrate many of life's most important events, to mark occasions that bear remembering. But no matter where beer is consumed, personal responsibility is a necessary part of the enjoyment. In the same way Miller encourages consumers to make informed choices and drink responsibly, so are its employees committed to brewing and marketing beer responsibly and supporting responsible consumption and alcohol awareness efforts. This is a mission shared wholeheartedly by Miller distributors and retailers.

Miller has made it a serious priority to be part of the solution to end drunk driving and underage drinking. The company has taken the lead for more than 20 years in stressing the importance of drinking responsibly. In addition to the national Think When You Drink™ advertising campaign, Miller has offered its full support to a wide range of responsible drinking programs and materials for consumers, distributors, and retailers.

A chief concern at Miller is the fight to stop underage drinking. Materials such as *Let's Talk: A Family Guide to Making Responsible Choices* serve as templates parents can use when they talk to their children about alcohol issues and responsible behavior. Other materials have been developed for distributors and

MILLER'S WORKFORCE IS MADE UP OF PEOPLE FROM ALL WALKS OF LIFE WHO HELP REPRESENT THE COMMUNITIES OF THE CUSTOMERS IT SERVES. MILLER BELIEVES THAT BY WORKING WITH PEOPLE OF ALL BACKGROUNDS, THE COMPANY CAN BETTER SERVE ITS CUSTOMERS.

City by the Waters

retailers to give them the tools they need to discuss appropriate methods for serving beer.

What's more, the company has created specific programs to help retailers serve beer with maximum responsibility. Wait staff training, ID checking, and other programs are all designed to ensure safe, responsible beer consumption. Miller sponsors safe-ride-home programs, and provides responsible drinking materials for law enforcement officers and college representatives. In short, the company is setting the standards for alcohol enjoyment, and is setting them high.

The people at Miller believe these initiatives go a great distance toward improving the quality of life for those who have chosen to enjoy its products. Beer is clearly a part of the company's heritage, but so is responsibility, and Miller takes both of these factors very seriously.

Responsible behavior involves many directions. Miller has also made it part of the company's corporate profile to be a steward for the environment. For more than 25 years, Miller has pursued an aggressive recycling program that today can boast that just about everything, from hard hats to the byproducts of the brewing process itself, is recycled. Miller's environmental and energy programs have yielded benefits in all company operations.

For example, the company has reduced the thickness of cans and bottles to save raw materials and reduce reprocessing activities. Miller has also achieved significant reductions in the amount of water it uses through conservation and re-engineering programs. From 1997 to 2000, water consumption dropped nearly 9 percent. In Milwaukee, the brewery has reduced emissions of greenhouse gases by 29,000 tons.

Frederick J. Miller always insisted on careful reuse of as many materials as possible. Today, his company takes him as seriously as ever.

The Milwaukee-Miller Connection

Perhaps because Miller and Milwaukee are joined together in so many ways, it seems natural that the company and the community would find opportunities to support each other. Milwaukee has given Miller some of the finest employees available anywhere, and, in return, those employees have seen fit to give back to their community whenever possible. Whether it is a program to help youngsters improve their reading, or an effort to improve inner-city housing conditions, or the opportunity to make the holiday season a bit brighter with gifts for children, volunteerism is as much a part of the day for Miller employees as coming to work.

Beyond these efforts, Miller serves as a corporate sponsor for many community organizations. The company is involved in social justice initiatives, job-training efforts, the fight against hunger, and programs to end domestic abuse. Miller has developed partnerships with organizations in Milwaukee—and with other cities where its employees live and work—to improve the quality of life. Some of Miller's long-standing initiatives include TOOLS FOR SUCCESS™, a program that gives technical school graduates the tools, technology, and support they need to get jobs, and FIGHTING HUNGER, which supports today's hunger relief efforts and contributes to future hunger prevention.

If there is one thing the people of Miller Brewing Company have learned during the past some 150 years, it is that people work best when they work together.

Miller: A Great Place to Work

In his first year of operation, Miller employed only a handful of people. So no doubt he would be shocked to find that today the Miller workforce is greater than 6,000 people in locations throughout the world. Miller has long enjoyed

MILLER HAS TAKEN A STRONG STAND IN SUPPORT OF RESPONSIBLE DRINKING. PROGRAMS SUCH AS MILLER FREE RIDES™, WHICH PROVIDES FREE BUS RIDES FOR THE PUBLIC ON NEW YEAR'S EVE AND ST. PATRICK'S DAY, HAVE BEEN MET WITH GREAT PUBLIC SUPPORT IN MILWAUKEE AND OTHER CITIES.

a reputation as a good employer, offering not only an excellent salary and benefits package, but professional growth opportunities that give employees both the responsibility to do the job and the support to do it well. While expectations are high, so are the rewards. And the facts make that point clear: Miller's workforce is solid, with some employees choosing to spend the bulk of their careers with the company.

Along with its employee base, Miller considers its network of nearly 500 distributors as strategic partners in the beer business. Distributors located throughout the country serve as the first contact for retailers obtaining Miller brands. As such, they represent a key constituency, a very important part of the way the company does business.

Developing a diverse workforce that represents the consumers it serves is a high priority at Miller. Since consumers come from all walks of life, it makes good business sense to create a workforce that represents that diversity. Miller has found that the more its employees are like its consumers, the better the company can understand its consumer base and what they expect. Ultimately, that means Miller can serve consumers better.

Living Out the Promise

Nearly 150 years. Seven breweries. Dozens of national and international offices. And thousands of employees. By virtue of its numbers alone, Miller Brewing Company is a fixture on the business landscape. Its brands have made it a worldwide name, and each year, more and more consumers come to identify Miller with great tasting beers, exciting marketing programs, good times, and great fun. Tours are available for visitors six days a week through the Miller Visitor Center to allow consumers to see the work involved in the production of Miller products.

But that's only part of the picture. The greater picture is one that includes a respect for the place this company came from, and a sense of where it needs to go to live out its promise in the future. Its future depends as heavily upon its shared mission as it did when Frederick J. Miller turned out that first barrel of beer a century and a half ago.

Whether it is a better brewing process, a smarter marketing plan, a stronger stand on responsibility issues, or a more tender approach to those who need help, the people of Miller Brewing Company know what they need to do to fulfill the promise Miller made to himself, to his employees, and to Milwaukee all those years ago.

"Quality, Uncompromising and Unchanging." It is a vow renewed every day, a motto etched not only on wooden carvings, but in the minds of the people who make this company what it is. Today, it is Miller's promise to Milwaukee– a promise each employee intends to keep.

A CHIEF CONCERN AT MILLER IS THE FIGHT TO STOP UNDERAGE DRINKING. MATERIALS SUCH AS *LET'S TALK: A FAMILY GUIDE TO MAKING RESPONSIBLE CHOICES* SERVE AS TEMPLATES PARENTS CAN USE WHEN THEY TALK TO THEIR CHILDREN ABOUT ALCOHOL ISSUES AND RESPONSIBLE BEHAVIOR.

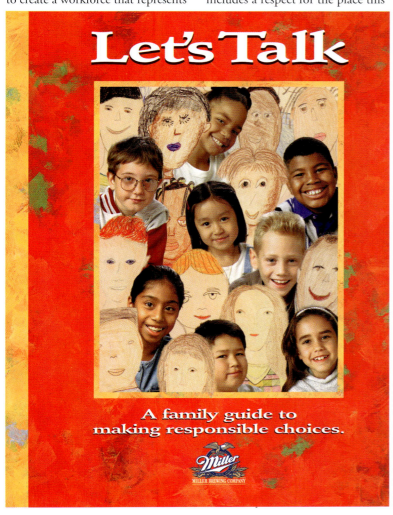

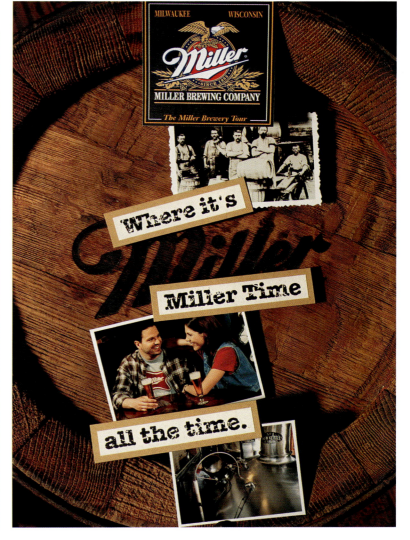

City by the Waters

· 295 ·

© JOHN J. BACIK III

1858-1896

1858
The F. Dohmen Co.

1858
YMCA of Metropolitan Milwaukee

1867
Vilter Manufacturing Corporation

1868
Catholic Family Life Insurance

1884
P&H Mining Equipment

1889
Emmpak Foods, Inc.

1894
Children's Hospital of Wisconsin

1896
Wisconsin Energy Corporation

THE F. DOHMEN CO.

When Frederick Dohmen helped found The F. Dohmen Co.—then known as Dohmen, Schmitt and Company—in 1858, he never imagined that it would one day be among the oldest wholesale pharmaceutical distributors in North America. One of three young German immigrants who established the company with an initial investment of just $400, Dohmen bought his friends out of the company when Schmitt returned to Germany and Meissner, the third founder, withdrew from the business.

The respect this wholesale pharmaceutical and health and beauty aid distributor has gained from customers is a direct result of ethical business practices, as well as a sincere interest in seeing customers use Dohmen's industry-leading services to become more successful. With more than 450 employees, The F. Dohmen Co. is one of the few U.S. companies in its field that can claim continuous family ownership and operation across five generations.

While other distribution companies tend to dwell on mission statements, company credos, and marketing philosophies, The F. Dohmen Co. Strategic Intent challenges each employee at every level. Using innovation as its guide, the company is dedicated to providing customers with value-added service and products.

Serving in Many Ways

Continuing its legacy as a leading supplier, The F. Dohmen Co. now comprises numerous divisions: jASCorp, PharmaSelect, Dohmen Medical, RESTAT, Comprehensive Pharmaceutical Services, DDN/Obergfel, Walsh Dohmen Southeast LLC, and Dot Connect.

jASCorp is an open-concept technology provider offering interfaces to specialty health care products and services. jASCorp's innovative solutions are designed as affordable packages that avoid large, up-front capital expenditures. Each jASCorp product or design is infused with the company's total commitment to quality.

PharmaSelect, located in Narragansett, Rhode Island, views its most important objective as increasing corporate sales and profits through multidivisional marketing, while simultaneously enhancing the customer service it extends to its clients. As a culmination of many years of acquiring business knowledge in the delivery of health services to manufacturers, PharmaSelect is in the distinctive position of having access to resources from its many operating systems, allowing it to offer a unique combination of experience and approach.

Supplying brand-name and private-label products, Dohmen Medical—located in Richfield, Wisconsin—fulfills its customers' specific needs. Among the product categories available through Dohmen Medical are skin care, wound care, diabetic supplies, needles and syringes, and a wide array of nursing supplies.

Since its founding in 1985, RESTAT has maintained the philosophy that the customer always

Frederick Dohmen was one of three German immigrants who founded The F. Dohmen Co.—then known as Dohmen, Schmitt and Company—in 1858.

Milwaukee

CONTINUING ITS LEGACY AS A LEADING SUPPLIER, THE F. DOHMEN CO. (TOP RIGHT) NOW COMPRISES NUMEROUS DIVISIONS, INCLUDING JASCORP (TOP LEFT) AND RESTAT (BOTTOM).

comes first. As one of the first prescription benefit managers to offer a flexible benefit plan, RESTAT boasts a client list that includes insurance companies, managed health care organizations, third-party administrators, pharmacy provider groups, private-label marketers, and self-funded employers. More than 2.5 million people are now served by RESTAT.

With offices in Germantown, Wisconsin; Memphis; and Vernon, California, DDN/Obergfel works closely with logistics professionals to offer cost savings to supply chain management programs. The success of its programs is guaranteed through simplified distribution services, reduced operating costs, maximized profitability, and exceptional customer service.

Walsh Dohmen Southeast LLC, located in the Pinson Valley area of Birmingham, Alabama, was the first company ever formed by linking wholesale distribution firms and a pharmaceutical buying group. The company formed when John Dohmen, president of The F. Dohmen Co., and Ron Nelson, president of Walsh Distribution Inc., joined with the Alabama Pharmacy Cooperative Inc. to form a regional alternative for pharmaceutical availability after a local drug chain sold its operations to a larger, national corporation.

Dot Connect links retail pharmacies to consumers, pharmaceutical companies, and third-party processors, assisting customers with strategic delivery of products and services. Combining advanced information technologies with health care expertise, Dot Connect provides its clients with the same technological and cost-saving benefits enjoyed by large pharmacy providers.

Keeping the Tradition Alive

Over time, The F. Dohmen Co. has achieved great success with small amounts of self-promotion, concentrating its efforts on anticipating the changing needs of customers while earning their loyalty and respect. The management team adheres to very basic values—truth, compassion, commitment to each other, and a shared sense of responsibility for the entire company—that continue to drive success in meeting the company's long-term goals.

The success of those who rely on The F. Dohmen Co. every day remains the company's number one objective. This success results from many new ideas, innovative programs, and technological tools that deliver outstanding value to customers across the health care spectrum.

The most rewarding challenge for The F. Dohmen Co. is anticipating customer needs and developing solutions to strengthen the company's customers and clients. Keeping this family tradition alive, The F. Dohmen Co. is moving ahead, keeping its place as a unique, family-owned and -operated wholesale pharmaceutical distributor. World-class services, evolving technologies, and constantly expanding product offerings represent the company's commitment to both the present and the future.

YMCA OF METROPOLITAN MILWAUKEE

Originally founded as the Young Men's Christian Association, the YMCA of Metropolitan Milwaukee is part of a larger nonreligious, nondenominational organization located in more than 120 countries and serving an estimated 30 million people. Offering opportunities for people of all ages to build character and values, the organization's mission reads simply "to put Christian principles into practice through programs that build healthy spirit, mind, and body for all."

Organized locally in 1858, the YMCA has its first building on North Fourth Street, just south of Grand Avenue. As it continues to grow every year, the organization now has a YMCA branch or program site within a 10-minute traveling distance of all Milwaukee residents. As a nonprofit, charitable organization, the YMCA derives more than 84 percent of its budget from membership and program fees, while the remaining 15 percent comes from contributed revenue. The YMCA of Metropolitan Milwaukee is one of the largest and most successful metropolitan YMCAs in the country.

Serving the Community

Operating 22 full-service facilities—including three camps, seven full-day child care centers, and 12 membership branches and program centers—the YMCA delivers both traditional and innovative programs to more than 140,000 residents of the metro Milwaukee area. The Milwaukee YMCA employs more then 2,500 people.

As well as offering the best of traditional YMCA programs, the Milwaukee YMCA is constantly developing new programs to meet the unique needs of the communities it serves. In 1996, the Milwaukee YMCA committed to better serve central city youth and families through enhanced facilities and programs. The City Agenda, as it was called, surpassed its original goals, becoming a valuable source for the families and communities of Milwaukee. Signature programs of the City Agenda include YMCA Youth Volunteer Corps, Black Achievers in Business and Industry, Milwaukee Mentors, One on One Mentoring, Safe Places, Sponsor-A-Scholar, Youth City Fun Card, Youth in Government, and the Youth Leadership Academy.

When more than 2,500 families turned to the YMCA for child care in 1998, the organization became the largest not-for-profit provider in the state of Wisconsin. That same year, membership reached an all-time high of 30,582 units, or 75,584 people.

John C. Cudahy YMCA

When local business leader and philanthropist Michael Cudahy donated 55 acres of land and a challenge grant to build a YMCA where he grew up, it was decided that the center would be named after his father, John C. Cudahy, a former attorney and U.S. ambassador to Ireland. This new YMCA reflects Cudahy's commitment to the arts and firm belief that, through the arts, children and families can grow stronger in spirit, mind, and body.

Opened in June 2000, the John C. Cudahy YMCA blends traditional YMCA activities with the arts. Many different features are available, such as a state-of-the-art child care center, outdoor pool, soccer field and scenic trails, outdoor amphitheater, music and dance practice rooms, arts-focused day camps, and youth super sports.

The $5.5 million project is the first of its kind in YMCA history. The site of the facility was a former Cudahy homestead, and features woods, wetlands, and fields that present unlimited options for environmental exploration and outdoor fun.

As well as offering the best of traditional YMCA programs, the YMCA of Metropolitan Milwaukee is constantly developing new programs to meet the unique needs of the communities it serves.

Extensive Programs, Extending Membership

YMCA leadership is deeply rooted within the community, with more than 3,000 volunteers forming its backbone. Members of the executive board of directors and the branch boards of managers are all dedicated volunteers with a strong sense of responsibility for the quality of life in their communities. While working together, YMCA volunteers, financial contributors, members, and professional staff determine the program direction and policies of the facilities.

Along with its association offices, there are 12 branches and program centers and three camps in the YMCA of Metropolitan Milwaukee. Camp Matawa is located in Campbellsport, Camp Minikani in Hubertus, and Triangle Y Ranch in West Bend. The YMCA Southtown Center and Holton Youth Center are located in Milwaukee. Among the membership branches are the West Suburban Branch in Wauwatosa; Tri-County Branch in Menomonee Falls; Southwest Branch in Greenfield; South Shore Branch in Cudahy; Schroeder Branch and Aquatic Center in Brown Deer; Feith Family Ozaukee Branch in Port Washington; and the John C. Cudahy, Parklawn, North Central, and Downtown branches in Milwaukee.

For those who are unable to afford the membership and program dues, the YMCA offers scholarships so that no person is turned away due to an inability to pay. The Strong Kids Scholarship Program provides those in need with support to participate in activities at the YMCA. Community volunteers raise program funds in an annual campaign, with more than 11,000 donors contributing.

Becoming involved with the YMCA means being part of an organization committed to building strong kids, families, and communities. Providing children with the skills and values necessary for successful adulthood, the YMCA protects the integrity of family life by fostering togetherness and responsible parenting. Placing emphasis on each person as a whole throughout the programs and activities develops healthy spirit, mind, and body in all who participate. For thousands of people, the YMCA of Metropolitan Milwaukee is a foundation, a haven, and an inspiration.

THE JOHN C. CUDAHY YMCA BLENDS TRADITIONAL YMCA ACTIVITIES WITH THE ARTS AND HAS MANY DIFFERENT FEATURES AVAILABLE, INCLUDING AN OUTDOOR POOL (LEFT).

THE YMCA FINDS INNOVATIVE WAYS TO REACH MORE THAN 140,000 RESIDENTS OF THE METRO MILWAUKEE AREA (RIGHT).

BECOMING INVOLVED WITH THE YMCA MEANS BEING PART OF AN ORGANIZATION COMMITTED TO BUILDING STRONG KIDS, FAMILIES, AND COMMUNITIES.

VILTER MANUFACTURING CORPORATION

In 1867—in the days when the only source of ice was frozen lakes—Vilter Manufacturing Corporation was established by Peter Weisel and Ernst Vilter. Carefully stored below ground in caves or icehouses, ice lasted through the rest of the year; however, a warm winter could result in ice shortages. It was during a particularly warm winter in 1879 that Vilter modified a steam engine to drive a compressor to make ice. Soon, there was a huge demand for this so-called artificial ice, particularly from local breweries and slaughterhouses.

Vilter Manufacturing originally supplied steam engines to local industries, but by 1882, the company was producing a horizontal compressor driven by a steam engine that was more efficient than its vertical compressor counterparts. The age of industrial refrigeration had begun.

Leading the Industry

Vilter equipment is used throughout the world, from the smallest cold storage room to huge food processing operations. Vilter is relied upon to satisfy the sophisticated cooling needs of the petrochemical and pharmaceutical industries as well. Ice rink operators use Vilter equipment to produce high-quality skating surfaces for hockey games, ice shows, and recreational use, such as Milwaukee's Bradley Center arena and Petit Center Olympic Speed Skating Training Facility. Whenever dependable, high-performance refrigeration is needed, Vilter's goal is to provide it.

As refrigeration technology has evolved, Vilter has always been at the forefront, whether utilizing steam, petrochemicals, natural gas, methane gas, microchip science, or other advances to produce refrigeration equipment. The company has five main product lines: compression equipment; industrial air-handling units; vessels, such as heat exchangers and oil separators; complex package systems that include everything from evaporators to compressors; and electrical computer control systems. The company also markets products under private label partnerships.

"Vilter is recognized around the world as the gold standard of refrigeration equipment," says Paul Szymaszek, president and CEO. "We sell our products based on demonstrable value. Throughout the life of our equipment, the customer will realize lower maintenance and energy costs, and, most important, fewer equipment failures. Companies that seek the best come to Milwaukee and come to Vilter."

Continual Innovation

A string of successes has followed the company right from the beginning. In 1910, the Santa Fe railroad contracted with Vilter to design an ice-making, precooling plant to produce 225 tons of ice needed to chill 150 carloads of fruit daily. In 1917, General John Pershing and the War Department needed a 500-ton ice plant to store 5,000 tons of beef for the troops in Europe. Vilter built it. During World War II, the company built pack ice machines for use in steamships moving foodstuffs to troops in both Europe and the Pacific.

In 1945, Vilter introduced the VMC 440 reciprocating compressor, which quickly became the refrigeration industry standard. This was followed by the 320 in 1962 and the 450XL in 1985. In 1982, Vilter acquired Gebhart Industrial Refrigeration, and began offering stainless steel and galvanized coil cooling units. In 1990, the company introduced the VSS 601 single screw compressor, to be followed by seven more models in various sizes. In 2000, the company introduced the revolutionary Vission micro-controller with touch screen color graphics.

Vilter has more than 400 employees at its 450,000-square-foot world headquarters and manufacturing plant in Milwaukee. The company has 13 sales offices around the country, and hundreds of distributors and service centers throughout the world. Approximately 30 percent of

Equipment produced by the Vilter Manufacturing Corporation is used throughout the world.

Milwaukee

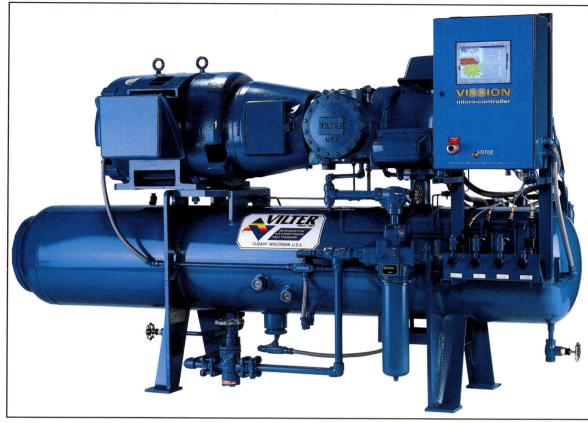

IN 2000, THE COMPANY INTRODUCED THE REVOLUTIONARY VISSION MICRO-CONTROLLER WITH TOUCH SCREEN COLOR GRAPHICS.

the firm's annual volume comes from international customers. There are only four companies in the world that can do what Vilter can, and they are large conglomerates built up through consolidation. Vilter has invested in its physical plant and workforce to emphasize that Vilter equipment is made—and will always be made—in America.

Employee Owned

Vilter is unusual among manufacturers in that it is 100 percent employee owned through an employee stock option plan. As a result, the company's employees understand that their decisions impact Vilter's financial performance. Szymaszek has an open-door policy, and visiting customers are invited to go onto the manufacturing floor and speak to employees. As their livelihood is connected to their performance, employees are dedicated to growing the company by putting customers first. This is particularly important because Vilter builds custom products rather than stocking off-the-shelf items.

Providing customer support in times of need is critical in an industry where refrigerated products can spoil in a matter of hours. Vilter guarantees shipment of replacement parts within 24 hours. The company offers the industry's longest warranty, the Vilter 5/15, on its screw compressors. In 1999, Vilter was awarded the Governor's Award of Excellence for the development of export markets using Wisconsin products. In 2000, the company was awarded *Start* magazine's Technology and Business Award for the best use of Windows CE in an industrial equipment application.

Made with pride in America, made with pride in Milwaukee— Vilter's products carry a brand name that signifies the company's excellent reputation across the nation and around the world.

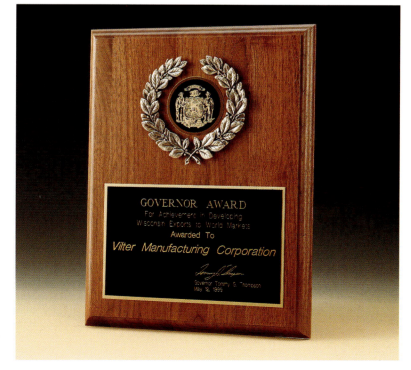

IN 1999, VILTER WAS AWARDED THE GOVERNOR'S AWARD OF EXCELLENCE FOR THE DEVELOPMENT OF EXPORT MARKETS USING WISCONSIN PRODUCTS.

City by the Waters

· 303 ·

Catholic Family Life Insurance

Catholic Family Life Insurance, the nation's oldest Catholic fraternal benefit society, was founded in 1868 upon the urging of the first Catholic bishop of Milwaukee, the Most Reverend John Martin Henni. The Family Protective Association, as it was known at the time, was organized to meet the financial needs of families devastated by the aftermath of the Civil War. Though Henni was the society's inspirational leader, the organizational efforts were left to dedicated Catholic businessmen, headed by John Traudt, a local dry goods merchant, who later became the organization's first president.

Over the years, this fraternal benefit society became a leader in its field, being the first to insure children, the first to adopt the legal reserve system, the first to pay dividends to members, the first to offer Masses for living and deceased members, and the first to provide whole family protection. This innovative spirit continues through the society's unique roster of life insurance plans and family-oriented, value-added benefits.

Today, Catholic Family insures approximately 5,000 people in the Milwaukee area, 25,000 throughout Wisconsin, and 65,000 nationwide. Members can be found in all 50 states and Canada.

Members' Loyalty and Confidence

Catholic Family, as a fraternal benefit society, provides members of the Roman Catholic faith with such financial plans as universal life insurance, annuities, term and whole life insurance, and disability insurance. Its membership benefits include tuition aid for Catholic school; a children's club; medic alert identification; a full-color, quarterly magazine; newborn and orphan assistance; home eye test kits; and financial aid for youth members attending summer camps.

The organization is a mutual insurer, owned by the policyholders, who every four years elect a board of directors and review its bylaws. Licensed in 21 states and the District of Columbia, Catholic Family has remained true to the faith of its founders by providing a wide range of benefits promoting baptism, first communion, confirmation, and religious retreats.

With more than $1.5 billion of life insurance in force, Catholic Family is the 11th-largest fraternal benefit society in the nation. In five years' time, the organization's insurance in force grew 13 percent, assets increased 17 percent, and surplus funds grew 39 percent. Annually, Catholic Family returns three-fourths of its revenue—approximately $20

At St. Mary Church in Milwaukee in 1849, Bishop John Martin Henni founded Milwaukee's first benevolent organization, the St. Pius Society. Members of this and other societies came together in 1868 to form the Family Protective Association, later named Catholic Family Life Insurance (left).

Catholic Family Life Insurance has long been supportive of the Milwaukee Archdiocese. The Very Reverend John Endejan (left) is pastor of the Cathedral of Saint John the Evangelist and Catholic Family's spiritual director, while the archbishop of Milwaukee, the Most Reverend Rembert G. Weakland, O.S.B., serves as the organization's national chaplain (right).

million—to members in the form of insurance or fraternal benefits.

"Catholic Family is financially stronger today than at any time during our rich and colorful history," says William L. Eimers, president and CEO. "Our strength lies in the loyalty of our members and their confidence in the society's ability to meet their financial needs when called upon to do so."

Thoughtful, Committed People

The mission of Catholic Family is to provide its family of members sound insurance products designed to meet their financial security needs while supporting programs fostering spiritual, social, and educational well-being. "Our organization is unique in that one of our primary purposes for existence is to help those less fortunate than ourselves, thereby improving the quality of life in the communities we serve," Eimers says. "We believe that one helping hand, one kind word, one person's call to action can make a profound difference in the lives of others."

Catholic Family funds its charitable efforts through the selling of insurance, as well as through prudent investments. The society's 95 lodges located in 11 states raise dollars for their favorite charities, while the national organization provides matching funds. Catholic Family donates approximately $500,000 each year through the matching funds efforts of its lodges. An average of 60 percent of these funds is donated to

Catholic causes. In addition, nearly 2,100 Catholic Family members log their volunteer activity, reporting some 142,000 hours of service to their parishes and communities.

Catholic education is Catholic Family's national cause. Since 1971, more than 4,500 young people have received tuition aid, totaling $1.4 million, to attend Catholic middle and high schools. College financial assistance is provided through Catholic Family's New England division, Union Saint-Jean-Baptiste, whose trust fund principal now exceeds $1.4 million. The organization has also established an education foundation that provides expanded financial assistance to its members and the Catholic community at large.

"As Catholic Family entered its second century of service," notes David L. Springob, chairman of the board, "we gradually shifted from total concentration on our membership to a mission that was expanded to include fraternal benevolence and outreach to the community at large."

Milwaukee-area Catholic Family lodges provide time, talent, and funding for such worthwhile efforts as the Child Abuse Prevention Fund, St. Francis Children's Center, Hunger Task Force, and Habitat for Humanity. One project involved purchasing, remodeling, and furnishing a home for a Laotian refugee family with nine children. With support from Milwaukee members, the parents were able to find jobs and enroll their children in school.

"Catholic Family members never doubt that a small group of thoughtful, committed people can change the world," says Eimers. "As they follow in the footsteps of our founder, Bishop Henni, they are examples of how a dedicated few can improve the lives of many."

CLOCKWISE FROM TOP LEFT: WILLIAM L. EIMERS (LEFT), PRESIDENT AND CEO, STANDS IN FRONT OF CATHOLIC FAMILY'S CURRENT HOME OFFICE WITH DANIEL T. LLOYD, EXECUTIVE VICE PRESIDENT AND TREASURER, AND MARY C. D'ARRAS, SENIOR VICE PRESIDENT AND SECRETARY.

IN 1991, CATHOLIC FAMILY PURCHASED A VACANT HOUSE FOR HABITAT FOR HUMANITY INTERNATIONAL. CHAIRMAN OF THE BOARD DAVID L. SPRINGOB PRESENTED A CHECK TO HABITAT REPRESENTATIVES, AND CFLI MEMBERS RENOVATED THE ENTIRE HOME IN A RECORD-SETTING TIME OF FOUR AND ONE-HALF MONTHS.

CATHOLIC FAMILY MEMBERS NATIONWIDE ARE INVOLVED IN A VARIETY OF CHARITABLE EVENTS, INCLUDING THE AMERICAN CANCER SOCIETY'S RELAY FOR LIFE.

P&H Mining Equipment

The mining industry is a rich and important part of Wisconsin history. In fact, the state's nickname comes from early miners who, reminiscent of badgers, dug caves in the hillsides to live in. Today, there are more than 100 Wisconsin firms that provide products and services to the mining industry around the world. P&H Mining Equipment is among those at the top of the list who are important and have made an impact.

From humble beginnings in 1884 as a manufacturer and servicer of overhead cranes, to introducing the first gas-powered excavator in 1917, P&H has grown to become a global leader in the manufacture and service of mining equipment.

Throughout the world, everything is either grown or mined—mining is a basic and critical industry. Approximately 56 percent of electricity generated in the United States is powered by coal made possible by mining. Each American is responsible for the consumption of about 7,000 pounds of coal a year, as well as for the annual use of 40,000 pounds of minerals in the way of materials used for highways, computers, and other goods.

"All enhancements to our lives require minerals," says Bob Hale, P&H president. "It is estimated, for example, that the popularity of the Internet has increased electric generation by 8 percent. The mining industry is vital to people's lives."

P&H Manufacturing

P&H's manufacturing operation consists of 1.2 million square feet of factory space in Milwaukee, Australia, Brazil, South Africa, and a Japanese affiliate plant. There are about 1,000 Milwaukee-based employees and some 2,500 globally. Among the machines manufactured by P&H is a walking dragline, the largest self-propelled machinery in the world. The dragline stands 22 stories high, is 400 feet long, weighs 5,700 tons, and takes 50 people 18 months to assemble at the mine site.

Not surprisingly, the machine tools used to manufacture such mining equipment—welders, boring machinery, and gear cutters—are the largest in the world. A highly skilled workforce averaging 23 years of service makes it possible for P&H to meet such impressive engineering challenges.

"Because mining equipment is so complicated, massive, and expensive, a full-size prototype can't be produced for testing," Hale says. "As result, the first one that comes off the line absolutely has to work properly." Sophisticated engineering tools make that possible.

The company's flagship product is the 4100 series of electric mining shovels, the fastest in its class. The shovel carries up to a 115-ton payload with one scoop. With three or four scoops, the shovel can fill the largest mining trucks made. The company also manufactures rotary blast hole drills. Ninety percent of the world's surface mines utilize P&H equipment. The equipment is used to

The powerful P&H 9020 dragline removes overburden at a coal mine in Australia with a 120-cubic-yard bucket on a 320-foot boom.

The bigger, faster, smarter P&H 4100XPB shovel is setting new world records at a Wyoming coal mine, loading more than 9,400 tons of overburden per hour.

Milwaukee

mine copper, coal, iron ore, silver, diamonds, phosphate, oil sands, molybdenum, potash, and gold.

Ironically, these massive machines require only one operator, thanks to P&H's sophisticated control systems. Information management systems allow the operator to take advantage of programmable logic controllers, a global positioning system, semiautomated tasks, and operator assists that are akin to cruise control. Sensors can even provide the weight of each shovel load, accurate to within 2 percent.

MinePro Services

Beyond manufacturing equipment that mines raw materials essential for the world's economy and human progress, P&H focuses on equipment life-cycle management. Life-cycle management is designed to maximize equipment availability by minimizing downtime. Mining equipment often operates 24 hours a day, seven days a week under incredibly difficult conditions, ranging from jungles and deserts to tundras and mountains. The company's far-flung equipment can be found in Africa, Australia, Canada, Chile, China, India, New Guinea, the United States, and scores of other nations. Equipment reliability is vital to a mine's success, given that mines operate around the clock. Minerals are sold on an open market where prices cannot be controlled. Thus, reducing costs may be the only way to increase profits.

P&H's MinePro Services division includes some 1,500 employees in the field who perform many sophisticated support services, such as operating state-of-the-art, predictive diagnostic systems at mine sites. Housed in vans, these computerized systems diagnose wear and predict potential breakdowns before they occur. In this way, mining equipment can be fixed at the most cost-effective point in its life cycle. Typically, a MinePro facility is constructed near major mining centers for quicker service to large mines.

Efficient repair service is one of the reasons that P&H mining equipment may be in use for decades at the same mine. While P&H forms partnerships with customers to anticipate their needs, the company has aligned itself with other leading allied equipment manufacturers in the industry to provide customers with one-stop shopping. In fact, there are some 250,000 types of parts in the company's inventory.

"For members of the surface mining industry," Hale says, "P&H is their local one-stop shop, providing productivity solutions throughout the mine."

Working at 11,000-foot elevation in a copper mine in Peru, a rugged P&H 120A drill puts down 13.75-inch-diameter blast holes.

P&H factory workers like this Milwaukee welder average 27 years of service. The big, 60-cubic-yard dipper is for a P&H 4100 series shovel.

City by the Waters

· 307 ·

Emmpak Foods, Inc.

At the turn of the 20th century, Morris Segel and his sister were young emigrants from Eastern Europe. A Sheboygan butcher sponsored their passage to the United States and, in return, Segel worked hard herding cows for him. He later sold newspapers, saving his money to buy his own cattle for butchering. In 1932, Segel founded Wisconsin Packing Co., which then became Wis-Pak Foods.

Over the years, Wis-Pak Foods remained a Segel family business. Morris Segel handed the company reins to his son, Floyd Segel, who in turn passed the firm on to his two sons, Justin and Robert. Today, Justin Segel, CEO, and Robert Segel, vice president, are the third generation of the family to successfully operate the business. It was natural for them to keep Wis-Pak thriving, says Justin Segel. "Not everyone is comfortable with the mechanics of meatpacking—the stockyards, boning floor, killing floor, rendering plant, et cetera," he says. "But my brother and I grew up in the business and were familiar with the operations."

Peck Foods was founded in 1889 by Bernhardt Peck, and was owned and operated by three generations of the Peck family before being sold to the Sara Lee Corporation in 1984. Peck Foods was sold in 1989 to George Gillete, who operated Peck Foods as Emmber Foods. In 1993, Emmber Foods was purchased by an investor group that included Wis-Pak. Subsequently, in 1996, the family-founded companies merged, creating Emmpak Foods, Inc., one of the nation's leading vertically integrated meat processing companies.

Lines of Business

Today, Emmpak employs nearly 1,900 workers, with projected annual revenues of $600 million by 2001. The company has six plants and distribution facilities, and slaughters some 430,000 cattle each year. Each week, the processed meat plant produces 2 million pounds of deli meats, including the only fat-free roast beef on the market. Emmpak's ground beef operation produces more than 1 billion hamburger patties a year.

A top priority at Emmpak is food safety. The company has invested $55 million in its operations in the late 1990s, including $7 million toward clean room facilities–among the nation finest–where cooked products are sliced and packaged in nearly sterile conditions. "Essentially there are five hospital-like operating rooms, complete with stainless steel walls, acid-treated floors, and special air-conditioning and filtration systems," says Segel, describing the clean rooms. As part of the clean room process, employees also go through a triple scrub-down procedure to prevent food-borne illnesses caused by bacteria such as *Listeria* or *E. coli*. "It is not just good business to go to the expense of a clean room," Segel says. "We have a moral obligation. Food safety is part of our corporate culture."

Emmpak's primary product lines include fresh meat produced by Peck Foods as a private label supplier; processed meats under various brand names such as Emmber Classic, Deli-Rite, Lean N Tender, and

Brothers Justin Segel (left), CEO, and Robert Segel, vice president, are the third generation of the family to successfully operate Emmpak Foods, Inc.

Each week, Emmpak's processed meat plant produces 2 million pounds of deli meats, including the only fat-free roast beef on the market.

Bernhardt Peck; heat-and-serve entrées for home meal replacement programs; precut steaks under the Wis-Pak label for steakhouse dinner chains; and private label ground beef products for prominent national quick service food chains and food service distributors. Emmpak Foods has also developed the TNT burger, a proprietary formula of ground beef and seasonings that retains its flavor and juices under a variety of cooking and serving methods.

Emmpak also has extensive research and development facilities, and can create more than 400 kinds of hamburger patties to meet customers' individual cooking and facility needs. Cooking time, equipment, and burger size, shape, texture, and binding vary among quick service food chains. Emmpak Foods provides each customer with consistent quality, flavor, and texture in its meat products. "For a company our size, we have an immense commitment to food research. We have food scientists and technicians with doctoral degrees developing and testing our foods," says Segel.

Service is another specialty for Emmpak Foods. The company offers the only technical support staff in the meat processing industry. If a customer's hamburger patty does not perform properly and consistently—if there's too much breakage, for example—Emmpak's technical staff will analyze everything from the meat to the customer's storage facilities and cooking temperatures to find the solution. In about 90 percent of these circumstances, the solution is in education: teaching customers how to better utilize their cooking equipment to attain the desired end product.

"Our business is more than just meat," Segel says. "We sell value in terms of a complete protein package. We provide product research, menu development, technical support, logistical solutions, and a deep commitment to food safety."

The Emmpak Difference

In the 1980s, it was typical for meat companies to specialize, which created a very segmented industry. One company never had total control or responsibility for the safety of the products. Today, Emmpak Foods has achieved that goal. The company is a vertically integrated meat supplier, which enables the firm to maintain product quality and food safety, from slaughter to customer delivery.

Emmpak Foods rounds out its value chain with Wispak Transport. The Emmpak Foods trucking and distribution system maintains control of delivery with approximately 160 tractors, 350 refrigerated trailers, and a new, state-of-the-art, 150,000-square-foot distribution center. This control of the processing and delivery chain ensures a safer, more consistent product for the customer.

Emmpak Foods, an old-line Milwaukee company with roots going back more than 100 years, and with its emphasis on quality and food safety, has strategically positioned itself for continued success well into the 21st century.

EMMPAK'S PRIMARY PRODUCT LINES INCLUDE FRESH MEAT, WHICH GOES THROUGH A BONING AND TRIMMING PROCESS AND IS PRODUCED BY PECK FOODS AS A PRIVATE LABEL SUPPLIER (LEFT).

EXTENSIVE TESTING AT EMMPAK'S STATE-OF-THE-ART LABORATORIES HELPS ENSURE PRODUCT SAFETY (RIGHT).

WISPAK TRANSPORT'S DISTINCTIVE TRAILERS, USED TO DISTRIBUTE EMMPAK'S PRODUCTS, DEPICT A WISCONSIN FARM LANDSCAPE AND CARRY THE PHRASE "SOMETHING SPECIAL FROM WISCONSIN."

CHILDREN'S HOSPITAL OF WISCONSIN

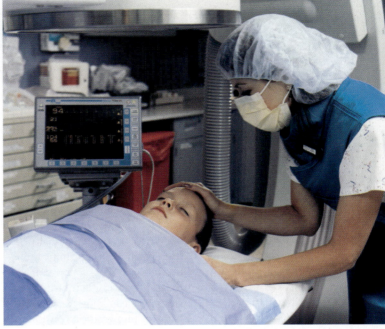

In 1894, seven Milwaukee women founded a children's hospital with 10 beds and one nurse in a small house on Brady Street. They were committed to caring for children, no matter how poor. In fact, the hospital initially was called Children's Free Hospital. Volunteer local doctors comprised the first medical staff. From these humble origins, Children's Hospital of Wisconsin has grown into a major institution beloved by countless families. Today, located at the Milwaukee Regional Medical Center in Wauwatosa, it is Wisconsin's only pediatric medical center, serving the sickest children from all over the state, as well as from northern Illinois and the Upper Peninsula of Michigan.

Children's Hospital of Wisconsin's 18,397 admissions in 1998 ranked first among U.S. pediatric medical centers. In southeastern Wisconsin, more than nine out of 10 children in need of hospitalization come to Children's Hospital.

Affiliated with the Medical College of Wisconsin and nine schools of nursing, Children's Hospital is a teaching center for general pediatricians, pediatric specialists, and pediatric nurses. Increasingly, the hospital also sponsors research.

Children's Hospital has grown tremendously, but its employees remember their roots. The small Victorian house where it all began inspired the design of the current lobby, which serves as a reminder of the past to all who enter.

Treating Children

When it comes to providing health care for children, all too often they are treated as if they were adults, with the same drugs, protocols, and equipment. But children are different—anatomically, physiologically, and emotionally. At Children's Hospital of Wisconsin, all aspects of patient care take these differences into account.

"Children are special," says Jon E. Vice, president and CEO. "They are not small adults, their medical treatments are not the same as adults, and they shouldn't be housed with adults."

Following that philosophy, Children's Hospital is designed with children in mind, and the staff relates to children in a special way, to create a reassuring and comforting environment, while providing the highest-quality care.

Major Initiatives

Children's Hospital is the state's leading center for pediatric heart care. About 600 children a year—many of them newborns—undergo heart operations at the hospital. The cardiovascular surgery team is a nationwide leader in safer, more effective ways to treat heart conditions in children.

Children's Hospital has also recently instituted research initiatives aimed at diabetes, birth defects, genetics, and pain management. Using the latest gene-mapping tools, scientists at the Max McGee National Research Center for Juvenile Diabetes are trying to find the genes and triggering events that lead to type 1 diabetes. The center works closely with one of the country's largest clinical diabetes programs (more than 900 patients enrolled).

Another genetics research project,

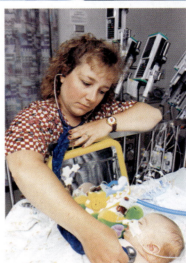

the Birth Defects Research Center, is exploring how genetic mutations and environmental toxicants interact to cause birth defects.

The Jane B. Pettit Pain Management Center is researching new ways to relieve pain in children. The Pettit Center supplements conventional medicine with alternative therapies such as acupuncture and meditation. In a related initiative, as a promise to minimize pain in

An interventional radiology nurse at Children's Hospital of Wisconsin comforts a patient who is about to undergo a procedure.

Nurse Karen Wilcox listens intently to the heart of month-old Kelsey Schneider.

all procedures, the hospital has declared itself the Comfort Zone™.

A Variety of Specialties

Children's Hospital has more than 80 specialty clinics, which handle about 180,000 patient visits per year, for everything from asthma to Zollinger-Ellison syndrome.

The hospital operates the state's only pediatric trauma center. Serving trauma patients—and all others in need of emergency transfer—throughout the region are the critical care doctors and nurses of Children's Transport.

The Pediatric Intensive Care Unit, providing state-of-the-art critical care to children with serious injuries or illnesses, is known as one of the finest in the Midwest.

The Blood and Bone Marrow Stem Cell Transplant Program, a collaborative effort with the Medical College of Wisconsin, pioneered use of nonmatched bone marrow donors, and is internationally known in the treatment of cancer and noncancerous blood disorders.

Children's Hospital is a full-service pediatric transplant center for livers, lungs, and hearts. In 1999, the state's first living-donor liver transplant was performed at Children's Hospital by a team of Medical College of Wisconsin surgeons.

The transplant program is supported by an ambitious general pediatric surgery program. Pediatric surgeons address everything from commonplace injuries to limb reattachment, and are leading the way with less-invasive approaches to problems such as funnel chest.

For epilepsy, the pediatric neurology program offers a promising new implant therapy called vagal nerve stimulation. For recurrent brain tumors, the program offers an experimental treatment—photodynamic therapy—that uses a photosensitive dye and high-intensity light to destroy hard-to-reach malignancies.

In a Class by Itself

Children's Hospital, as the flagship entity of Children's Health System, participates in the health system's ongoing effort to improve pediatric health care in local communities. As a first step, in 1994, the health system founded Children's Medical Group, which today operates 17 community and school-based pediatric clinics in southeastern Wisconsin.

Bringing specialty services to families in northeastern Illinois, Children's Hospital Clinics-Gurnee opened for patients in 1998. Also that year, the health system acquired the Children's Health Education Center. Located in Schlitz Park in downtown Milwaukee, the center offers youth and adult health and safety classes, and is a popular field trip destination for schools.

In 1999, the health system opened Children's Hospital of Wisconsin-Kenosha, a 31-bed, general pediatric hospital-within-a-hospital at Kenosha Hospital and Medical Center. A similar venture is planned at Theda Clark Medical Center in Neenah.

Children's Hospital has come a long way from that little house on Brady Street more than a century ago, with the story far from over. As the state's only hospital dedicated to pediatric health care and research, and to educating the doctors and nurses who care for sick children, Children's Hospital of Wisconsin truly is in a class by itself.

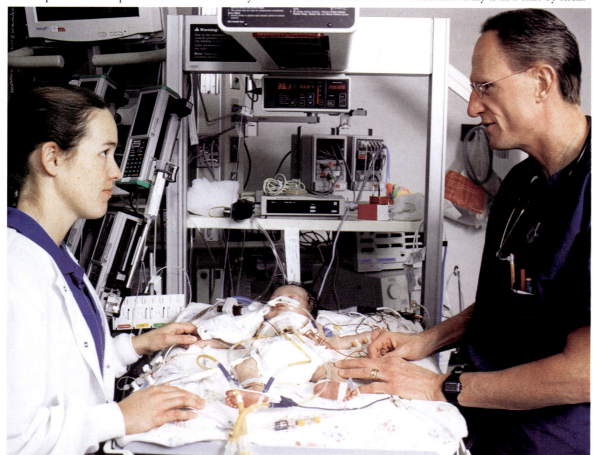

PEDIATRIC INTENSIVE CARE UNIT STAFF MEMBERS MONITOR NEWBORN MIZEL BRADLEY-BIRTS, WHO HAS JUST UNDERGONE EMERGENCY OPEN-HEART SURGERY (LEFT).

IN THE JANE B. PETTIT PAIN MANAGEMENT CENTER, DR. LYNN RUSY, PEDIATRIC ANESTHESIOLOGIST, USES ACUPUNCTURE TO RELIEVE THE SHOULDER PAIN OF FIBROMYALGIA PATIENT NICOLE NELSON (RIGHT).

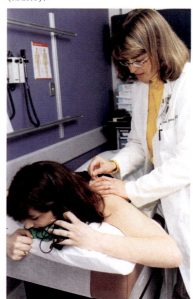

WISCONSIN ENERGY CORPORATION

WISCONSIN ENERGY CORPORATION (WEC) AND ITS SUBsidiaries have a long history of pioneering innovation. Formed in 1986, WEC was one of the first utility holding companies in the nation to have nonutility subsidiaries, which have allowed the corporation to pursue opportunities outside the regulated utility industry.

However, the backbone of the corporation remains its two major energy utilities—Wisconsin Electric and Wisconsin Gas.

Wisconsin Electric

Wisconsin Electric is the state's largest electric utility, serving 1 million residential, commercial, and industrial customers. The utility also serves about 450 steam customers in downtown Milwaukee and more than 400,000 natural gas customers. Wisconsin Electric's service area encompasses some 13,000 square miles, including the Milwaukee, Appleton, and Prairie du Chien areas, as well as portions of northern Wisconsin and the Upper Peninsula of Michigan.

Wisconsin Electric has 24 power plants, including 14 hydroelectric plants, six coal-fired plants, two natural-gas-fired plants, one nuclear plant, and one that is oil or gas fired. Of electricity generated by Wisconsin Electric in a typical year, more than 60 percent is provided by coal-fired plants and about 25 percent is provided by nuclear power. The rest comes from plants powered by natural gas, renewable resources, and purchased power. Wisconsin Electric's award-winning green power program promotes the use of renewable energy sources, such as hydroelectric power and wind power.

Formed in 1896, Wisconsin Electric was originally named The Milwaukee Electric Railway and Light Co. In its early years, the company operated electric streetcars and an interurban railway, in addition to providing utility services. In 1919, the company developed the use of pulverized coal as a boiler fuel, which made low-cost central station electric service possible. In 1935, the company's Port Washington Power Plant began its 13-year reign as the world's most efficient power plant.

In the 1940s, Wisconsin Electric was among the first utilities to outfit its power plants with equipment to capture fly ash from stack emissions. In the 1970s, the company was one of the first utilities to undertake major energy conservation efforts to help customers make their homes and businesses more energy efficient. In the 1980s, Wisconsin Electric pioneered technology to recycle fly ash, a power plant waste product, for use by the construction industry.

Wisconsin Gas

Founded in 1852, Wisconsin Gas is the state's oldest and largest natural gas utility, serving some 540,000 customers in more than 531 communities throughout Wisconsin. The company's largest concentration of customers is located in southeastern Wisconsin, including the metro Milwaukee area.

WISCONSIN ELECTRIC'S PLEASANT PRAIRIE POWER PLANT IN KENOSHA COUNTY HELPS TO ENSURE THE AVAILABILITY OF ADEQUATE POWER TO MEET THE INCREASING DEMANDS OF THE AREA'S EXPANDING ECONOMY.

THE PUBLIC SERVICE BUILDING IN DOWNTOWN MILWAUKEE SERVES AS CORPORATE HEADQUARTERS FOR WISCONSIN ENERGY CORPORATION (WEC) AND WISCONSIN ELECTRIC. OPENED IN 1905, THE PSB WAS RENOVATED AND RESTORED IN THE MID-1990S, AND IS LISTED ON THE NATIONAL REGISTER OF HISTORIC PLACES.

Wisconsin Gas began operations to meet the street lighting needs of the City of Milwaukee. As uses for natural gas grew with home heating, water heating, cooking, and clothes drying, so did Wisconsin Gas. The company has been adding about 10,000 customers a year. In 1998, in an effort to leverage its expertise in energy delivery, metering, and billing, the company launched Wisconsin Gas Water Services, which now provides municipal water services to portions of the Milwaukee area.

The Wisconsin Gas name is also behind a successful natural gas equipment commercial leasing business and PowerNow!, which installs and maintains residential and commercial natural-gas-fired generators.

Edison Sault Electric

Another WEC subsidiary, Edison Sault Electric, serves about 22,000 customers in upper Michigan. Edison Sault, based in Sault Ste. Marie, Michigan, was formed in 1892.

Combined, WEC's utilities have about 6,500 employees, and own and maintain some 30,000 miles of power lines and 16,000 miles of gas mains.

Other Subsidiaries

In addition to utilities, Wisconsin Energy also includes several nonutility subsidiaries. FieldTech is a subsidiary that offers meter reading technology and services to gas, water, and electric utilities nationwide. Hypro Corp. manufactures pumps and fluid-handling equipment for a variety of markets.

Minergy develops and markets proprietary technologies designed to convert high-volume industrial and municipal wastes into value-added products. SHURflo Pump Manufacturing Company makes small, high-performance pumps and fluid-handling equipment.

Sta-Rite Industries manufactures pumps and water processing equipment for residential, industrial, and agricultural markets. Major markets are water systems, pools, and spas. WICOR Energy is a marketing subsidiary selling a variety of energy-supply-related services, including gas purchasing and storage and risk management.

Wispark is a real estate development subsidiary emphasizing brownfield development, primarily in southeastern Wisconsin. Wisvest is an energy services subsidiary that builds, owns, operates, and maintains energy production facilities. Wisvest also invests in other energy-related projects.

Planning for Progress

Nationwide, the utility industry is changing. New regulations aimed at increasing competition among utilities and providing consumers with more energy choices have been implemented in some areas of the country and are expected in Wisconsin in the future. Wisconsin Energy is positioning itself for the industry's potential changes.

The company is in the process of implementing a 10-year, $6 billion growth strategy to improve the supply, reliability, and quality of electricity in Wisconsin. Elements of the program include construction of new power generation units, refurbishment or retirement of older generation units, and substantial improvements and additions to the company's electric distribution system.

"As the largest energy company in Wisconsin, we are dedicated to helping the state meet its critical electric and natural gas energy needs by providing reliable, quality, and reasonably priced energy services to our customers," says Richard A. Abdoo, WEC chairman, president, and CEO. "In today's energy industry, success also can be measured by embracing change and bringing new ideas to the marketplace. We have had great success in both of these areas."

CLOCKWISE FROM TOP LEFT: DEDICATED CUSTOMER SERVICE AND CONTACT TEAMS MAKE A DAILY DIFFERENCE IN THE LIVES OF THE UTILITIES' CUSTOMERS.

WEC'S ELECTRIC DISTRIBUTION EXPERTS WORK HARD UNDER NORMAL AND STORM CONDITIONS TO KEEP THE POWER ON.

MORE AND MORE CUSTOMERS ARE TURNING TO WISCONSIN ELECTRIC AND WISCONSIN GAS TO PROVIDE CLEAN-BURNING NATURAL GAS TO HEAT THEIR HOMES AND BUSINESSES.

1900-1920

1900
Fortis Heath

1903
Milwaukee School of Engineering

1906
Waukesha Engine

1908
Western States Envelope Company

1912
Thomas A. Mason Co., Inc.

1914
Brady Corporation

1920
Grede Foundries, Inc.

1920
Lincoln State Bank

Fortis Health

IN TRUE MILWAUKEE FASHION, FORTIS HEALTH HAS QUIETLY become an industry giant through a combination of solid business values and innovation, while also providing a health conscious workplace with strong community ties for almost 2,000 local employees. ■ Anchoring the corner of Fifth and Michigan streets downtown, Fortis Health is the nation's leading provider of health insurance products for individuals and small businesses. In addition to its Milwaukee headquarters, the company employs 1,000 people at regional offices in Miami; Minneapolis; Boise; Kansas City, Missouri; and Dublin, Ohio. The firm is a member of the Fortis worldwide group of insurance, banking, and investment companies that together make up one of the world's largest corporations.

History and Vision

Fortis Health's visionary work to help others develop health care financing solutions is a long-standing tradition. In 1892, the La Crosse Mutual Aid Association was formed by 100 business owners in La Crosse, Wisconsin, as means of protection from the loss of income due to accident or sickness. This meant a great deal to policyholders in the days before workers' compensation, Social Security, and employee benefits. With its growing success, the company moved to Milwaukee in 1900 and changed its name to Time Insurance Company.

Later acquired by the Fortis family of companies, the company became Fortis Health in April 1998. The company's tradition of using innovative solutions to help those in need continues to guide Fortis Health into its second century of leadership and community involvement.

A Healthy Work Environment

While the company is a leader in insurance products, Fortis Health is also a leader in providing employee benefits and workplace wellness initiatives. The firm has received the prestigious Silver Well Workplace Award from the Wellness Councils of America, recognizing Fortis Health as one of the healthiest work environments in the nation. Wellness programs include voluntary screenings for a variety of health concerns, as well as Healthy Choice menu items in the company cafeteria, Weight Watchers meetings, a walking club, and reimbursement for outside health club memberships, among other programs.

Fortis Health recognizes the importance of work-life balance and child care issues. Employees enjoy flexible work scheduling plans, with a variety of starting times throughout the day and options for telecommuting. Fortis Health employees can buy extra vacation time if needed or sell time back to the company, bank their unused sick days for paid sabbatical leave, and participate in flexible savings accounts for medical expenses and child care. The company provides an excellent tuition reimbursement program and a variety of professional development courses.

"When it comes to your job, a good fit means more than being good at what you do," says Ben Cutler, president and CEO. "It means feeling compensated for your contributions to the company, and comfortable with its culture and environment."

A Partner in the Community

Fortis Health is a leader in community outreach programs, supporting initiatives such as the

FORTIS HEALTH COO DAVE MCDONOUGH (LEFT), AND PRESIDENT AND CEO BEN CUTLER STAND IN FRONT OF THE FORTIS BRANDMARK. THE LOGO SYMBOLIZES COMMUNITY AND THE FORTIS COMPANIES' SERVICE TO CUSTOMERS, AGENTS, EMPLOYEES, AND COMMUNITIES WORLDWIDE.

· 316 ·

Milwaukee

YMCA's award-winning One-on-One mentoring program, where middle school students come to Fortis Health once a week to receive academic tutoring from company volunteers. Fortis Health also hosts blood drives throughout the year, and supports many runs/walks and other annual charity events. As an incentive to encourage community involvement, Fortis Health compensates all employees for up to eight hours of volunteer time each year. Additionally, the Fortis Insurance Foundation contributes hundreds of thousands of dollars to community causes annually, both directly and through the Employee Matching Grant Program.

Innovation in a Challenging Business

Fortis Health already insures more than 1 million people through its three major divisions. The growing company has become an industry leader by continually developing innovative products that fulfill specific customer health insurance needs.

Fortis Health is the largest provider of individual medical insurance in the nation, serving individuals with high-quality health care solutions in nearly every state. The company's Small Group division is the nation's leading independent provider of health insurance to small-business owners.

Short Term Medical products provide solid health insurance options for individuals with gaps in health insurance–people between jobs, recent college grads, people starting home-based businesses, and temporary or seasonal workers. The company sells as much of this product as all of its competitors combined. Likewise, the firm's Student Select plan is a leader in providing coverage for full-time college students who are no longer covered by their parents' plan. Fortis Health has successfully reached out to these specialized audiences through its groundbreaking marketing programs on the Internet and elsewhere. The company was also one of the first to offer medical savings accounts nationally.

This position of leadership brings responsibilities. Cutler points out that health care costs in the United States are already the highest in the world–more than double that of any other country–because Americans demand the finest doctors, technology, and expensive prescription drugs. At the same time, Americans are not getting healthier. Current trends reveal that by 2020, the United States will be spending one of every four dollars of gross domestic product on health care. That would put the country at a serious disadvantage in the global economy. Add to this the fact that almost one out of five Americans have no health insurance, and it's easy to see why Cutler and Fortis Health use every opportunity to challenge Americans to improve their personal health, urge corporate leaders to promote work site wellness initiatives, and encourage politicians to develop legislation that allows more Americans to choose appropriate health insurance.

CLOCKWISE FROM TOP LEFT: THE CUSTOMER MANAGEMENT CENTER AT FORTIS HEALTH EMPLOYS 250 STAFF MEMBERS WHO PROVIDE QUALITY SERVICE TO CUSTOMERS ACROSS THE NATION.

FORTIS HEALTH HAS BEEN A BUSINESS AND EDUCATION PARTNER WITH SHOLES MIDDLE SCHOOL FOR MANY YEARS. THE COMPANY HAS RECEIVED COMMUNITY AWARDS FOR ITS COMMITMENT TO THE ON-SITE MENTORING PROGRAM.

FORTIS HEALTH EMPLOYS MORE THAN 1,700 PEOPLE AT ITS HEADQUARTERS IN DOWNTOWN MILWAUKEE, WITH AN ADDITIONAL 1,000 EMPLOYEES LOCATED IN OFFICES ACROSS THE COUNTRY.

Waukesha Engine

Back in 1906, internal combustion engines were a relatively new, unproved technology. Engines were not only difficult to start, but also to be kept running. That same year saw the creation of the Waukesha Motor Company, started by three men—Harry Horning, Fred Ahrens, and James Remington—with ideas on how engines could be improved.

In a small garage in Waukesha, Horning, Ahrens, and Remington studied existing engines, and found ways to make an engine of their own that would start easily and run well. Their engines were field tested—driving pumps and oil drills in the harsh, remote areas of faraway Texas.

With the engine's robust design and ability to operate on abundant natural gas, the application proved ideal and even inspired new methods of drilling and production. Customers soon realized the engine—with its demonstrated reliability and wide power range—could drive a compressor as well as drilling equipment. The Waukesha soon became the engine of choice in the oil fields—an honor the company can still claim nearly a century later.

Today, Waukesha Engine remains focused on clean-burning, gaseous-fueled engines that provide reliable, versatile power worldwide. In addition, the company's ability to respond to changing market demands and ever tightening emissions requirements keeps it at the top of the industry, while its customers continue to find new and innovative ways to use Waukesha's broad engine line.

"Waukesha engines still drive pumps, but they also are used to power massive gas compressors along with powerful generators, chillers, and more, providing electricity, heating, and cooling to facilities around the globe," says Bill O'Connor, president.

Reasons for Success

Outstanding durability and minimal downtime are the key reasons why customers specify Waukesha engines in critical installations such as gas compressing stations and stations that provide prime electrical power. Through decades of experience, Waukesha has found ways to deal with engine noise, heat, and exhaust in sensitive environments. Waukesha engines can be installed indoors or out, in new or existing buildings. Waukesha Power Systems, the company's engine/generator packaging division, can build customized generator packages to power almost any application or facility.

As the company has expanded into myriad diverse applications, its product line has grown as well. Today, Waukesha offers a full line of natural gas engines to meet virtually every power demand. Along the way, the firm's continual product improvements literally have advanced engine technology. By incorporating stronger and higher technology components and computerized controls, Waukesha has modified its proven design to meet modern demands for higher speed without sacrificing durability or compromising emissions standards.

"We have developed lean-burn versions of our most popular engines, thereby ensuring low emissions and combustion stability across a wide load and speed range," O'Connor says. "As a result, our engines meet or exceed stringent environmental standards the world over."

Waukesha engines can run on almost any kind of gaseous fuel, from natural gas to propane to digester and landfill fuels. Natural gas is a cleaner-burning fossil fuel—today's fuel of choice. Waukesha continues to make improvements in emissions technology, providing a better environment for future generations.

Waukesha Engine began as Waukesha Motor Company, originally established by its founders at the Blue Front Garage at 139 North Street in Waukesha, located a few miles west of Milwaukee. Later, the name was changed to the Waukesha Engine Company.

Waukesha engines are in use at natural gas sites around the world.

· 318 ·

Milwaukee

Digester and landfill gases, normally waste products, can also fuel Waukesha engines. This fuel flexibility can make landfills and waste treatment plants nearly self-sufficient by using the gases they generate to power their facilities.

Decades of Experience

Waukesha's many years of experience have shown that engines can power just about anything. Customers, who are always seeking ways to control costs, recognize that Waukesha engines are cost effective and can run all sorts of equipment.

Waukesha Engine employs more than 1,000 people. The headquarters are in Waukesha, Wisconsin, and include more than 1 million square feet of manufacturing, engineering, laboratory, and service training space. The company's 150,000-square-foot facility in Appingedam, Netherlands, is responsible for supplying product for the European continent. All manufacturing facilities have received the Lloyd's Register of Quality Assurance quality ISO 9001 certification, an international standard which reflects the continuous effort of the company's workforce toward the production of quality products. Waukesha's Certified Product Training Center is a state-of-the-art facility offering instruction in engine technology and operation.

Waukesha engines are exported to some 147 nations and nearly a million Waukesha engines are currently operating around the world. "Wherever there is gas, you'll find a Waukesha engine," O'Connor says. "Decades of experience in engine technology, together with excellent engineering skills, will make Waukesha Engine the reliable power source for years to come. Waukesha powers the world, today and tomorrow."

DEPENDABLE WAUKESHA ENGINES OPERATE IN ALL CLIMATES, WHETHER IN THE DESERT OR IN EXTREME COLD, WHEREVER NATURAL GAS NEEDS TO BE COMPRESSED AND SENT TO REGIONAL OR NATIONAL DISTRIBUTION HUBS.

PRECISION BUILT AND ENGINEERED FOR MANY YEARS OF SERVICE, WAUKESHA ENGINES CONTINUE TO SET THE PACE IN GASEOUS-FUELED, RECIPROCATING-ENGINE TECHNOLOGY.

City by the Waters

Milwaukee School of Engineering (MSOE)

At the request of local industry, German immigrant and engineer Oscar Werwath founded the Milwaukee School of Engineering (MSOE) in 1903. Milwaukee companies were looking for a resource for mechanical and electrical engineers with an applied science orientation to harness the technologies of the day. That same interface between MSOE—a private, coeducational, nonsectarian university—and local business and industry is still one of the university's most outstanding features.

"Our graduates are ready to hit the ground running," says Hermann Viets, Ph.D., MSOE president. "They are extremely focused and dedicated, and they do not require a big learning curve. They can contribute to the bottom line immediately."

MSOE has a definite technological focus in preparing its 2,700 students for the real world. Each freshman is required to have a laptop computer. Students who lease a laptop from MSOE receive Internet access, maintenance, software, and insurance. After two years, these laptops are replaced and the students get to keep them upon graduation. MSOE was the first university in the state to require laptop computers of its students, and the first to establish a software engineering program as well.

"We are always in tune to what the marketplace is looking for, whether it means requiring a laptop or founding the first fluid power engineering program in the country," Viets says.

Mastering the Challenge

Engineering is not MSOE's only focus. In addition to several engineering degrees, the university offers undergraduate programs in nursing, business and computer systems, construction management, management systems, and technical communication, plus master's degrees in various engineering disciplines, medical informatics, engineering management, and perfusion. MSOE also offers international programs with universities in the Czech Republic, Germany, and India.

The university's location in downtown Milwaukee provides some advantages to students. As part of the lower East Side, MSOE's 13-acre campus is located in a rich, vibrant neighborhood, and the close proximity of the campus to area businesses provides easy access to employment opportunities, sometimes within walking distance. As a result, students don't need cars, and the university doesn't need a formal co-op program, as many other colleges and universities do.

"Virtually every student who graduates from MSOE has work-related experience on their résumé, whether it's part-time during the school year or full-time during the summer," Viets notes. Work-related experience often leads to full-time employment, as many employers groom MSOE interns to join the firm upon graduation.

MSOE's slogan is "Master the Challenge. Experience the Rewards." For their drive and dedication, students are rewarded. Ninety-nine percent of graduates are employed in their professional field within six months at an average starting salary of more than $44,000. Along with a 12-to-1 student/faculty ratio, the university provides many services to help students master the challenge.

In fact, MSOE is the only educational institution in the state offering a four-year guarantee. Students who are on track will be able to take the necessary course work and graduate in four years—guaranteed—even if it means opening a class for just a handful of students. This is particularly important for the engineering and nursing curriculum, where other universities may offer core courses only on a cyclical basis.

The Milwaukee School of Engineering's (MSOE) Student Life and Campus Center not only serves students, but has been utilized for such large events as Governor Tommy Thompson's St. Patrick's Day Party; a reception for world-famous architect Santiago Calatrava, who designed the Art Museum Expansion; and the National Trade Education Tour of U.S. Secretary of Commerce William M. Daley.

MSOE's Rapid Prototyping Center is the only center in the world that houses all major rapid-prototyping machines for undergraduate student use.

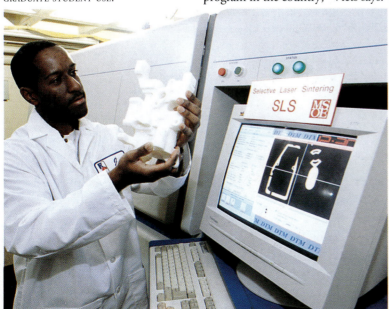

· 320 ·

Milwaukee

But MSOE is more than academics. "Our students are here, first and foremost, for academics," Viets says. "If they don't come in with a strong work ethic, they're not going to make it. But there are other parts of student life that are critical to their personal and professional development." Education takes precedence, but the university offers a slate of 18 NCAA Division III sports, plus intramural sports and 50 student organizations.

Advanced Laboratories

The advanced engineering laboratories that are integrated into the curriculum comprise one of MSOE's true strengths. The labs use the latest full-size industry equipment, and are frequently sponsored by companies that have a particular interest in a specific area of science or engineering.

Perhaps the most prominent MSOE laboratory is the Rapid Prototyping Laboratory. As the name implies, this laboratory prepares products or concepts for market well before traditional means would normally allow. The concept-to-design process takes hours, rather than weeks or months. In medical applications, certain brain surgeries have been reduced from 15 to seven hours. Advanced computer modeling programs are the key. MSOE is the only university in the world to have four rapid-prototyping machines—an advanced and expensive technology—for use by undergraduates. The lab made headlines in 2000 when the technology was used to help solve a murder; the lab's equipment helped reconstruct what the victim's face looked like, based on the remains found by authorities.

MSOE is helping provide a solution to the state's brain drain in which high-tech, highly trained individuals go elsewhere for jobs. While the university hosts students from 30 nations, nearly two-thirds of its alumni live in Wisconsin, particularly in Milwaukee. Part of the reason for the university's ability to attract and retain local talent is that MSOE recruits heavily in Wisconsin, and Wisconsinites are happy to stay close to home when they graduate. When they do venture from the state, expect big things: MSOE alumni helped found Apple Computers and Compaq Computers, as well as a myriad of other companies and organizations.

As Viets says, "The work ethic, the commitment, the focus: these touchstones at MSOE reflect what Milwaukee is all about."

STUDENTS UTILIZE THEIR ENGINEERING SKILLS WHILE HAVING THE OPPORTUNITY TO BECOME DJS, VOLUNTEERS, AND BROADCAST ENGINEERS AT MSOE'S "FRONTIER RADIO" STATION, WMSE 91.7-FM. THE AWARD-WINNING STATION NOW HAS CONTINUOUS LIVE BROADCASTS ON THE WEB (LEFT).

SENIOR PROJECTS PROVIDE THE OPPORTUNITY FOR STUDENTS TO SYNTHESIZE THE MATERIAL THEY HAVE LEARNED DURING THEIR FIRST THREE YEARS AT MSOE. PNEUMAN, AN ANIMATRONICS (LIFELIKE ROBOTIC) FIGURE WAS CREATED TO HIGHLIGHT THE LATEST IN ELECTROPNEUMATIC TECHNOLOGY (RIGHT).

MSOE STUDENTS WON THE SOCIETY OF AUTOMOTIVE ENGINEERS (SAE) AERO DESIGN COMPETITION THREE YEARS IN A ROW.

City by the Waters

Western States Envelope Company

Since 1908, Western States Envelope Company has specialized in analyzing and satisfying the unique envelope and stationery needs of the graphic arts industry. Today, as one of the largest envelope manufacturers in the nation, the company maintains four full-service plants, which are located in Butler, Wisconsin; Maplewood, Minnesota; Erlanger, Kentucky; and Wallbridge, Ohio. The Butler headquarters facility has some 235,000 square feet and 500 employees.

"With an unparalleled inventory, innovative approaches, and leading-edge equipment," says Mark Lemberger, president, "Western States provides a quality product and superior service."

The company has the largest and most diverse finished paper-goods inventory in North America, which allows for immediate shipment of most items. Western States' 24-hour-a-day production, state-of-the-art facilities, and comprehensive service provide the flexibility to support today's need-it-now marketplace.

Innovation, Efficiency, and Reliability

Western States is constantly reinventing itself to provide the latest and greatest improvements in its field. The company develops new processes, designs innovative approaches, and invests in the most advanced equipment. In conjunction with Western States' in-house engineering capabilities, these practices allow the company to offer the fastest possible turnaround of even one-of-a-kind designs.

"Our goal is to set the standard," Lemberger says. "We use only the finest raw materials from suppliers that produce to our specifications. And our continually improving quality-control processes go beyond industry requirements." This ensures that the final product runs perfectly on customers' printing and inserting equipment, thereby improving operational efficiency.

Western States provides such services as die cutting, printing, window punching, folding, and adhesive application, as well as envelope conversion. The company frequently works directly with machine manufacturers to develop new equipment that increases efficiency and cost-effectiveness.

"We will make envelopes of any size and description, in any quantity," Lemberger notes. "Our machinery runs the gamut from the latest high-speed, all-in-one presses to older machines that are perfect for smaller runs. We also have the in-house capability to fold and create specialized, small-quantity envelopes by hand."

One area of particular emphasis at Western States is customer service. With one phone call, customers can receive instant, accurate estimates; reliable advice about more cost-effective or innovative ways to approach their projects; or up-to-the-minute information about the status of an order. Western States' customer service representatives undergo thorough training that is unique to the industry. They work as a team with the sales, manufacturing, and production departments, ensuring that customers always get the best products for their needs when they need them.

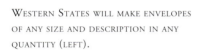

Western States Envelope Company's Butler headquarters facility has some 235,000 square feet and 500 employees.

Western States will make envelopes of any size and description in any quantity (left).

Western States Envelope Company was founded in 1908 (right).

· 322 ·

Milwaukee

BRADY CORPORATION

For nearly a century, Brady Corporation (NYSE: BRC)—one of Milwaukee's most innovative companies—has maintained its position as the leading manufacturer and marketer of complete identification solutions. The company produces more than 30,000 products ranging from high-performance labels, safety signs, and precision die-cut materials to printers, software, and data-collection systems. Brady serves a wide-range of markets including telecommunications, electronics, electrical, manufacturing, transportation, warehousing, and education.

The company was founded by William H. Brady Sr. in 1914 in Eau Claire, Wisconsin, producing advertising specialty products such as calendars and punch cards for banks, feed mills, and other local businesses. During World War II, the firm, under the direction of Brady's sons Fred and Bill, began manufacturing pressure-sensitive labels to mark wires in military equipment and the electrical industry. Under Bill Brady, the company grew from about $3 million in sales in 1960 to about $200 million in 1990. Today, the company's sales are near $600 million, with Brady employees striving to increase sales by 15 percent a year.

With more than 3,100 employees in operations in more than 20 countries, and distribution in more than 70 countries, Brady provides local support and manufacturing to a wide range of customers, including Airbus Industries, Boeing, Cisco, Dell, Ericsson, General Motors, IBM, Johnson & Johnson, Lucent, Motorola, Nokia, Siemens, Solectron, Texas Instruments, and more than 300,000 others. With dozens of Web sites, including its corporate site at www.bradycorp.com, Brady is reaching out to more businesses around the globe, providing access to its products and information with the click of a mouse.

Brady meets customers' needs in many ways. Brady helps companies comply with safety and environmental regulations with its high-performance signs, pipe markers, lockout/tagout devices, and regulatory consulting. Brady identification products remain in place and readable even under demanding conditions, such as exposure to harsh chemicals, abrasion, weathering, extreme temperatures, static-sensitivity, and more. Brady's automatic identification and data collection solutions—including bar code and radio frequency labels and scanners, software, and services—increase companies' productivity by providing the tools needed to seamlessly gather and use information across an entire enterprise. Inside cellular phones and other electronics devices, Brady precision die-cut materials improve product performance by protecting, filtering, adhering, and identifying.

"Brady products and services help customers increase safety, security, productivity, and performance, says Katherine M. Hudson, president and CEO. "Our focus is always on creating value—value for our customers, our employees, and our shareholders. This focus has helped Brady to achieve impressive growth and profitability."

Named one of the 100 Best Corporate Citizens by Business Ethics Magazine, Brady is also committed to creating value in the communities

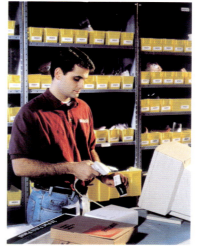

where it operates. In Milwaukee, for example, Brady's annual Academic All-Stars program has honored more than 1,250 high school scholar athletes and awarded more than $270,000 in college scholarships.

"As we look ahead, we recognize that Brady's future, and that of so many other businesses, rests with the educational opportunities given to today's young people," Hudson says. "Brady is proud to play a part in opening more educational doors and working with area schools to enhance the learning experience."

BRADY CORPORATION'S IDENTIFICATION SOLUTIONS, INCLUDING BAR-CODE LABELS, SCANNERS, AND SOFTWARE, HELP COMPANIES INCREASE PRODUCTIVITY BY MANAGING CRITICAL DATA QUICKLY AND ACCURATELY.

BRADY CORPORATION HAS OPERATIONS IN 20 COUNTRIES AND DISTRIBUTION IN MORE THAN 70. ITS GLOBAL HEADQUARTERS ARE IN MILWAUKEE.

THOMAS A. MASON CO., INC.

In 1912, Thomas Macaione, a recent emigrant from Sicily, founded a painting company in Milwaukee based on his old-world painting skills and experience with fine finishes. Shortly after establishing the business in the United States, he changed the family name to Mason. Mason used a horse-drawn wagon to carry paint and equipment to his jobs, mostly at local residences. Despite personal tragedy and the lean years of the Great Depression, Mason and his firm persevered, and he enjoyed a reputation for work well done.

Upon his death in the late 1950s, Mason's son Domenic took over the business, heading the firm through the early 1980s. Representing the firm's third generation, Thomas A. Mason, named after his grandfather, and his younger brother Steven J. Macaione—who reverted back to the family name—learned the painting trade working in the family business while teenagers. Eventually, Thomas and Steven gravitated to office positions.

At that time, the company was a father-son business with six employees and sales of about $250,000 a year. For years, the firm continued to operate out of the offices built in the basement of the founder's downtown home. The company did mostly high-end, single- and multi-family residential painting for decades before gradually advancing to commercial painting, its primary area of business today. Thomas A. Mason Co., Inc. is now a $9 million firm located in a two-story, renovated brick building on Martin Luther King Drive at the outskirts of downtown Milwaukee.

In the past decade, the company has provided all of the painting and wall coverings at the Midwest Express Convention Center, in addition to painting the rotunda and south wing for the restoration of the Wisconsin state capitol. Thomas A. Mason Co., Inc. also provided finishes for the parking structure and Concourse D at General Mitchell International Airport. And for Miller Park, the firm provided painting services and wall coverings, as well as carpeting and resilient flooring—including rubber, vinyl, and linoleum. In both public and private sector jobs, the company specializes in wood finishing, special coatings, and hard tile.

"Steve and I were born and raised in the Midwest," Thomas Mason says. "We watched our father get up and go to work, work all day, and come home with sweat on his brow. We learned a lot from him."

Expanding beyond Milwaukee

The company has expanded the scope of its work beyond the Milwaukee area to Racine, Kenosha, and Madison. In 1997, Thomas Mason relocated his family to a mountain resort area of Colorado, where he runs a satellite office from his home. He soon found that his was the only union painting contractor in the area, and that there was a shortage of skilled and dedicated workers. As a solution, he flies in his Milwaukee-office tradespeople and houses them in a 12-person lodge that his firm purchased and renovated. His Milwaukee labor force and its phenomenal work ethic make it cost effective for large-scale jobs in Colorado, including a new resort, large residences, and several school

Thomas A. Mason Co., Inc. has painted such areas as the UW Center on Grand Avenue (top) and the IMAX Dome Theatre (bottom).

projects, where quality and scheduling are essential.

"The Milwaukee work ethic allows us to be more competitive in the mountain area," Mason says. "Our productivity per hour is greater for Milwaukee workers than for most of our Colorado workers, which means we get more done in a shorter period of time. And it's quality work. Our Milwaukee workers provide the manpower for larger jobs, and their efficiency helps offset travel costs."

Mason's tradespeople, for example, have provided painting and wood finishing services at the Zephyr Mountain Lodge under construction in Winter Park, Colorado, which includes condominiums as well as a ski resort.

The Art and Science of Painting

Thomas A. Mason Co., Inc. continues to build on its nine decades of knowledge and maintains state-of-the-art commercial painting equipment, from the latest paint sprayers to different types of rigging, plus the best new products from waterborne acrylics to unique floor coverings.

The firm has 60 union tradespeople on staff, which allows the company to bid on even the largest jobs. With one telephone call, a client has access to the in-house, on-staff expertise of skilled tradespeople, including members of the United Brotherhood of Carpenters of America and the International Brotherhood of Painters and Allied Trades. Because it does not need to subcontract to other firms to perform work, Thomas A. Mason Co., Inc. maintains control of quality, budget, and timing.

The company is sought after for its service and dependability. It can handle any project, from a small retail space to a convention center, on schedule and on budget. The firm is often chosen for high-end finishing work because of its reputation for quality, which has lasted nearly 90 years.

"There are some buildings in downtown Milwaukee," says Mason, "that our grandfather helped finish when they were new and that our father would later help renovate. As the third generation, we may help finish a new building that replaces an original. Through the years, our family has considered the downtown skyline to truly be our own."

THE FIRM IS OFTEN CHOSEN FOR HIGH-END FINISHING WORK BECAUSE OF ITS REPUTATION FOR QUALITY AS IN ITS WORK ON THE RIVERWALK PLAZA CONDOMINIUMS (TOP LEFT), THE MIDWEST EXPRESS CENTER (TOP RIGHT), AND MILLER PARK (BOTTOM).

City by the Waters

GREDE FOUNDRIES, INC.

THE FUNDAMENTAL FOUNDRY PRACTICE OF POURING MOLTEN metal into sand molds has not changed significantly since the industrial revolution. But, through the decades, there has been a fairly steady technological evolution in how this work is done, with much of the process once accomplished by muscles now performed by machines. Grede Foundries, Inc. has been at the forefront of this advancement.

Founded in 1920, when Milwaukee native William J. "Bill" Grede, at the age of 23, purchased the Liberty Foundry, Grede Foundries has continuously expanded its facilities and its expertise. Today, with 5,000 employees in 12 plants, Grede is the largest privately held foundry headquartered in the United States. An international firm, Grede has a facility near Birmingham, England, and has plans for a joint venture in Monterrey. The company pours gray iron, ductile iron, and steel in order to manufacture items such as valves, engine parts, axles, and crankshafts.

State-of-the-art automation, mechanization, and use of computers require employees to possess a level of knowledge and technical sophistication greater than ever before. "Today, we're hiring more for brains than for brawn," says W. Stewart Davis, vice president of human resources and a third-generation member of the family-owned business. Davis and his cousin Bruce Jacobs, president and CEO, are principals in the firm.

The Changing Face of the Industry

Through more than two decades with Grede, Jacobs and Davis have seen major transformations in the foundry industry. From about 6,000 U.S. foundries in the 1970s, only some 2,500 remain today. The general globalization of business has affected the industry, and many foundry customers have shifted their operations overseas in order to cut costs and remain competitive—causing foundries and

THE PRACTICE OF POURING MOLTEN METAL INTO SAND MOLDS IS DONE VERY DIFFERENTLY TODAY THAN IT WAS DURING THE 1950S AND MILWAUKEE-BASED GREDE FOUNDRIES, INC. HAS BEEN AT THE FOREFRONT OF THIS ADVANCEMENT SINCE ITS FOUNDING IN 1920.

GREDE RECOGNIZES THAT ITS EMPLOYEES ARE RESPONSIBLE FOR ITS SUCCESS. UNDER THE LEADERSHIP OF PRESIDENT AND CEO BRUCE JACOBS (TOP, ON RIGHT) THEY ARE HELPING THE COMPANY ACHIEVE GREATER INNOVATIION.

other suppliers to do the same.

But, as advances in metallurgy have yielded new alloys and increased quality requirements, Grede has kept pace. The company has achieved the international quality standard rating ISO 9000 and the U.S. automotive quality standard QS 9000. Comprising about 50 percent of revenues, the automotive industry represents the largest segment of Grede's business. In addition to auto manufacturers and auto component suppliers, major customers include Caterpillar, J.I. Case, John Deere, and Allied Signal.

Although some things have changed, much at Grede remains the same. The privately held company operates on the guiding principles of integrity, honesty, and hard work. Intrinsic to the Grede philosophy is the fair treatment of employees. Productive employees are well rewarded through merit pay, performance bonuses, incentive compensation, employee benefits, education reimbursements, and more.

"Employees are the competitive advantage we've concentrated on for 80 years," Davis says. "And we don't see any reason why that needs to change now. The investment we make in people is significant. We hate to see someone walk out the door, knowing how much effort went into preparing that employee to be a contributing member of the team."

Loyal Employees, Loyal Customers

Typically, a company balances the size of its workforce with customer orders. But Grede long ago recognized that the expense of recruiting and training far outweighed the cost of keeping employees on the payroll during times of reduced customer orders. Unusual among large manufacturers, the company has a no-layoff policy. Despite fluctuations in customer orders, Grede employees can count on job security, and as a result, Grede can respond quickly to new orders with a well-trained and knowledgeable workforce.

"We are a responsible employer who treats people with the dignity and respect we all deserve as individuals," Davis says. "At Grede, employees have many opportunities to advance their careers as far as possible, based on their performance and willingness to work. Many employees spend a lifetime with us."

Grede is also unique in that it prefers to choose its customers rather than be chosen by them. The company conducts market research and actively solicits new accounts that best fit its capabilities and philosophy. With strict quality controls and integrated information systems, everything is designed to facilitate a long-term, mutually beneficial relationship with customers.

The results are obvious. For more than 80 years, Grede Foundries has played a key role in Milwaukee's industrial base—a position it plans to fill throughout the years to come.

City by the Waters · 327 ·

Lincoln State Bank

In 1920, Lincoln State Bank was founded as a single branch by Polish businessmen in the southside neighborhood of Milwaukee, along Lincoln Avenue. Like the Milwaukee community, the bank has shown remarkable growth, with nearly $200 million in assets and branch locations in several communities throughout the area. Its mission remains the same: to serve the community—its residents, schools, churches, organizations, and businesses.

A subsidiary of Merchants & Manufacturers BanCorp (MMBC), Lincoln State Bank today has its main office on South 13th Street, just 20 feet from its original building. In addition, the bank has branches in Brookfield, Muskego, New Berlin, and Pewaukee, as well as eight Convenience Centers located in senior care facilities in Milwaukee, Hales Corners, Greenfield, West Allis, and Muskego. Other subsidiaries of MMBC include Franklin State Bank, Grafton State Bank, Lincoln Community Bank, and Lincoln Neighborhood Redevelopment Corporation. A new name, Community BancGroup, and symbol have recently been adopted to help customers identify all MMBC member banks.

Service before Size

A full-service financial institution, Lincoln State Bank offers neighborhood banking, whereby customers can perform transactions at any one of the corporation's 12 locations. In addition to its retail banking focus, Lincoln State Bank provides commercial banking for small and medium-sized businesses. "We offer the financial strength of four banks within our network," notes Michael J. Murry, chairman of MMBC, "while maintaining our emphasis on local decision making in the communities we serve." To prove the bank's readiness to go the extra mile for its customers, Murry accompanied a local businessman to Poland to examine a company the customer was considering buying.

Not content to wait for the community to come to the bank, Murry developed a strategy whereby commercial lenders work from within

The original Lincoln State Bank, located on Lincoln Avenue near 13th Street, was built in 1920 (top).

Lincoln State Bank today has its main office on South 13th Street, just 20 feet from its original building (bottom).

Milwaukee

customer establishments—instead of from their own desks—so they can take bank services and loans directly to their customers. This customer-centric program caught the eye of *The Wall Street Journal*, which ran an article about the bank that makes "house calls."

Historically, Lincoln State Bank has been unusually innovative. For years, it has provided multi-lingual banking services, including Polish and Spanish, in addition to English. In 1950, it opened Milwaukee County's first drive-in auto bank. In 1990, it introduced Convenience Center banking located in senior living centers. Bank staff provide on-site financial services so seniors do not have to leave the residence.

Focus on the Community

Even with its remarkable success and expansion, the bank still maintains the warmth and family-oriented approach of its founders. Banking at Lincoln State Bank has become a social occasion, with free coffee, cookies, and popcorn, as well as holiday visits from Santa Claus and the Easter bunny. In keeping with this community focus, the bank offers accounts for nonprofit organizations, as well as for minors and senior citizens. It also continues to issue one of the vestiges of another era—passbook savings.

Today, Lincoln State Bank strives to bring together businesses and residents in the neighborhoods it serves. The bank has always offered what the modern banking industry calls high-touch service. When customers call the bank, for example, they talk to an actual person rather than being confronted with an endless menu of automated telephone options.

If some improvement is going on in its neighborhood, Lincoln State Bank is very likely to be involved. The institution works closely with the Lincoln Neighborhood Redevelopment Corporation, providing financing for small businesses and an affordable housing program.

The bank has earned a reputation for its innovation in structuring loans and banking services that enable its customers to become successful. "We look beyond the numbers," explains Cynthia A. Loew, president and CEO of Lincoln State Bank. "We strive to know our customers and understand their banking needs. These are people from a neighborhood we are committed to, so our judgment factors are not limited strictly to statistics."

Lincoln State Bank's leaders continually find new ways to reach out to the community, whether spearheading the restoration of St. Josephat's Basilica or serving on the board of directors of organizations such as hospitals, colleges, and fund-raising events. "We have a close working relationship with educational and religious institutions in the area," Loew notes. "Besides working in a professional capacity within the communities they serve, our employees often participate in citywide events and volunteer for charitable activities.

"What began as a neighborhood bank has flourished," Loew continues, "while maintaining its character and loyalty to the community."

"What began as a neighborhood bank has flourished," says Cynthia Loew, president and CEO of Lincoln State Bank, "while maintaining its character and loyalty to the community." (top)

In 1950, Lincoln State Bank introduced the auto bank concept to Milwaukee (bottom).

City by the Waters

· 329 ·

© JOHN J. BACIK III

1921-1928

1921
Grubb & Ellis | Boerke Company

1925
Pereles Brothers, Inc.

1927
Klement Sausage Co., Inc.

1928
Helwig Carbon Products Inc.

1934
Kalmbach Publishing Co.

1935
Plunkett Raysich Architects

1936
Dafoss Graham

1939
Andrus, Sceales, Starke & Sawall, LLP

GRUBB & ELLIS | BOERKE COMPANY

FOUNDED IN 1921, THE BOERKE COMPANY IS A LEADER in Milwaukee's real estate markets. Formed by Edison M. Boerke, the firm was the first in the city to specialize in the marketing of commercial properties. During World War II, the company served as a part of a select group that represented the U.S. government in its efforts to find and convert industrial facilities in support of the war effort. Boerke was a cofounder and past president of the Society of Industrial and Office Realtors (SIOR). In the 1950s, the company was among the first specialty firms in the country to promote corporate parks—then a pioneering concept.

Since 1997, the firm has been known as Grubb & Ellis | Boerke Company, reflecting the company's affiliation with Grubb & Ellis, a member of the New York Stock Exchange. Boerke's alliance with this market-leading firm, which serves commercial real estate interests worldwide, gives the company the ability to offer real estate services on both a national and international platform. Grubb & Ellis has the collective resources of nearly 7,000 people in 200 offices in 27 countries.

"This partnership offers us the most advanced information technology infrastructure available anywhere," says David Boerke, principal and son of the company's founder. "We can access significant Grubb & Ellis resources without leaving our office. This includes in-depth market data in every geographical area that Grubb & Ellis covers. We firmly believe that only companies with this type of connectivity will survive and flourish."

The arrangement with Grubb & Ellis allows The Boerke Company to better meet its clients' real estate needs, which include a broad array of services ranging from facilities management to sales of existing assets to creating new facilities. In addition, Grubb & Ellis also provides a private university function, offering just under a 100-course curriculum to continually educate its professionals. Moreover, The Boerke Company has developed its own unique program to recruit, mentor, and retain promising young brokers and prepare them for the partnership track.

Growth through the Years

David Boerke grew up in the real estate business, attending the real estate program at the University of Wisconsin-Madison. From a two-person firm in 1967, he has seen The Boerke Company grow to its present size of some 20 brokers and seven support staff members. From one generation to the next, the company has witnessed many changes in the real estate business. Industrial buildings have shifted from locally owned, multistory facilities to separate, institutionally owned facilities—wired and flexible—on corporate campuses. In the past, major Milwaukee corporations and institutional investors had in-house real estate departments; today, most companies outsource much of their real estate functions. Unlike the past, Grubb & Ellis | Boerke Company now provides an ongoing consultative approach to guiding clients to a more favorable future.

In the early 1990s, in order to complement its other divisions, the firm merged with Brian Riordan Company, a company specializing in the retail real estate sector. In 1998, Boerke acquired the Harrigan Company, Inc., essentially a 100 percent industrial real estate firm. And in 1999, the Jaymes Company, also focusing on industrial real estate, was added to the firm. Today, The Boerke Company continues as a full-service real estate firm, servicing the industrial, office, retail, and investment markets.

SINCE 1997, THE FIRM HAS BEEN KNOWN AS GRUBB & ELLIS | BOERKE COMPANY, REFLECTING ITS AFFILIATION WITH GRUBB & ELLIS, A MEMBER OF THE NEW YORK STOCK EXCHANGE (TOP).

GRUBB & ELLIS | BOERKE COMPANY'S EXPERTISE ENABLED IT TO BE RETAINED BY AN INSTITUTIONAL OWNER TO FIRST LEASE AND THEN ADVISE IN THE SALE OF THE MILWAUKEE CENTER (BOTTOM).

Milwaukee

Areas of Specialty

During the office boom of the late 1970s and 1980s, the firm was involved with development groups that brought new ideas and products to Milwaukee. By the early 1980s, The Boerke Company was doing as much office business as industrial, reflecting the Milwaukee economy's shift from a manufacturing base. "The firm's expertise in the office segment has progressed to the point that, in 1998, we were retained by an institutional owner to first lease and then advise in the sale of the Milwaukee Center, a 375,000-square-foot, 27-story office tower," says Andrew Jensen, principal and manager of the company's office group.

In 1984, the company introduced the concept locally of a tenant's representative, also known as a buyer's broker. Today, large transactions have become much more complex; each side has the need for an advisor. "This new component of service has mushroomed in recent years, and is expected to continue to do so in the future," Boerke notes.

The firm's most recent involvements include Mitchell International Business Park, a state-of-the-art, airport-oriented corporate center that was developed in cooperation with the City of Cudahy, Wisconsin; Milwaukee County Government; and Wisconsin Energy. The company also assembled the land and helped coordinate the development and marketing of the 350-acre West-ridge Corporate Park and the 200-acre Silver Spring Corporate Park, anchored by the 650,000 square foot Kohl's Corporation Headquarters facility.

The Road Ahead

Ever vigilant to stay on the cutting edge of the real estate industry, Grubb & Ellis | Boerke Company will continue to grow in its role as a real estate advisor by combining its well-known transactional capabilities with an ongoing consultative approach to real estate. The company's objective is always to turn complex issues into simple solutions that look beyond an existing requirement to long-term goals for the firm's clients. More than anything else, this approach has made the company a leader in its industry.

"When it comes to commercial real estate, nothing is accomplished without the cooperation of the Milwaukee community," Boerke says. "For this reason, we encourage our professionals to become leaders in their local communities. Creating value in today's commercial markets requires cooperation and trust between local officials, our clients, and an experienced real estate advisor such as Grubb & Ellis | Boerke Company.

THE FIRM ASSEMBLED THE LAND AND HELPED COORDINATE THE DEVELOPMENT AND MARKETING OF THE SILVER SPRING CORPORATE PARK (TOP LEFT).

MITCHELL INTERNATIONAL BUSINESS PARK IS AMONG THE FIRM'S MOST RECENT INVOLVEMENTS (TOP RIGHT).

PRINCIPALS (LEFT TO RIGHT)—JACK PRICE, KEVIN RIORDAN, ANTHONY WELLS, TERENCE MCMAHON, ANDREW JENSEN, DAVID BOERKE, JAMES BABIASZ, CHAD VANDE ZANDE. NOT PICTURED— BRIAN RIORDAN (BOTTOM LEFT).

AS A TRUSTED ADVISOR, GRUBB & ELLIS | BOERKE COMPANY NOT ONLY IDENTIFIED A PREMIER LOCATION ON MILWAUKEE'S LAKEFRONT FOR THE HAMISCHFEGER CORPORATION, THEY ASSISTED IN THE ACQUISITION AND DEVELOPMENT OF THE PROPERTY (BOTTOM RIGHT).

City by the Waters

PERELES BROS., INC.

Pereles Bros., Inc. (PBI) is a venerable Milwaukee firm specializing in plastic injection molding and related services. Brothers Joe and Al Pereles founded the firm in 1925 as a light manufacturing operation, and got into plastic fabricating in the 1930s. The company produced lenses for military vehicles during World War II. ■ After the war, PBI produced sunglasses, drafting scales and templates, and slide rules for engineering applications. The company also produced electric power components for Milwaukee's Allen Bradley Co., and camera components and lenses for Bell & Howell and Polaroid. An important contract in the 1960s came from locally owned Badger Meter; PBI converted many of Badger Meter's cast and machined metal parts to molded-to-size plastic.

In 1970, Al Pereles sold PBI to Beatrice Foods, and at that time Keith Tracy began managing operations. In 1981, Tracy and his partner, Don Biesecker, purchased PBI from Beatrice. At the time, PBI had about $4 million in annual sales and produced, among other things, ice-cream containers. The partners rebuilt the firm, and Tracy bought out Biesecker in 1991, when sales had reached nearly $9.5 million. Today, with 140 employees working around the clock in a 47,000-square-foot facility, the company records annual sales of about $13 million.

Tracy retired in 2000 after serving 30 years of leadership with the company. Upon his retirement, he assured management continuity of the company by transferring ownership to the salaried employees and

three key executives through an employee stock ownership plan. While Tracy remains involved in a consulting capacity, the three key executives—Ted Muccio, president; Les Wilson, vice president/CFO, and Bill Chase, vice president/chief engineer—are the firm's officers, directors, and trustees.

Products and Processes

Key to PBI's success in the last decade was its entrance into the parts market of the power tool industry. The company has provided parts to Emerson Electric, Milwaukee Electric Tools, and Snap-On Tools. Other PBI customers include Chilton Products, Bemis Manufacturing, John Deere & Company, the generator division of Kohler Co., Sanyo, Siemans/Furnace Controls, Miller Electric, Thomas Industries, Elco-Textron, and Wells Manufacturing. PBI products include automotive parts, electronics, medical products, and parts for consumer durables such as appliances and lawn and garden equipment.

In addition to plastic injection molding, the company offers ancillary finishing processes such as hot stamping, sonic welding, pad printing, assembly, and packaging. PBI has developed a unique custom machine that provides the molding of two colors and/or materials at the same time. The process is often used in overmolding, in which a molded part encases another part, as in soft-touch grips on handles. This process has been added to the

CLOCKWISE FROM TOP:
PERELES BROS., INC. (PBI), ESTABLISHED IN 1925, SPECIALIZES IN PLASTIC INJECTION MOLDING AND RELATED SERVICES.

AFTER WORLD WAR II, PBI PRODUCED SUNGLASSES, DRAFTING SCALES AND TEMPLATES, AND SLIDE RULES FOR ENGINEERING APPLICATIONS, AS WELL AS ELECTRIC POWER COMPONENTS, CAMERA COMPONENTS, AND CAMERA LENSES.

KEY TO PBI'S SUCCESS IN THE LAST DECADE WAS ITS ENTRANCE INTO THE PARTS MARKET OF THE POWER TOOL INDUSTRY. THE COMPANY ALSO PRODUCES AUTOMOTIVE PARTS, ELECTRONICS, MEDICAL PRODUCTS, AND PARTS FOR CONSUMER DURABLES SUCH AS APPLIANCES AND LAWN AND GARDEN EQUIPMENT.

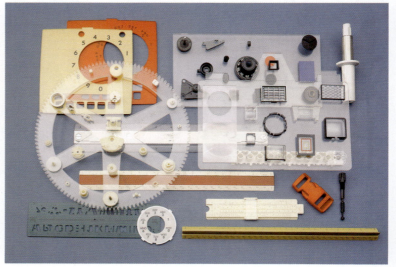

traditional plastic molding capabilities of PBI.

A significant market for PBI is insert molding in which another part, such as a metal switch component, may be inserted into a plastic mold and surrounded by a plastic material; a switch could then have electric conductivity at one end and be insulated to a larger assembly by its plastic area. Insert molding provides quality assemblies, and increases the opportunity for cost efficiencies through the elimination of excess labor, equipment, and inventory management expenses.

"This process has become an excellent choice for items previously produced with multiple components," notes Tracy. "For example, insert molding can fabricate several individual pieces into one component permanently and automatically with no further assembly required." Insert molding simplifies the assembly process by decreasing the manufacturing steps required to produce a finished product. Where a component once required multiple stages of assembly, it can now be accomplished by PBI with insert molding in one integrated operation.

Product appearance is enhanced with PBI insert molding through the elimination of unsightly joints. Additional fasteners and adhesives are no longer necessary with the use of insert molding, allowing the assembly to remain compact. The result is a sleek, attractive product devoid of any unnecessary parts or seams. The company's insert-molded components also withstand extreme temperatures, moisture, vibration, and corrosion, which makes injection-molded parts applicable to a wide range of environments.

Innovations and Quality Assurance

PBI was an early adapter of computer-aided design (CAD) technology. Today, the company uses CAD to develop plastic parts, prototypes, and design tools to create plastic parts. Customers simply transmit technical data via the Internet and CD-ROM. Furthermore, PBI can transmit engineering data electronically to its suppliers and tooling vendors as needed. The company also has a program management system that allows tooling and molding development to be integrated to assure timely completion with quality results.

Another valuable quality assurance program is PBI's design audit in which all PBI disciplines involved in a project audit both the product designs and the tool designs before tooling is started and during tooling development. PBI utilizes standardized management tools for maintaining process and quality control. The firm's computerized process control monitors temperatures and repetitive movements of molding machines so manual adjustments are seldom necessary. This system provides a consistent product and improves quality as well. The company is certified ISO 9002, having met stringent criteria for the international quality standard.

"We consider ourselves a one-stop shop, from design services through tooling manufacture, product fabrication, and assembly," Muccio says. "We offer a wide range of machines that can produce parts that are extremely small or very large." The company also has unique, high-temperature molding abilities. These molds are oil heated to high temperatures and provide molding challenges that many injection molding firms do not want to participate in. But at PBI, it's just another level of expertise.

PBI's consistent pursuit of new products and processes has allowed the company to expand its client base and its record of success in the Midwest and in its industry.

PBI USES THE LATEST TECHNOLOGY TO OBTAIN STATISTICAL DATA (LEFT).

PBI HAS DEVELOPED A UNIQUE CUSTOM MACHINE THAT PROVIDES FOR THE MOLDING OF TWO MATERIALS OR TWO COLORS AT THE SAME TIME (RIGHT).

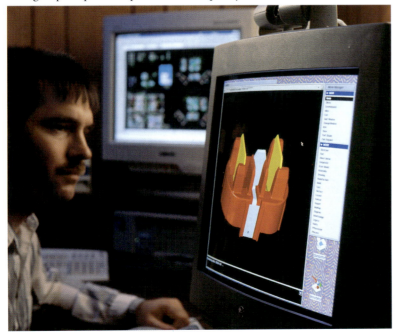

PBI WAS AN EARLY USER OF COMPUTER-AIDED DESIGN (CAD) TECHNOLOGY, AND NOW USES CAD TO DEVELOP PLASTIC PARTS, PROTOTYPES, AND DESIGN TOOLS TO CREATE PLASTIC PARTS.

City by the Waters

KLEMENT SAUSAGE CO., INC.

KLEMENT SAUSAGE CO., INC. IS MILWAUKEE'S LARGEST PRODUCER of fine, old-fashioned sausage products. The company makes more than 700 varieties of sausages for delicatessen, self-service, food service, and snack use. ■ More than four decades ago, the three Klement brothers—John, George, and Ron—purchased a small sausage company in a highly European area on the south side of Milwaukee. Each brother brought his own area of expertise to the company: John was the executive presence that provided for expansion and growth, George was a highly skilled sausage maker, and Ron was the sales organizer necessary to ensure the company's future growth. Today, each of the founders has children involved in the business. There are six second-generation relatives holding key positions in the company.

In the early days, the Klement brothers were fortunate to have European-trained sausage makers—including their father, Frank, who came out of retirement from a competitor sausage company—to help formulate recipes that appealed to the sausage lovers of the south side of Greater Milwaukee. The company's German bratwurst, Italian sausage, and savory Polish sausage soon became the basis upon which the business prospered.

From its earliest days, Klement Sausage Co. had easy access to the Wisconsin beef and pork herds that provided the boneless chucks and rounds needed to produce some of the freshest sausage America had to offer. As the business grew, the pork and beef products from feed lots throughout the Midwest—including Illinois, Iowa, and Wisconsin—continued to provide the sausage makers with fresh ingredients for a superior product.

After 40 years and five company expansions, Klement Sausage Co. has grown from a small sausage kitchen with six employees into a nationwide sausage product supplier with two state-of-the-art plants and equipment, and more than 300 employees. From the delivery of product to small meat markets on the south side of Milwaukee with half-ton trucks, the company's fleet of refrigerated trucks today services stores throughout Wisconsin twice each week. In addition, Klement Sausage Co. delivers its products to chain store warehouses throughout the United States.

Klement Sausage Co.'s emphasis on product quality and freshness has earned the company several industry awards. Most recently, the firm won the Seal of Excellence Award at the Wisconsin State Fair for its four-by-six-inch cooked ham, and has won

the Award for Meat Snack Sticks, Turkey Breast & Hams.

Quality Sausage at a Value Price

What makes Klement Sausage Co. truly successful is the quality and value of its sausage. From the leaner and tastier cuts of meat to the flavorful, natural seasoning and spices to the natural casings, Klement Sausage Co. sets a high standard that few companies achieve. In addition, the company has a USDA-certified laboratory on the premises that aids greatly in achieving product uniformity, and ensures that government-set standards for sanitation are met, which guarantees long-term shelf life for the firm's many products.

The company utilizes three separate and distinct sausage kitchens to produce its sausages. One kitchen produces only sausage from pre-rigor pork meat, which provides a lean, flavorful sausage with a shelf life that guarantees freshness both at the retail level and on the consumer's dinner table.

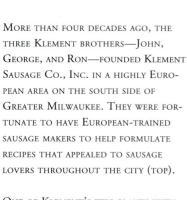

MORE THAN FOUR DECADES AGO, THE THREE KLEMENT BROTHERS—JOHN, GEORGE, AND RON—FOUNDED KLEMENT SAUSAGE CO., INC. IN A HIGHLY EUROPEAN AREA ON THE SOUTH SIDE OF GREATER MILWAUKEE. THEY WERE FORTUNATE TO HAVE EUROPEAN-TRAINED SAUSAGE MAKERS TO HELP FORMULATE RECIPES THAT APPEALED TO SAUSAGE LOVERS THROUGHOUT THE CITY (TOP).

ONE OF KLEMENT'S TWO PLANTS WITH THE MOST MODERN CONSTRUCTION AND STATE-OF-THE-ART EQUIPMENT AND WHOSE PRODUCT QUALITY IS CONTROLLED BY A USDA HACCP CERTIFIED LABORATORY (BOTTOM)

· 336 ·

Milwaukee

Klement Sausage Co.'s second kitchen is the cooked and smoked kitchen, where curing ingredients are added to natural hardwood smoke for consumer protection and flavor. And in the company's third kitchen, which is used to manufacture semidry sausage, summer sausages of every size and flavor are naturally smoked with hardwoods to ensure taste and long-term shelf life.

This division of sausage-making processes sets the standard for the industry. As a result, Klement Sausage Co.'s sausages are now sold at either the supermarket level or in gift boxes to all 50 states and several countries overseas. In fact, the company supplies sausage to virtually every gift box company in Wisconsin, a state famous for national and international distribution of cheese and sausage.

Perhaps the most important ingredient in Klement Sausage Co.'s success is the company's team of workers, from supervisors to plant union employees dedicated to the best quality at a competitive price. The workforce is directed and controlled by a group of people known as key employees. Special dinner meetings are held to inform these key people on the progress of the company; they also participate in a year-end bonus depending on the progress made on sales, engineering, production, and administrative needs. For nonunion staff, Klement Sausage Co. has a profit sharing plan, and for union workers, a retirement pension plan is offered.

Klement Sausage Co. also has yearly Christmas parties for current and retired employees and their spouses. Various awards are distributed, and a short update of the company's progress is presented. Once every five years, the company holds a summer picnic for the families of current and retired employees. The event features fun, food, games, and prizes.

With state-of-the-art equipment and engineering, a committed labor force, and a dedication to achieving maximum quality at a value price, Klement Sausage Co. has grown to become a leader in its industry. From bratwurst to Italian sausage and Polish sausage to frankfurters, the company's products will continue to be among the finest sausages in the United States for decades to come.

KLEMENT SAUSAGE CO.'S SAUSAGE HAUS PROVIDES TASTY SAUSAGES TO BASEBALL FANS AT MILWAUKEE'S MILLER PARK (TOP).

PERHAPS THE MOST IMPORTANT INGREDIENT IN KLEMENT SAUSAGE CO.'S SUCCESS IS ITS TEAM OF WORKERS, WHO ARE PROVIDING THE BEST QUALITY AT A COMPETITIVE PRICE (LEFT).

ONCE EVERY FIVE YEARS, THE COMPANY HOLDS A SUMMER PICNIC—COMPLETE WITH FUN, FOOD, GAMES, AND PRIZES—FOR THE FAMILIES OF CURRENT AND RETIRED EMPLOYEES (RIGHT).

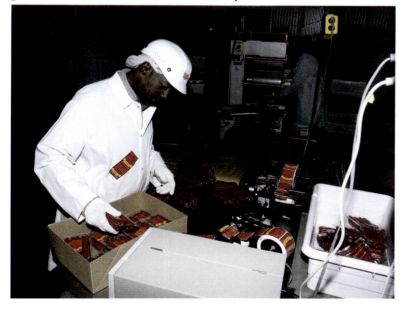

City by the Waters

· 337 ·

KALMBACH PUBLISHING CO.

Kalmbach Publishing Co. and its nearly 300 employees publish magazines, books, and videos that focus in large part on hobbies, science, and other leisure-time interests. Kalmbach's hallmark has long been its publications' beautiful illustrations, outstanding photography, and authoritative editorial content. Altogether, there are 14 magazine titles that account for 80 percent of Kalmbach's business. The company, which has an extensive Internet presence, also produces hobby exhibitions, predominantly on the East Coast where its Greenberg Shows division is located. Kalmbach distributes nearly 50 magazines for other publishers through hobby shops or specialty retail stores as well.

The company has grown through acquisitions of other publishers and launches of new magazines. Since 1995, eight such magazine titles have been acquired or launched. The firm's recent acquisitions include *The Writer* and *Plays*, and a recent launch was *Classic Trains*. Kalmbach does not print its own magazines, but is otherwise responsible for concept through completion, including editorial content, design, advertising sales, circulation, and marketing.

Unique among Publishers

Albert "Al" Kalmbach began the company that today bears his name as a depression-era college graduate in 1934 with no job prospects who sought to combine his hobbies of model railroading and printing. *Model Railroader* was developed as Kalmbach's first title–one that continues today as one of the company's leading magazines. His passion for quality in his magazines and customer service remains a very important part of the Kalmbach tradition and culture.

Upon entering Kalmbach's corporate office, one is reminded of the customer's importance by a quote from Kalmbach inscribed on the lobby wall: "The customer is the real boss of us all. Not a cent can be paid out for payroll unless it comes in from the customers, and not one of us would have a job for long if we didn't please the customer."

Employees, advertisers, and readers are all seen as key company customers, and are treated as VIPs, according to Gerald "Butch" Boettcher, president. "Our goal is to develop a lifelong relationship with our customers," Boettcher says. "When we get new customers, we usually retain them for life, losing few via cancellation. They're valued that way in the quality products we offer, the customer service we provide, and the manner in which we respond to customer expectations."

When readers call the company, they speak to knowledgeable Kalmbach customer service representatives, not third-party call centers. The latest information-sharing technology is emphasized to provide speedy, accurate customer service. The firm's Customer Focus Program sets service standards, including same-day shipment on orders, as well as prompt response to customer phone calls and mail inquiries.

Unlike some group publishers, Kalmbach specifies an editorial staff for each of its magazines. Ranging from three to eight members, these editorial groups are supplemented by a full complement of in-house graphic designers and illustrators, as well as outside freelance writers and contributors—all of whom are acknowledged experts in their respective fields. The advertising sales and circulation staffs are teamed by magazine title as well.

"In this way, staff members are experts and specialists on the topic of their magazine," says Boettcher. "They develop a specific knowledge and expertise regarding their readers and interests. If it isn't picture perfect and absolutely correct, our customers will know it."

KALMBACH PUBLISHING CO.'S NEARLY 300 EMPLOYEES SHARE FOUNDER ALBERT KALMBACH'S PASSION FOR QUALITY IN HIS MAGAZINES AND HIS BELIEF IN THE IMPORTANCE OF CUSTOMER SERVICE (LEFT).

KALMBACH PUBLISHING CO. OUTGREW ITS DOWNTOWN MILWAUKEE CORPORATE HEADQUARTERS IN 1989 AND MOVED INTO A SPACIOUS OFFICE IN NEARBY WAUKESHA (RIGHT).

Milwaukee

Kalmbach's family of magazines includes *Astronomy, Bead & Button, Birder's World, Classic Toy Trains, Classic Trains, Dollhouse Miniatures, FineScale Modeler, Garden Railways, Model Railroader, Model Retailer, Plays, Scale Auto Enthusiast, Trains,* and *The Writer.*

Caring for Employees

Kalmbach's employees are respected as customers, as well. When they are paid each week, a member of the company's senior management personally delivers their paycheck. Here, a family-oriented work environment calls for a 37.5-hour workweek, and employees are provided the technical and staffing resources necessary to succeed. When Kalmbach's five-year business strategy is updated each year, it is revised from the ground up with a grassroots approach that involves all departments and publications. There is an active profit-sharing plan for employees, and quarterly employee meetings are held to communicate the latest information about company finances and current business issues, and to provide an opportunity for employees to ask questions.

As part of Kalmbach's mission to provide exceptional magazines and products for its customers, all employees are encouraged to participate fully in a vibrant Customer Focus program that emphasizes the highest standards of service both internally and externally. Under the program, which debuted in 1992, each of the company's 30 departments holds meetings to identify customers' expectations, and to design and monitor performance measurements that lead to enhanced customer relationships.

In this way, the company fulfills and enriches the mission of its founder to provide the best service and the best magazines for its customers. The mission is as fresh today as it was almost 70 years ago when Kalmbach first planted the seeds of the company.

CLOCKWISE FROM TOP LEFT: KALMBACH EMPLOYEES HANDLE ALL ASPECTS OF MAGAZINE PUBLISHING INCLUDING DESIGN, ILLUSTRATION, AND PRODUCTION.

THE COMPANY PUBLISHES 14 MAGAZINES AND A VARIETY OF BOOKS AND CALENDARS RELATING TO THE SUBJECTS COVERED BY THE MAGAZINES. ALL PUBLICATIONS ARE ON DISPLAY IN THE LOBBY.

THE HEADQUARTERS IS A POPULAR SPOT FOR VISITORS WHO HAVE INTEREST IN MODEL RAILROADING OR THE OTHER HOBBIES COVERED BY KALMBACH'S PRODUCTS. A COLORFUL, INFORMATIVE, AND INTERACTIVE LOBBY DISPLAY COVERS THE HISTORY OF THE COMPANY.

City by the Waters

PLUNKETT RAYSICH ARCHITECTS

PLUNKETT RAYSICH ARCHITECTS TRACES ITS ROOTS BACK TO 1935, when Henry Plunkett began to specialize in education and medical design work. That design work became the backbone of the future of the firm. ■ James Plunkett joined the firm in 1955, after graduating from Cornell University with a degree in architecture, and David Raysich joined in 1975 with a master's degree in architecture from the University of Wisconsin-Milwaukee, becoming a partner in 1987. Kim Dale Hassell, Michael Scherbel, and Mark Herr became partners in the late 1990s, forming the five-person partnership. The company has grown through new business and various acquisitions, including that of Architects III (Schuett Design Associates) in 1998. In 1999, Plunkett Raysich formed a strategic alliance with Deutsch Associates—a Phoenix firm steeped in the design trends of the fashionable Southwest and its growing number of high-tech facilities. Combined with the firm's Madison office, Plunkett Raysich currently has some 120 employees, quite a difference from the 25 the firm employed in 1987. This includes some 40 registered architects, 30 architectural designers, and 15 interior designers.

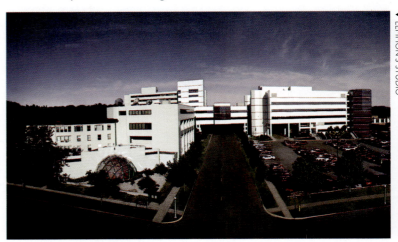

Client Success

For years, Plunkett Raysich's primary focus has been health care and education design. The company's 1992 decision to expand its focus has led to a broader base of clients, including corporate office buildings, churches, and assisted living facilities.

Plunkett Raysich's design philosophy is to go beyond delivering what the client wants, on time and on budget. Simply stated, the company seeks to exceed expectations and do each job right. "A majority of the time, a new client becomes a repeat client because they are happy with our work," Raysich says. "Our existing clients provide great references for us as well."

The majority of the firm's projects are new buildings and additions to existing structures. For example, Plunkett Raysich designed headquarters for the ProVantage Corporation, Snap-On Tools, and Badger Meter. The company's work has taken it into 12 states throughout the country with projects for ShopKo and Cumulus Broadcasting. Plunkett Raysich also designs tenant build-outs within existing buildings, such as the offices of Michael Best & Friedrich in Madison, Milwaukee, and Chicago.

Partner Participation

In a typical year, Plunkett Raysich's construction projects approach $250 million in value. Each partner in the firm heads a specific division: Scherbel handles health care, Hassell directs education and long-term care projects, and Herr supervises corporate and religious projects. Plunkett and Raysich take the lead on a variety of projects. Specifically, health care projects total about 40 percent of the firm's

CLOCKWISE FROM TOP: PLUNKETT RAYSICH ARCHITECTS' RENOVATION OF MARQUETTE GENERAL HOSPITAL IN MARQUETTE, MICHIGAN, INCLUDED AN EXPANSION PROJECT LINKING TWO BUILDINGS ON CAMPUS; THE ADDITION WAS CONSTRUCTED AS A BRIDGED STRUCTURE OVER COLLEGE AVENUE.

DESIGNED BY PLUNKETT RAYSICH, HIGH CROSSINGS—A RESIDENTIAL CARE APARTMENT COMPLEX IN MADISON—HAS AS ITS CENTRAL FOCUS A COMMUNITY DINING AREA THAT LEADS TO A SECOND-FLOOR LIBRARY.

THE CORPORATE OFFICE BUILDING FOR SNAP-ON TOOLS INCORPORATED IN KENOSHA, DESIGNED BY PLUNKETT RAYSICH, FEATURES A SWEEPING OUTDOOR WOOD DECK, ACCESSIBLE FROM THE BOARDROOM AND SECOND-FLOOR OFFICES.

Milwaukee

PLUNKETT RAYSICH'S RENOVATION OF DOWNTOWN MILWAUKEE'S FEDERAL COURTHOUSE, ORIGINALLY DESIGNED IN A RICHARDSONIAN ROMANESQUE STYLE, WAS DONE IN CONSULTATION WITH THE STATE HISTORICAL SOCIETY AND FEDERAL HISTORIC PRESERVATION GUIDELINES (LEFT).

OUR LADY OF LOURDES CATHOLIC CHURCH IN DePERE, WISCONSIN, WAS A $5.5 MILLION PROJECT—DESIGNED BY PLUNKETT RAYSICH—WHICH INVOLVED THE MERGING OF THE PARISHES OF ST. BONIFACE AND ST. JOSEPH INTO A NEW PARISH COMMUNITY (RIGHT).

business, while education and corporate offices account for about 30 percent each. The Phoenix alliance specializes in retail, manufacturing, and high-tech projects.

Plunkett Raysich sets itself apart by providing exceptional service to customers, and the company's commitment to detail and design makes it a favorite of contractors. The firm's architectural drawings are known for their accuracy and their effective use of a database of 1,000 technical details that have proved successful from church designs to office buildings.

While giving prominence to the time the firm spends on architectural design and interpreting a client's vision, Plunkett Raysich is also very conscious of quality control within the office—effectively using a series of internal review steps before a drawing is sent to a contractor. This minimizes mistakes and misunderstandings, and provides better construction details, better design documentation, and higher-quality design solutions, resulting in happy clients.

Commitment to Quality

Measuring the quality of an architectural firm requires looking at its buildings in terms of functional and human qualities, as well as of context and overall appearance. Award-winning architecture makes a positive contribution to the community. For decades, Plunkett Raysich has felt the responsibility to contribute a level of excellence to the area's common environment. Now Milwaukee's largest architectural firm, Plunkett Raysich has won a succession of awards along the way.

The American Society of Interior Designers has given awards to the firm for projects including the Firstar Building's Lakeview Market, Columbia Hospital's clinical building, and the offices of Michael Best & Friedrich. American School and University has granted awards to the firm for its Rawson Elementary School in South Milwaukee and its Medical College of Wisconsin Health Research Center. Plunkett Raysich won both national and state awards for its renovation of the federal courthouse in downtown Milwaukee.

Plunkett Raysich Architects' staff of professionals, comprising architects, designers, and planners, is dedicated to a philosophy of design excellence and sensitivity to each client's unique needs. Partner participation in every project guarantees that each client will receive the company's highest level of service and quality from design through post-occupancy.

For more than six decades, Plunkett Raysich's experienced professionals have produced award-winning work while establishing a reputation for understanding their clients' needs. The firm expects to maintain this tradition as it continues to define architectural excellence.

THE SCHOOL DISTRICT OF SOUTH MILWAUKEE UTILIZED THE TALENTS OF PLUNKETT RAYSICH WHEN SEVERE SPACE, MECHANICAL, AND ACCESSIBILITY PROBLEMS REQUIRED THE REPLACEMENT OF THE EXISTING 1930S BUILDING FOR RAWSON ELEMENTARY SCHOOL (LEFT).

PLUNKETT RAYSICH'S AWARD-WINNING PROJECT FOR MICHAEL BEST & FRIEDRICH INCLUDED A 32,000-SQUARE-FOOT, TOTAL RENOVATION AND EXPANSION OF THE FIRM'S EXISTING LAW OFFICES IN MADISON'S FIRSTAR BUILDING (RIGHT).

City by the Waters

Danfoss Graham

Founded in 1936 as a manufacturer of metallic traction drives, Danfoss Graham has progressed to produce today's energy efficient electronic adjustable frequency drives. Becoming a member of the Drives Division of the Danfoss Group in 1995, Danfoss Graham is the company's North American headquarters for HVAC adjustable frequency drive systems.

With world headquarters in Denmark, Danfoss' major worldwide markets include refrigeration and air-conditioning controls, compressors, components for burners and boilers, valves, hydraulic components, industrial controls, and industrial instrumentation, as well as electronic drives and controls. With more than 20,000 employees throughout the world, Danfoss Graham is known as a leading producer of intelligent control systems and precision mechanical and electronic devices.

Several additional Danfoss operations are headquartered in the Milwaukee facility. Nessie® water hydraulic products offer a complete range of hydraulic components that use ordinary tap water as the hydraulic medium with no additives. Nessie products are used by industries that need hydraulic power and also have important hygiene, fire risk, and environmental considerations.

Danfoss Drives Global HVAC is known and recognized as the global leader in variable speed drive solutions for the HVAC market, encompassing technology, products, application expertise, and value-added services.

Danfoss Drives for Water provides a product range covering all water processes—from abstraction to final effluent returned to nature. The company's U.S. and global business units are both located at the Milwaukee facility.

In addition to Milwaukee, Danfoss factories are located in Canada, Denmark, France, Germany, Great Britain, Mexico, Poland, Slovenia, and elsewhere in the United States. These production facilities—all geared for efficient production and all making use of the most advanced manufacturing techniques—are capable of producing more than 80,000 components daily.

Meeting the Needs of Customers

The Danfoss North American network provides customers with the vast experience and resources of the company's global organization. Field sales representatives, skilled applications engineers, and service technicians on hand at dozens of facilities provide comprehensive support.

Among Danfoss' wide range of products of precision engineering are electronic drives. The company's VLT® electronic drives provide speed control of three-phase air-conditioning motors. These units convert the fixed frequency and voltage from input power to variable frequency and voltage, precisely varying the speed of motors and enabling them to be used with maximum efficiency.

Other products offered by the company are refrigeration and air-conditioning controls, compressors for commercial refrigeration, compressors for refrigerators and freezers, thermostats for refrigerators and freezers, industrial controls, comfort controls, heating and ventilating controls, system controls, components for burners and boilers, instrumentation, SOCLA valves, and mobile hydraulics.

The Danfoss Mission

Danfoss seeks to achieve market leadership through technology, product and application expertise, and value-added services. "Today, Danfoss Drives are recognized as the world leader in

The Milwaukee facility provides headquarters for several Danfoss Graham business units (top).

Danfoss Graham's executive management team—(from left) Dawn Riley, Curt Monhart, Ralph Ewert, Al Drifka, Chuck Manz, and Bill Mudge—provides leadership for the company's operations (bottom).

drives for HVAC," says Curt Monhart, vice president, Global HVAC Business. "Our mission is to be known and recognized as global specialists, providing drive solutions for our markets."

Danfoss Graham embraces the four components of the Danfoss mission that are vital to the company's work and are evident in its operations and practices. First is its insistence on producing and delivering products to the total satisfaction of customers in global markets with a high degree of environmental consciousness. Danfoss Graham supports this goal with ISO 9001 and ISO 14000 certifications.

Danfoss operates as a committed group of people with meaningful working lives. Danfoss strives to create a professional working environment for all employees that supports and allows further development and fulfillment both as a team and as individuals. Acknowledging that satisfied employees are more productive and create better results for customers, Danfoss reinforces this statement in day-to-day operations.

Danfoss pledges that it will globally promote the Danfoss culture while supporting and respecting local values. Danfoss encourages the creation of a corporate culture based on shared values concerning human relations, quality, products, technology, and environment. At the same time, Danfoss aims to strengthen the self-respect, pride, and initiative of local entities.

Lastly, Danfoss seeks to bolster the societies in which the company plays an active role. The firm works to strengthen the community by encouraging and supporting the pursuit of economic growth and stability for its local entities and the Danfoss Group in its international activities.

Environmental Policy

In addition to focusing on producing quality products, Danfoss Graham emphasizes environmental awareness and management. Fully committed to improving environmental performance and preventing pollution, the company ensures that all activities are planned and performed with the utmost respect for the environment. Annual environmental performance improvement objectives and targets have long been established, and environmental concerns are openly discussed in a positive atmosphere.

Danfoss Graham has established the Environmental Management System to inform employees of their environmental responsibilities, ensure compliance with environmental regulations, and minimize undesirable environmental effects. This system supports the Danfoss corporate mission and environmental policy as well. After succeeding in lowering its consumption of electricity and raw materials while reducing the emissions of wastewater and other pollutants, Danfoss has received several major environmental awards for its efforts.

With industry facing a tough challenge—how to ensure continued economic growth while protecting the environment against resource depletion and pollution—Danfoss Graham is playing an important role. The company's products help to conserve energy, increase industrial efficiency, and improve living standards worldwide. Creating unique products and maintaining good practices, the company will continue on its course of success for years to come.

DANFOSS DRIVES PROVIDES THE PRECISE CONTROL OF PUMPS AND FANS TO KEEP THE MIDWEST EXPRESS CENTER COMFORTABLE YEAR-ROUND (TOP).

THE DANFOSS GRAHAM PRODUCT LINE INCORPORATES A FULL LINE OF ADJUSTABLE SPEED DRIVES, AS WELL AS SOFT STARTERS AND OPTION PANELS (BOTTOM).

City by the Waters

ANDRUS, SCEALES, STARKE & SAWALL, LLP

To protect their intellectual properties through patents, trademarks, and copyrights, inventive Milwaukeeans and corporations alike turn to the law firm of Andrus, Sceales, Starke & Sawall, LLP. With a team of 14 intellectual property attorneys, Andrus/Sceales is Wisconsin's largest law firm devoted exclusively to the practice of intellectual property law, including patents, trademarks, copyrights, trade secrets, and related matters.

Elwin A. Andrus and Merl E. Sceales founded the firm in 1939, after serving as patent attorneys at A.O. Smith Corp. The firm has grown steadily since then, and today, its distinguished list of clients includes Wisconsin Electric; Mercury Marine and other divisions of Brunswick Corp.; Waukesha Engine; Great Northern Corp.; Krueger International, Inc.; Wisconsin Alumni Research Foundation; Fleetguard/Nelson; ATO Findley, Inc.; U.S. Filter Corp.; and Datex-Ohmeda, Inc.

Special Expertise

In addition to passing the general practice bar exam, intellectual property attorneys must have a science or engineering degree and must pass a separate bar exam. Andrus/Sceales attorneys specialize in fields as diverse as biotechnology, chemistry, data processing, electromechanical engineering, pharmaceuticals, and physics.

"We can cover every possible intellectual property situation," says Gary A. Essmann, a partner with the firm. "We have a substantial pool of legal talent that offers specialties within specialties. We have the education and experience to handle anything." Half of the firm's attorneys have been with Andrus/Sceales for more than 15 years.

An important part of intellectual property law is litigation to enforce patents, trademarks, and copyrights. The firm's attorneys prosecute infringements of intellectual properties for their clients and defend clients alleged to be violators. As much as 30 percent of the firm's business is comprised of litigation issues.

Approximately 80 percent of the firm's work deals with patent issues, and about 15 percent deals with trademarks. The remainder involves copyright and other issues.

"From the guy in his garage who invents a new fishing apparatus to a major corporation that wants to trademark the name of a new product or patent a living organism, our legal expertise truly runs the gamut," says Essmann.

Often, Andrus/Sceales receives new business referred by general interest law firms that do not offer intellectual property expertise. The firm also acts as local counsel for corporations represented by out-of-state law firms. Large companies come directly to Andrus/Sceales because of its reputation for advanced knowledge and experience with all areas of intellectual property law, including international issues.

Letter of the Law

In the case of a trademark, a client may select a name and ask Andrus/Sceales to determine if the trademark is available for use. The firm searches state and federal records, and provides its opinion on whether the trademark may be used as the client intends. Such a decision involves both how the trademark will look and what products it will appear on. For example, the name of an automobile may be trademarked, but

ELWIN A. ANDRUS AND MERL E. SCEALES FOUNDED THE FIRM OF ANDRUS, SCEALES, STARKE & SAWALL, LLP IN 1939, AFTER SERVING AS PATENT ATTORNEYS AT A.O. SMITH CORP (TOP).

LOCATED ON THE RIVERWALK, THE FIRM CAN BE FOUND IN ONE OF MILWAUKEE'S MOST PRESTIGIOUS LOCATIONS (BOTTOM).

if a dairy company wanted to use the same name for its brand of cottage cheese, it probably could, as long as the trademark artwork could not be confused with that of the car.

If the trademark appears to be available, Andrus/Sceales attorneys will file the necessary application at the state or federal level. The application itself can be a complicated document. Using an experienced firm like Andrus/Sceales, a client knows that every issue will be addressed in the application, making approval of the application more likely and the litigation to protect the trademark easier. Should the trademark application be rejected, the firm will rewrite the application and guide it through the appeal process.

The patent process is similar to the trademark process, but the application is even more complex, as it includes detailed drawings of the new product. In essence, a patent application provides written and illustrated directions for the manufacture and use of the product. Obtaining a patent—from the time an application is submitted until its final approval—currently takes more than two years.

A patent application must be prepared in such a way that it can be defended against infringement, an area in which Andrus/Sceales' attorneys are experts. Their respective science and engineering backgrounds provide a great asset to clients. With Mercury Marine engines, for example, one attorney specializes in carburetor patents. Patents for other engine components are handled by other attorneys in the firm, based on their specializations.

With copyright law, educating the client is key. Ideas, for example, cannot be copyrighted. Therefore, an idea for a screenplay cannot be copyrighted, but the screenplay itself, which shows how the idea is developed and expressed, can be copyrighted. Thus, the idea for Romeo and Juliet has been the basis for many dramatic productions through the ages without protection. Technically, copyright exists as soon as something is written. However, it is much easier to enforce a copyright in court if it has been registered with the Library of Congress.

"We've been doing nothing else but intellectual property for more than 60 years and we have developed a lot of expertise," says Essmann. "Unlike other firms, intellectual property is our specialty. We don't do real estate, traffic accidents, or wills on Thursday, and then patents on Friday. Intellectual property is the only hat we wear, and we think we wear it well."

ANDRUS/SCEALES ACTS AS LOCAL COUNSEL FOR CORPORATIONS REPRESENTED BY OUT-OF-STATE LAW FIRMS (TOP).

APPROXIMATELY 80 PERCENT OF THE FIRM'S WORK DEALS WITH PATENT ISSUES, AND ABOUT 15 PERCENT DEALS WITH TRADEMARKS (BOTTOM).

City by the Waters

HELWIG CARBON PRODUCTS, INC.

Helwig Carbon Products, Inc. manufactures carbon brushes, brush holders, electrical contacts, and mechanical carbons. Carbon brushes, the company's primary products, are used throughout the industry on motors and generators. Some of the firm's trademark innovations include the Red Top multiflex brush that improves brush contact, quick-disconnect terminals that make brush maintenance easy, brush wear indicators, and brush holders that optimize brush life.

Walter O. Helwig founded the firm in 1928. He began selling carbon brushes in Milwaukee for a Pennsylvania firm, and then started manufacturing them in a garage behind his parents' flower shop. John Koenitzer, Helwig's son-in-law, came on board in the 1950s, and was largely responsible for the development of the sales force, rapid sales growth, and several innovative product features. Koenitzer is now serving as chairman of the board. Jeff Koenitzer, president, and Jay Koenitzer, vice president of marketing, represent the third generation of the family to lead Helwig Carbon Products.

Sales with Attention to Service

"Our products are not well understood, and it's not easy to select the proper brush for a given application," says Jeff Koenitzer, a professional engineer. "It's important that we build trusting relationships with our customers. We do this by manufacturing carbon brushes that are at least as good as those of the original equipment manufacturer, if not better. We also provide on-site service, trouble shooting, and the quickest deliveries because our customers need to keep their equipment operating."

With annual revenues exceeding $30 million, more than 250 employees, and a 130,000-square-foot facility in Milwaukee, Helwig is a world leader in its business. The company manufactures and sells approximately 100,000 carbon brush variations to giants of industry and mom-and-pop businesses alike.

Helwig directly serves about 15,000 customers throughout North America, although its products are shipped worldwide as components on a variety of machines and equipment. Its aftermarket customer base includes steel and paper mills, as well as the mining, metal processing, electric power, and transportation industries. Most of the orders Helwig handles are for fewer than 50 pieces, but a large OEM may order 200,000 carbon brushes at once. Helwig keeps more than 2,000 brush styles on hand, along with raw materials and hardware for fast fabrication.

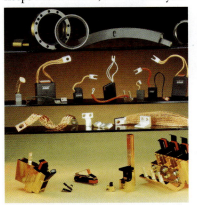

As a family-owned and privately held company, Helwig Carbon Products realizes that maximizing profits every year does not need to be a top priority. Every year, the company contributes at least 4 percent of profits to charities concentrated in the Milwaukee area, and it even donated its former facility on 30th Street to the Next Door Foundation. Helwig Carbon has also been recognized by Wisconsin Manufacturers & Commerce with awards for community commitment and for a history of employee concern.

Exceeding customer needs; providing comfortable, satisfying employment; and supporting the community have constituted the primary focus of the company, and these goals will continue to make Helwig Carbon Products successful in the future.

HELWIG CARBON PRODUCTS, INC. MANUFACTURES A VARIETY OF CARBON BRUSHES, BRUSH HOLDERS, ELECTRICAL CONTACTS, AND MECHANICAL CARBONS.

FROM ITS CORPORATE HEADQUARTERS IN MILWAUKEE, HELWIG CARBON PRODUCTS DIRECTLY SERVES ABOUT 15,000 CUSTOMERS THROUGHOUT NORTH AMERICA, AND SHIPS ITS PRODUCTS WORLDWIDE AS COMPONENTS ON A VARIETY OF MACHINES AND EQUIPMENT.

Milwaukee

1944-1953

1944
Western Industries, Inc.

1946
A.N. Ansay & Associates, Inc.

1947
Voss Jorgensen Schueler Co., Inc.

1948
GE Medical Systems

1948
Manpower Inc.

1948
STS Consultants, Ltd.

1953
HUSCO International, Inc.

1954
Corrigan Properties, Inc./Bayshore Mall

WESTERN INDUSTRIES, INC.

tto Boeheim founded Western Industries, Inc. in 1944 when he purchased an existing contract metal manufacturer that produced railroad car heaters, septic tanks, and components of larger assemblies. Today, the company is a unique blend of seven manufacturing divisions that provide plastic molding, metal fabrication, assembling, and packaging to leading original equipment manufacturers (OEMs) and retail customers. OEM client companies typically incorporate components and subassemblies into finished products, such as an appliance or tractor, while retailers direct-sell finished goods into home, garden, and leisure markets. Western's client base includes household names like Case/New Holland, Deere & Co., General Electric, Newell-Rubbermaid, Wal-Mart, and Home Depot.

The Boeheim family owned the company until the mid-1980s, when it was taken over by First Chicago Venture Capital, who sold the company to the Exor Group in 1994. Currently owned by B-G Western Holdings, LLC, a newly formed limited liability company controlled by Brera Western, LLC, and Graham Western, LP, who purchased the firm in 1999, the company's annual sales are approximately $235 million. The new owners intend to aggressively acquire complementary outsourcing businesses, as well as fuel organic growth by capitalizing on a general pattern of production outsourcing among large industrial OEMs.

Seeking the Source

Many Fortune 500 companies turn to us when they outsource a component, a subsystem, or a complete product," notes Jerry Sorrow, president and CEO. "They look to Western Industries for quality parts, continuous cost reduction, waste elimination, speed, and flexibility. We offer a lean enterprise methodology that examines the entire manufacturing process for continuous improvement."

OEMs are looking for partners like Western Industries to act as a resource for value-added services. These include design, engineering, and die tooling capabilities, as well as the components that Western produces. Some OEMs are seeking complete assemblies of Western components that can be simply bonded together to form the final product.

Following the lead of the auto industry, most OEMs seek a few fully integrated suppliers that can manage a supply base and coordinate various suppliers, rather than expecting the OEM to deal with many smaller companies. Ideally, efforts are coordinated between two key partners, similar to one-stop shopping.

One of Western's strategies for growth is to expand its engineering capability in process development and product design. The company is moving from being a contract supplier to providing a strategic supply relationship that supports an OEM's production capabilities, making it seem as if Western and the manufacturer were in the same building.

Electronic Advantages

Anyone can stamp metal once it's been designed and tooled," Sorrow says. "From a value-added standpoint, we want to get involved in the initial concept of a product under development. We have the capability to help develop product specifications, performance and material standards, and manufacturability." Western Industries would then select and procure the tooling used to make a component, and stamp the component. Western would also coordinate smaller supply

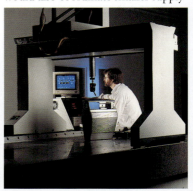

CLOCKWISE FROM LEFT: WESTERN INDUSTRIES, INC.'S ROBOTIC WELDING ENSURES DIMENSIONAL ACCURACY.

WESTERN'S DIMENSIONAL CHECKS CONFIRM DESIGN TOLERANCES.

WESTERN'S CAD/CAM/DNC NETWORK SIMPLIFIES AND IMPROVES THE DESIGN AND MANUFACTURING PROCESS.

Milwaukee

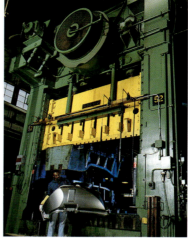

WESTERN'S AUTOMATED LASER-CUTTING FABRICATION SYSTEM PROVIDES UNATTENDED OPERATION AND MULTITASKING TO REDUCE COSTS (LEFT).

WESTERN'S LARGE PRESS AND DEEP-DRAW EXPERTISE ENABLE THE COMPANY TO MANUFACTURE A WIDE RANGE OF PRODUCTS (RIGHT).

firms; select, test, and procure their components; and assemble all components into a final subsystem sent to the OEM. In some cases, when it leaves Western's doors, the product would be ready for retail sale.

E-commerce allows the company to work closely and in a timely manner with its customers. Using Web-based technology, Western extracts data directly from customers' files, reviews prints, and makes suggestions for design and process changes. These changes can improve the product while reducing manufacturing costs.

Electronic data interchange facilitates the electronic transmission of orders, and advances shipping notices and invoicing. Similar communication extends to Western's computer-assisted design and manufacturing equipment, expediting the design and production of prototype parts.

Vision and Sales

The company's mission is "to be a profitable, world-class manufacturer of the highest quality products and services that meet or exceed our customers' needs; to be the low cost producer in our market areas; and to create a positive environment where all employees have the opportunity for growth and reward."

About 70 percent of Western's business is the stamping and molding of metal and plastic products. Western is one of the few firms in southeastern Wisconsin that manufactures plastic parts. The company expects to expand its presence in the plastics market through existing operations and acquisitions. Most of Western's some 2,000 employees are based in Wisconsin, but the company also has facilities in California and Kansas. With plants in Milwaukee, Watertown, Menomonee Falls, and Chilton, Western has more than 850,000 square feet of office and manufacturing space in Wisconsin alone.

Home and outdoor products, such as propane cylinders for the camping industry and small engine components for lawn and garden equipment, account for about 40 percent of Western's sales. Appliances and office products, including residential and commercial components for garbage disposals, cooktops, and ventilator range hoods, comprise another 40 percent. Agriculture and construction markets, including components for backhoes and tractors, comprise the remaining 20 percent of sales. Western produces proprietary products that it markets and sells, including camping equipment under the Chilton and Western Outdoors labels, and garbage disposals under the Sinkmaster and Waste King labels.

Western's competitive advantages, according to Sorrow, include its size and financial resources, as well as its ability to supply both metal and plastic components. But it may be the company's investment in equipment that really sets it apart. "We have a wide array of capital equipment assets related to plastic and metal processing," Sorrow says. "Outside of Detroit, you won't a find better array of such equipment anywhere else in the Midwest."

Focusing on quality products and innovative processes, Western Industries creates its own brand of success in a dynamic industry.

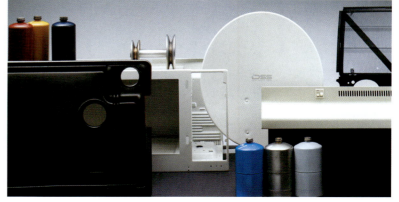

WESTERN HAS THE EXPERTISE TO HANDLE A WIDE VARIETY OF PLASTIC MOLDING JOBS (LEFT).

WESTERN USES METAL FABRICATION AND STAMPING FOR CONSUMER AND INDUSTRIAL APPLICATION (RIGHT).

Voss Jorgensen Schueler Co., Inc.

When he was just 12 years old, Gary Jorgensen got his start in construction as a water boy for the family's general contracting firm in Iowa. Today, he serves as chairman of Waukesha-based Voss Jorgensen Schueler Co., Inc. (VJS), one of Wisconsin's largest construction firms. VJS provides general contracting and construction management services for a broad array of renovation, restoration, revitalization, and new construction projects.

VJS grew out of Voss Hrdlicka Co., a firm established in 1947 by two former Allis-Chalmers engineers, Harold Voss and John Hrdlicka. As the initial founders moved toward retirement, Jorgensen joined as a principal in 1976. In 1978, he enlisted the talents of former coworker Tom Schueler.

Initially, Jorgensen and Schueler paid themselves very little and poured all the profits back into the company. As a result, VJS was able to hire additional employees, purchase more advanced equipment, and increase its bonding ability, which enabled the company to compete for large-scale projects. The financial risk was enormous, and the two partners put everything they had into the business, including a second mortgage and a loan from an insurance policy.

But their gamble paid off. The firm has grown from $2.5 million in revenues in 1976 to more than $60 million in 1999, with nearly 130 employees. Jorgensen's sons, Craig and David, serve as president and vice president/treasurer, respectively, while Jorgensen's brother, Jack, works as a project manager. Schueler's stepson, Jeff Stoll, is also a vice president with the company.

Reputation and Experience

For almost all the work VJS undertakes, the company acts as a team member, helping to develop a budget and schedule, and working with the architect to develop plans for the building. VJS analyzes the plans, and recommends the most appropriate systems and construction materials to provide optimum quality and value. "We consider ourselves an extension of the client, and we work to ensure the client receives a building that will stand the test of time," says Jeff Stoll, vice president.

"We have developed advanced in-house methodologies that create efficiencies in labor and enhance budget management without compromising quality or interfering with the client's operation," notes Craig Jorgensen. "We assist owners throughout the evolution of a project, even before it commences, through preliminary budgets and value engineering, as well as establishing the appropriate construction schedule."

During the 1960s and 1970s, VJS was known as a church builder. The firm has completed more than 100 church projects in southeastern Wisconsin for congregations including St. James Catholic Church, St. John's Lutheran Church, Grace Lutheran Church, and Falls Baptist Church.

But the firm does not limit itself to churches. VJS has completed projects for numerous long-term care facilities, including San Camillo Retirement Community, Village at Manor Park, Milwaukee Jewish Home, and Three Pillars; approximately 80 public and private schools throughout the area; and medical facilities such as Community Memorial Hospital, Sinai Samaritan Hospital, and Covenant Healthcare

(Clockwise from right) The Voss Jorgensen Schueler Co., Inc. VJS has completed more than 100 church projects in southeastern Wisconsin for congregations, including St. James Catholic Church in Menomonee Falls.

Approximately 80 public and private schools throughout the area have encountered the VJS touch, including Lannon Elementary.

Much of the firm's high-profile work is finishing tenant space in commercial office buildings, such as for Landaas & Company.

· 352 ·

Milwaukee

Systems-Franklin Medical Center. VJS' influence can also be seen in industrial construction, including work for Husco International, Cooper Power Systems, Allen Bradley, Seaquist Closures, and Waukesha Engine; and many retail/restaurant developments, such as Brownstones Shopping Center, Harvard Square, Zita, Southridge Mall Food Court, Mimma's, and Saz's.

Other prominent VJS projects include the Sharon Lynne Wilson Center for the Arts in Brookfield and a number of high-end private residences. Much of the company's high-profile work involves finishing tenant space in commercial office buildings, such as downtown Milwaukee's Firstar Center, International Corporate Headquarters for Rockwell International and Universal Foods, Milwaukee Center, and 411 East Wisconsin Center. Starting with the shell of the building, VJS works with the client to develop and build unique, customized offices that capture a company's personality. For many projects, this involves adding special features, such as wooden trim and cabinetry, wall and floor coverings, lighting, and custom ceilings.

"We are hired based on our reputation, our quality of work, and our experience," says David Jorgensen. "We're seeking not only to execute a single job, but to develop a relationship with clients. Each year, more than 70 percent of our business comes from satisfied customers asking us to build for them again."

VJS' many successes throughout the Milwaukee area have not gone unnoticed. The firm has twice won prestigious awards from the American Institute of Architects, including one for its renovation of Henni Hall on the St. Francis Seminary campus. Other prominent awards include Constructor of the Year from the American Institute of Constructors and Outstanding Contractor of the Year from the American Subcontractors Association of Greater Milwaukee. And for its work on the Federal Building-U.S. Courthouse in downtown Milwaukee, VJS won the Public Heritage Award from the U.S. General Services Administration recognizing outstanding achievement in historic renovation.

Giving Back to the Community

The company's projects are not limited to for-profit ventures. VJS places a high priority on community service. The members of the firm's succession team are active on numerous charity boards, as well as members of organizations within the industry. VJS also allocates a generous portion of year-end profits to charitable organizations within the community.

"My upbringing instilled in me the importance of giving back to the community," Craig Jorgensen says. "And it's nice to share our success by helping others."

(CLOCKWISE FROM LEFT)
THE INFLUENCE OF VJS CAN BE SEEN IN INDUSTRIAL CONSTRUCTION, SUCH AS WORK DONE FOR HUSCO INTERNATIONAL IN WHITEWATER.

VJS WAS AWARDED THE 2000 WISCONSIN GOLDEN TROWEL AWARD FROM THE INTERNATIONAL MASONRY INSTITUTE RECOGNIZING EXCELLENCE IN MASONRY CONSTRUCTION FOR THE CEDARBURG PERFORMING ARTS CENTER.

VJS WON THE PUBLIC HERITAGE AWARD FROM THE U.S. GENERAL SERVICES ADMINISTRATION RECOGNIZING OUTSTANDING ACHIEVEMENT IN HISTORIC RENOVATION FOR ITS WORK ON THE FEDERAL BUILDING-U.S. COURTHOUSE IN DOWNTOWN MILWAUKEE.

GE Medical Systems

G E Medical Systems is much more than a leading manufacturer of high-tech imaging equipment such as ultrasound and magnetic resonance technology. More and more, the company is a developer of all-encompassing systems that help hospitals raise their standard of health care to a new level. ■ GE Medical is a $6 billion business, as well as a subsidiary of General Electric, with about 20,000 employees in more than 150 countries. Approximately 20 percent of the firm's workforce is in Wisconsin, including its corporate headquarters in Waukesha and 10 additional facilities in the Milwaukee area. GE Medical is a global leader in medical diagnostic equipment and services, including conventional and digital X ray, computerized tomography (CT), magnetic resonance (MR), ultrasound, patient monitoring systems, positron-emission tomography (PET), nuclear medicine, and health care information management.

GE Medical's equipment and software products require an advanced level of sophistication in both development and maintenance. Developing CT scanning or ultrasound equipment is equivalent in its complexity to building and launching a satellite, requiring the highest-quality standards. And in the health care arena, it may be a matter of life or death.

As a rapidly growing company, GE Medical contributes to the health of the economy wherever it does business. By 2000, the company had doubled its 1996 revenue. It had added more than 1,000 employees by 1997, and, by 2000, had acquired Marquette Medical Systems, another Milwaukee-area company. In a three-year period, it acquired more than 30 medical technology companies around the world.

"We continue to selectively acquire companies that can further broaden our portfolio of products and services," says Charles H. Young, manager of global communication and public relations. "It is more efficient and cost effective for the hospital to have one turnkey provider of services than deal with many different vendors."

Systems and Services

GE Medical is reconceptualizing its business around core areas such as cardiology and women's health. One of the greatest areas of expansion since 1990 is in the related services the company offers. For example, hospitals can contract with GE Medical Systems to service all diagnostic and monitoring equipment, regardless of the manufacturer.

GE Medical also offers an asset management service in which fleets of equipment, whether simple or sophisticated, portable or stationary, are inventoried and tracked. For example, a 400-bed hospital might have 600 wheelchairs alone; efficiency and cost savings can be optimized with both computer and physical inventories.

Perhaps the most startling use of GE Medical's high-tech capabilities involves monitoring and repairing its equipment without a service call. When a child in San Francisco was rushed to a hospital with a head

GE MEDICAL SYSTEMS' EDUCATION CENTER IN WAUKESHA, WISCONSIN, HOUSES ITS EXPANSIVE EDUCATIONAL OFFERINGS, INCLUDING THE TRAINING IN PARTNERSHIP CURRICULUM FOR GE CUSTOMERS AND THE SERVICE CURRICULUM FOR GE FIELD ENGINEERS.

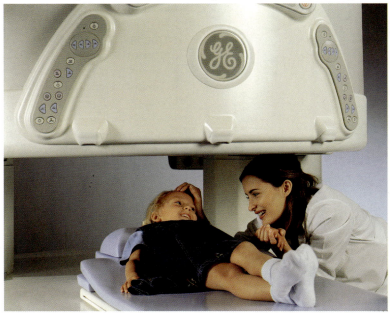

THE SIGNA OPENSPEED MRI PROVIDES A MORE COMFORTABLE EXAM FOR THE PATIENT WHILE PRODUCING HIGH-QUALITY IMAGES FOR DIAGNOSIS.

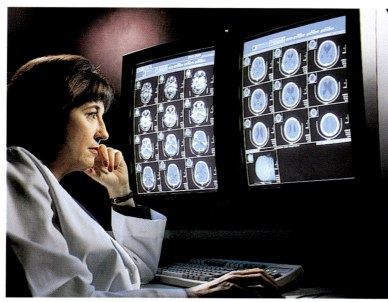

injury, he underwent a CT scan, which malfunctioned. The technician called GE Medical's Milwaukee headquarters at 1 a.m., and the call was passed to the Paris office. There, the CT software was uploaded from the San Francisco hospital, the Paris technician discovered the problem and downloaded the fix, and the CT scan was up and running again—within 15 minutes.

"This is a remarkable outcome of the functionality and sophistication built into our equipment's systems," says Young. "This level of sophistication is unmatched in the industry." Much of the GE Medical equipment at hospitals around the world is connected to the company's remote diagnostic centers. In 40 percent of cases, GE technicians can fix the problem remotely—without a service visit—because of the unique software embedded in the equipment.

GE Medical Systems is taking this unique advantage one step further with its Web-enabled Insite interactive system to monitor and maintain equipment. Through Insite, the company can solve equipment problems before a customer even knows there's a problem. Through an Internet connection, GE Medical and its far-flung equipment are in constant contact to maintain optimal performance of equipment operating systems.

A Number-One Choice

But GE Medical's efforts to improve the efficiencies of hospital management don't stop there. It has a separate satellite broadcast facility from which it offers video training for health care professionals. Through GE Medical's Training in Partnership (TIP) network, 6,000 hours of training programs can be beamed directly to conference rooms at 2,000 hospitals in the United States.

It should be no surprise then that GE Medical's services are expanding even more rapidly than equipment sales. "Never has there been more technology available in the health care field, but no health care system can afford it all," Young notes. "Our services help hospitals become more productive by controlling costs and increasing efficiencies."

With its all-digital equipment, GE Medical is moving the industry closer to the ideal administrative efficiency: a paperless and filmless office. Each year, hospitals spend millions of dollars on real estate to store seven years' worth of patient information and images. Digital information, however, can be stored on CD-ROMs, shared via the Internet, or quickly accessed with a computer terminal.

When *Medical Imaging Magazine* conducted a recent reader's choice survey, it polled 3,100 radiology professionals at the top 60 companies in the field. The number 11 reader's choice company was Marquette Medical Systems, a GE Medical subsidiary. The number-three choice was OEC Medical Systems, a recent GE Medical acquisition. And, in recognition of the company's extremely high standards, the number-one choice was GE Medical Systems itself.

CLOCKWISE FROM TOP: GE MEDICAL SYSTEM'S INTEGRATED IMAGING SOLUTIONS OFFERINGS PROVIDE THE BEST IN MEDICAL INFORMATION MANAGEMENT SYSTEMS TO FACILITIES AROUND THE WORLD.

GE'S ELFUN VOLUNTEER ORGANIZATION ENCOURAGES EMPLOYEES TO MAKE A DIFFERENCE IN THE COMMUNITY THROUGH VOLUNTARISM AND COMMUNITY SERVICE ACTIVITIES.

GE MEDICAL SYSTEM'S TIP-TV NETWORK BROADCASTS EDUCATIONAL PROGRAMMING THROUGH ITS OWN SATELLITE NETWORK TO CUSTOMER FACILITIES AROUND THE COUNTRY.

City by the Waters

MANPOWER INC.

As the landscape of the 21st century labor market continues to change, workforce management becomes key to successful business strategies. Manpower Inc.—a leading global provider of workforce management services—is keeping one step ahead to provide innovative solutions for the challenging human capital needs of the new economy. ■

WITH MORE THAN 50 YEARS OF EXPERIENCE AND A GLOBAL NETWORK OF MORE THAN 3,600 OFFICES, MANPOWER INC. CONTINUES TO LEAD THE WAY IN PROVIDING PREMIER STAFFING SOLUTIONS TO MORE THAN 400,000 CUSTOMERS AROUND THE WORLD.

MANPOWER PROFESSIONAL SERVICES HAS MORE THAN 250 OFFICES WORLDWIDE THAT SPECIALIZE IN THE ASSIGNMENT OF INFORMATION TECHNOLOGY, TELECOMMUNICATIONS, ENGINEERING, SCIENTIFIC, FINANCE, MARKETING, AND OTHER PROFESSIONALS.

For decades, the company built its reputation on the timely provision of skilled workers who were meticulously matched to customer requirements. Today, the company does that and much more. Manpower's customers require assistance not just in filling positions, but also with their overall workforce design and resource management strategies.

"Manpower has been the premier staffing and employment brand for more than 50 years," says Jeffrey Joerres, president and chief executive officer. "We have grown organically, through a steady increase in business and offices. With recent strategic acquisitions and mergers, we'll continue that growth by providing the most highly skilled professionals, customized workforce solutions, and e-commerce tools through our global network."

Putting People to Work

On any given day, some 500,000 Manpower supplemental employees are at work, and approximately 40 percent of the company's assigned workers transition to permanent positions. With more than 3,600 offices in some 54 countries, Manpower has more than 2.1 million workers servicing some 400,000 client companies worldwide, including 96 percent of Fortune 500 companies. More than 850 people are employed at Manpower's international headquarters in Milwaukee.

The company's core functions are built around two business units—Manpower Staffing Services and Manpower Professional Services. Manpower Staffing provides administrative, industrial, and call center staffing, while Manpower Professional, a fast-growing business segment, provides information technology (IT), engineering, scientific, finance, telecommunications, marketing, and human resource professionals.

Prepared to meet the staffing needs of companies across all industries, Manpower offers innovative staffing services and solutions that include professional, technical and traditional staffing resources; on-site management of supplemental staffing; quality assessment, testing, and training processes; flexible staffing to meet fluctuating business cycles; and outsourcing capabilities designed to staff and manage entire departments or business functions.

Leading the Way

Since its establishment in 1948, Manpower has been a pioneer in the staffing industry. With a philosophy that there is no such thing as an unskilled job—or an unskilled worker—Manpower developed groundbreaking assessment tools that identify the skills that each worker has to offer. As office technology moved from typewriters to word processors in the early 1980s, Manpower developed software training programs that have expanded into the comprehensive set of training programs the company offers today. These assessment and training tools form the basis of Manpower's proprietary system for matching workers with customer needs.

While anticipating the labor shortages of the 1990s, Manpower recruited and trained participants in welfare-to-work programs, people with disabilities, and other traditionally underemployed populations. In addition, Manpower was one of the first global service firms to achieve ISO 9002 certification, the international quality standard.

Manpower's ability to provide organizational performance consulting services to major corporations worldwide was recently enhanced through the formation of a new division, The Empower Group. Key services include consulting support on strategic human resource initiatives; organization design and development; and internal branding and communication strategy. The group also helps companies assess and

Manpower supports more than 1,500 call centers nationwide and has more than 50,000 call center agents working daily worldwide (left).

With its proven set of assessment tools and training programs, Manpower successfully matches the right worker to the right job, satisfying the needs of its two sets of customers—its employees and the companies it services (right).

maximize competence, develop leaders, and enhance individual performance and growth.

Blazing the E-Commerce Trail

To better serve the skill development needs of its growing workforce and customers, Manpower's extensive library of training programs is accessible through the company's on-line university, the Global Learning Center (GLC). Available anytime, anywhere, the GLC provides nearly 1,500 software and IT training modules, and more than 100 business skills courses, at no cost to Manpower employees. In addition, résumé development, career building, and skill assessment tools are available to Manpower employees, as well as to the general public.

The GLC is just one way in which Manpower utilizes the Internet to enhance the employment process for the benefit of its employees and customers. The company continues to explore and implement the power of the Internet across the entire spectrum of its service offerings, including e-procurement tools, on-line training for employees and customers, Internet-based recruiting, and on-line job orders.

"The advent of Internet usage by business and consumers has had a major impact on the way we do business," says Joerres. "Manpower has taken the industry lead in e-thinking every aspect of our work. We seek to enhance and simplify the employment process for the benefit of both our candidates and our customers."

Reaching Out

Manpower has developed numerous relationships across the country with nonprofit, community-based, and government organizations as part of its workforce development efforts. These partners provide recruitment services and assist candidates in overcoming barriers to employment. In recent years, the company has focused its attention on school-to-work educational initiatives, and has taken an active role in promoting such programs on a national basis.

In addition, Manpower was one of the first members—as well as one of the first service firms—to participate in a core group of Fortune 500 companies that make up the National Employer Leadership Council.

The company's active community involvement is a reflection of its core value: work is for everyone. Manpower's philosophy and practices are based on the premise that all adults of whatever age, gender, race, belief, or disability should, given the appropriate skills, have the chance to work. "Work can make an essential contribution to the development, self-esteem, fulfillment, and well-being of every human being," says Joerres. "At Manpower, we strive to help our employees reach their fullest potential, and provide our customers with innovative products and services that meet their business goals now and in the future."

Industrial staffing is one of Manpower's core service offerings, with thousands of Manpower employees helping companies get their products to market each day.

City by the Waters · 357 ·

STS Consultants, Ltd.

The foundation—and inspiration—behind Milwaukee's skyline lies well beneath the surface, for both the city and its skyline embrace a rich history and an impressive range of architectural design, materials, and diversity. But the city goes much deeper than that. What lies beneath these magnificent buildings can be every bit as spellbinding as the bluish-orange sunset silhouetting the skyline.

Building Milwaukee from the Ground Up

Just as everything else requiring solid foundations, the subsurface is Milwaukee's base. This is also where the expertise of STS Consultants, Ltd. lies—in the subsurface. Since 1948, STS has applied its knowledge of the underground to help developers, engineers, architects, and contractors understand these issues to effectively design structures and amenities.

As the fifth-largest engineering firm in Wisconsin, STS Consultants knows what is involved in making Milwaukee's skyline vision a reality. The firm opened its local office in 1971 to provide engineering support for the First Wisconsin (now Firstar Corporation) office building, still the tallest building in the state. In fact, STS has provided similar engineering services for seven of the 11 tallest buildings in the world.

Locally, other projects followed, including the Bradley Center, 100 East Wisconsin Avenue, the Milwaukee Center, 1000 North Water Street, Miller Park, the Marcus Amphitheater, and the Milwaukee Art Museum. STS was involved with the construction of each of these buildings, all contributors to Milwaukee's skyline.

Innovations to Match Diverse Needs

A combination of complex geology and extensive land improvements—ongoing since the 1800s—has literally transformed the foundation of the city. Before the land improvements, a series of swampy valleys and adjacent bluffs bordered the Milwaukee and Menomonee rivers. In order to improve building conditions and traffic flow, the bluffs were excavated to fill the valleys. The swampy areas were compressed under the weight of the excavated soil. It is on this material and the remaining high ground areas that the city's downtown was built.

Summarizing the approach, Paul Tarvin, professional engineer and regional vice president, says, "The Milwaukee Center is a good example of how, quite literally, STS helps build Milwaukee from the ground up." As part of the design/build team for the center, the STS construction team recommended the top-down method of construction, seldom used in the area. After a concrete slab was laid down, a seven-level parking structure was excavated and installed 50 feet below grade. In addition, a structural slurry wall was installed to prevent the adjacent river from flowing into the lower levels.

Today, visitors in the underground parking structure can observe the concrete columns, which are the original caissons drilled into the soil during construction. What may look

As part of the design/build team for the Milwaukee Center, STS Consultants, Ltd. recommended the top-down method of construction, seldom used in the area (top).

STS provided steel inspection services at 36 fabrication shops in the United States, China, and Japan for Miller Park, the new home of the Milwaukee Brewers (bottom).

· 358 ·

Milwaukee

like an unfinished exterior wall is actually the imprint of the soil that formed the inside face of the slurry wall.

The Greener Side

The firm's expertise doesn't end with the geotechnical aspects of new facilities. As a comprehensive engineering consulting firm, STS also provides a full suite of environmental services ranging from environmental assessments to the investigation and cleanup of contaminated properties, including brownfields redevelopment. Brownfields are abandoned or underutilized properties where environmental contamination—either real or perceived—has complicated development plans. The development of brownfields is growing in importance because of the limited space cities have for future development. STS works with clients to clean up sites, manage health risks, and develop sites to their full potential.

Such was the case of the shuttered Allis-Chalmers tractor plant in neighboring West Allis. STS defined geotechnical issues, investigated environmental conditions, and developed cleanup strategies for the property. Just as important to the regional community, STS also supported the city in negotiating the sale of several parcels of the former industrial site, resulting in a revitalized business district.

Be Civil

When the geotechnical and environmental evaluations are under way, it's time to be civil and constructive. During this phase of a project, the firm provides full-service civil engineering and construction management services to its broad client base.

For example, when a local developer required a multidisciplined firm for a 120-acre commercial and retail development, it hired STS. As one of the largest developments of its type in southeastern Wisconsin, the project required civil design, geotechnical, environmental, and field services, all delivered seamlessly through one project team. The site consists of three major anchor tenants, local retailers, detached restaurants, and an additional 25 acres of office development, as well as 30 acres of wetlands, floodplain, and natural areas, all located within the property boundaries.

In addition, when the construction project team needed a firm to provide complete steel fabrication/erection inspection and testing associated with Miller Park, the Milwaukee Brewers' new stadium, STS was hired. The retractable, domed stadium required more than 24,000 tons of steel. The firm's inspectors visited 36 domestic and foreign steel fabrication shops to ensure that the necessary materials met quality standards.

Reputation and Reliability

When surveyed, our clients cite our technical expertise, reputation, reliability, and broad capabilities as reasons for selecting STS," Tarvin says. "Realizing that, we hire professionals in diverse, yet complementary fields to offer services that cover every aspect of a site development or restoration."

The firm's vision of providing world-class engineering and science from the Midwest will continue well into the future. Its commitment to personal integrity and professional ethics drives its employees to become the best-in-class among their peers and in the eyes of their clients.

STS WAS INVOLVED IN THE CONSTRUCTION OF ONE OF THE MOST RECENT HIGH-RISE BUILDINGS IN MILWAUKEE, 100 EAST WISCONSIN AVENUE (TOP).

THE MILWAUKEE SKYLINE PROVIDES A BROAD SPECTRUM OF PROJECTS HIGHLIGHTING STS INVOLVEMENT.

A.N. Ansay & Associates, Inc.

Adolph Ansay began A.N. Ansay & Associates, Inc. in 1946 to provide insurance to his banking customers in Belgium, Wisconsin. Since Ansay sold the business to his sons Mike and John in 1980, the company has grown from $200,000 in premiums to about $70 million. Currently based in Port Washington, the firm has some 85 employees, and is among the largest and fastest-growing independent insurance agencies in the Milwaukee area. At a time when many independent insurance agencies are disappearing, Ansay consistently records double-digit growth.

Quality Service

Ansay offers full-service insurance solutions for businesses and individuals, including commercial property and casualty insurance, employee benefits, and personal insurance, as well as administration of retirement and 401(k) plans. The company has a safety and loss control affiliate and a real estate investment company for both industrial and residential properties. The first independent agency in the state to offer on-line instant auto insurance rates, Ansay has more than a 95 percent retention rate of its customers.

"Our father was always working, even on weekends," recalls Mike Ansay, president. "His philosophy was that you had to give something to get something to be successful. He also believed that honesty is the best policy. We recognize that his philosophy and work ethic are central to our success."

The Ansay brothers are quick to note that the insurance companies that A.N. Ansay & Associates represent have supported the firm in its growth and invested in its future. This partnership results in innovative insurance products and superior value to customers. Ansay shares proprietary data, technology, and plans with its client companies, as well as the firms that supply its insurance. Ansay even holds free seminars for clients on topics unrelated to insurance, but important to the success of the customers' businesses.

Remarkable Creativity

The Ansay brothers offer their salespeople the opportunity to become partners in the firm. This relationship was implemented some 20 years ago and brings stability to client relationships, as well as motivation for employees. Ansay also awards a quarterly bonus to associates, based on sales and customer service results. The company's WOW Committee rewards extraordinary customer service. Such incentives, as well as investments in technology and relationships, provide an entrepreneurial drive to solve customer problems quickly.

"Our business is about creativity and providing solutions to our clients," John Ansay says. "Insurance is more than a policy, more than a premium. We represent our clients as much as the insurance companies whose products we sell. We want our clients to succeed."

Different insurance companies provide different programs. Mike Ansay notes, "As an independent agency, we can creatively tailor and negotiate programs to best meet the needs of our clients. We represent nearly 30 top-rated insurance companies and have had relationships with some of them for 40 years. Each one offers competitive advantages on certain insurance products. For our clients, we select the best of the best."

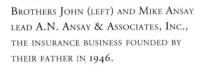

Clockwise from top:

Brothers John (left) and Mike Ansay lead A.N. Ansay & Associates, Inc., the insurance business founded by their father in 1946.

Ansay's creed is to "serve customers with integrity, respect, and a sincere desire to build lasting relationships."

Today, Ansay is among the largest and fastest-growing insurance agencies in southeastern Wisconsin.

Milwaukee

CORRIGAN PROPERTIES, INC./BAYSHORE MALL

SINCE CAUSING MASSIVE TRAFFIC JAMS AND ATTRACTING more than 85,000 people from all over Wisconsin when it opened in Glendale in April 1954, Bayshore Mall has consistently been one of the North Shore's retail jewels. Today, this outstanding facility is owned and managed by Corrigan Properties, Inc., one of the premier realty companies in Milwaukee. Corrigan also manages Hilldale Mall in Madison, as well as office buildings, apartment complexes, and retail centers in the Dallas area.

Leo Corrigan III is president and CEO of the firm, succeeding his father, Leo Corrigan II, who purchased Bayshore Mall in 1956. Alice Corrigan, who lives in the Dallas area, is Leo Corrigan III's sister and a partner in the company.

Bayshore Mall

Half a century after opening, Bayshore Mall today offers 75 stores, complete with an attractive tenant mix of department stores such as Boston Store and Sears, specialty women's clothing stores like Aversa and Lise & Kato's, men's clothing stores including Structure and Fox's, and unisex clothing stores such as The Gap, Banana Republic, and Eddie Bauer. In addition, Bayshore Mall retains its uniqueness because of the many locally owned stores that occupy the mall's retail space.

Bayshore Mall offers uncommon shopper convenience with its 15 entrances, immediate access to I-43, and easy, free parking. The single-level layout of the mall makes it a comfortable, easily navigated shopping center, and includes a food court with seating for more than 100 people. Altogether, there is about 500,000 square feet of space, including 36 professional office tenants such as attorneys and dentists.

Bayshore Mall is located on the North Shore, a solid community with high property values and strong housing stock. The stability of its neighborhood, plus its proximity to I-43 and downtown Milwaukee, has provided Bayshore Mall with a consistent base from which to operate. The median age of the shopping center's primary market is 36 years, with a median household income

of more than $66,000 a year. Average drive time to the mall for this group is just seven minutes.

"We are perceived as a safe place to be, day or night," says Mike Mesenbourg, vice president. "It's a good place to bring the kids, too. For the last few years, we have carved a niche for shoppers with children through convenient child care and retailers like Zany Brainy, an educational toy store."

Mesenbourg joined the firm 25 years ago, when Bayshore Mall was merely an unenclosed retail center that had fallen to only 60 percent occupancy. Since then, he has seen a myriad of changes and upgrades as the shopping center has evolved with its customers, including the mall's enclosure in the late 1970s.

"The Corrigan family has made numerous investments in the property, and is willing to do what's necessary to keep Bayshore fresh and attract the best retailers," Mesenbourg notes. "Corrigan and Bayshore have been synonymous for more than 40 years. The continuation of ownership offers further stability in the property, as the Corrigans have an ongoing, vested interest in keeping the shopping center thriving."

CLOCKWISE FROM TOP:
BAYSHORE MALL ATTRACTED MORE THAN 85,000 PEOPLE FROM ALL OVER WISCONSIN WHEN IT OPENED IN GLENDALE IN APRIL 1954. SINCE THEN, IT HAS CONSISTENTLY BEEN ONE OF THE NORTH SHORE'S RETAIL JEWELS.

UNCOMMON CONVENIENCE FOR SHOPPERS IS OFFERED AT BAYSHORE MALL WITH ITS 15 ENTRANCES. THE SINGLE-LEVEL LAYOUT OF THE MALL MAKES IT A COMFORTABLE, EASILY NAVIGATED SHOPPING CENTER.

ALTOGETHER, BAYSHORE MALL HAS ABOUT 500,000 SQUARE FEET OF SPACE, INCLUDING 36 PROFESSIONAL OFFICE TENANTS.

City by the Waters

HUSCO International, Inc.

The Hydraulic Unit Specialties Company, now known as HUSCO International, Inc., began in 1946 when Dana Schneider set up a drill press in his Painesville, Ohio, garage. Schneider designed the company's first product, a hydraulic power unit largely for agricultural applications. Net sales that year for the one-man operation were $4,750. The company was moved to Waukesha in 1953.

Growth Strategy

When manufacturers of construction and material handling equipment began converting from mechanical to hydraulic designs, HUSCO's sales grew. From its inception, HUSCO products were engineered for customer specific applications. Direct sales to major original equipment manufacturers have always accounted for the majority of the company's business.

HUSCO established its first international licensee, Kayaba Co. Ltd., in Japan in 1967. Koehring Company acquired HUSCO in 1968, and AMCA International, a Canadian-Pacific subsidiary, acquired Koehring in 1980. Agustin A. Ramirez, an AMCA executive, became HUSCO's vice president and general manager in 1984, and purchased the company—together with the management team—in 1985. Today, Ramirez is HUSCO's chairman and CEO.

"Our growth strategy is to provide custom-designed products with a focus on customers that are leaders in their industry," Ramirez says. "These include John Deere, DaimlerChrysler, Komatsu, CNH, JCB, NACCO, Kubota, Bobcat, INA, Tenneco Automotive, and Caterpillar. Our international business orientation, superior custom-designed products, and strategic market development initiatives have been the key to our continued success."

Products and Efficiency

HUSCO manufactures hydraulic and electrohydraulic controls and related electronic products used in both on- and off-road vehicles for the automotive, agricultural, construction, utility, mining, and material handling industries. HUSCO controls are used in backhoes, excavators, tractors, bulldozers, and other equipment. The company also makes electrohydraulic ride control systems and engine management controls for the automotive industry. HUSCO has grown 500 percent since 1991, making the firm one of the fastest-growing major manufacturers in its industry.

"The opportunities we pursue are typically applications that are difficult to engineer and often require a great deal of investment," Ramirez says. "HUSCO invests more than three times the industry average in engineering but controls other expenses to below industry average to ensure that financial results are among the best in the industry."

HUSCO's state-of-the-art factories and facilities are located in Waukesha and Whitewater, Wisconsin; the United Kingdom; Germany; Brazil; and Shanghai, and are among the most productive and cost effective in the industry. HUSCO has maintained its low-cost, high-quality manufacturing position by designing and manufacturing specialized production machines unique to the manufacturing requirements of its products. Nearly half of the company's sales come from international markets, including strong positions in Europe, South America, Korea, China, and Japan. HUSCO has a 40 percent market share of its served off-highway market in North America and a 20 percent market share in Europe.

HUSCO International, Inc. world headquarters is located in Waukesha, Wisconsin (right).

HUSCO's facility in Whitewater, Wisconsin, is among the most productive and cost effective in the industry (bottom).

Engineering Prowess

Because HUSCO differentiates itself based on its engineering expertise, the company employs almost as many engineers as the rest of its domestic competitors combined. The firm's research and development personnel are able to evaluate conceptual and prototype applications of advanced control systems. Proprietary test and evaluation software enable HUSCO engineers to conduct dynamic product performance modeling and analysis before manufacturing prototypes.

HUSCO has been the first in its industry to receive supplier certifications from companies such as CNH, Caterpillar, DaimlerChrysler, JCB, and John Deere. HUSCO was recognized as Wisconsin Manufacturer of the Year in 1989, and received an award for International Business Excellence from Price Waterhouse, now known as PricewaterhouseCoopers. Ramirez received the 1995 Master Entrepreneur of the Year Award sponsored by Ernst & Young, Merrill Lynch, and *Inc.* magazine. The company received its ISO 9001 certification in the United Kingdom in 1990 and in the United States in 1994. QS 9000 certification has been obtained by HUSCO's Automotive Division.

For five decades, HUSCO engineers have successfully adapted traditional hydraulic control valves to hundreds of varied customer applications. After four years of design and development, the company recently introduced its revolutionary electrohydraulic poppet valve (EHPV) patented technology. This electronically controlled poppet valve replaces hydraulic valves and spools, each of which—before the introduction of EHPV—had to be designed and machined to meet a particular hydraulic application. This engineering effort overcame a series of challenges by creating standard designed units able to serve many needs through customized electronics, often offering capabilities unavailable before EHPV.

"With EHPV, the features that exist within hydraulic valves are customized by software programming," Ramirez explains. "In addition to fewer hardware variants being required, there is the potential for lower control system costs." Control sequences can be memorized and recalled to more efficiently accomplish repetitive motions. The power and reach of a machine, such as an excavator, can be controlled with software instructions. For example, control parameters can be created to make working in tight spaces, or use by a less experienced operator, easier.

HUSCO's latest major accomplishment has been the successful introduction of the suspension controls on the newly introduced ABC (active body control) system for Mercedes CL and S Class vehicles, which has resulted in a $100 million, life-of-vehicle contract. Several new automotive projects, including new engine management technology, commenced production in 2001, leading to the creation of a major new business unit for HUSCO.

Geared toward innovative solutions and meeting the diverse needs of its clients, HUSCO expects to continue to lead its industry for years to come.

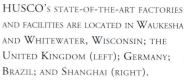

HUSCO'S STATE-OF-THE-ART FACTORIES AND FACILITIES ARE LOCATED IN WAUKESHA AND WHITEWATER, WISCONSIN; THE UNITED KINGDOM (LEFT); GERMANY; BRAZIL; AND SHANGHAI (RIGHT).

HUSCO MAINTAINS ITS LOW-COST MANUFACTURING POSITION BY CUSTOM DESIGNING AND PRODUCING SPECIALIZED PRODUCTION MACHINES UNIQUE TO PRODUCT REQUIREMENTS.

1956-1973

1956
Yale Equipment & Services, Inc.

1957
TEC

1961
Kaerek Builders Inc.

1961
North American Clutch Corporation

1969
Ultra Tool & Manufacturing, Inc.

1970
Milwaukee Brewers Baseball Club

1972
DeRosa Corporation

1973
Earth Tech

1973
Shoreline Company, Inc.

© JOHN J. BACIK III

YALE EQUIPMENT & SERVICES, INC.

At Yale Equipment & Services, Inc. there is a familiar saying, "If you drive it, sit on it, walk on it, wear it, live it, or eat it, it's probably been handled by a lift truck." The company supplies and services lift trucks, as well as personnel carriers, aerial platforms, and forklifts, for industries that typically use them to lift and move items throughout a warehouse.

President Cliff Anglewicz has been in the lift truck business for 35 years. In 1990, he purchased the local Yale dealership, which was originally founded in 1956 as the Hugh Ayers Company. Anglewicz moved the company to its current 52,000-square-foot facility in Menomonee Falls in 1993. Before purchasing the Yale dealership, Anglewicz served for six years as president of Volvo Automotive Systems in Detroit, and prior to that as a sales manager at a Caterpillar lift truck dealer.

"My whole life has been material handling," Anglewicz says. "It's a complex business. There are many different utilizations of equipment by different types of industries in different types of facilities, ranging from hospitals to foundries to water filter manufacturers to distributors of Green Bay Packers merchandise. Each presents its own challenges."

New equipment sales make up about 30 percent of the company's income, with parts and service equaling another 40 percent, and equipment rentals comprising the remainder. Anglewicz's Yale dealership serves most of southern Wisconsin, and grew from 32 employees in 1990 to more than 70 in 2000. As the business has moved more toward service and rentals, Yale has grown from five service vans and 12 rental lift trucks in 1990 to 30 service vans and 450 rental lift trucks in 2000. In the same time period, the company has grown from a $6 million to a $20 million business.

Stable Growth

In contrast to the volatile economy in eastern Michigan, governed by the peaks and valleys of the auto industry, southeastern Wisconsin offers a consistent, growing economy based on a melting pot of industry, Anglewicz says. He points to tractor, lawn mower engine, mining equipment, and toilet fixture manufacturers as examples of industries that contribute to a strong, consistent economy in the area.

"Investing properly and planning for growth are the main concerns," Anglewicz says. "What's allowed me to take risks and grow the business is being able to count on the economy in Milwaukee. Plus, we are sure to take care of our customers."

Yale Equipment offers high-quality, American-made products backed by an international company, one of the largest in the industry. Some competitors have farmed out production and, years later, the necessary parts are unavailable. By manufacturing and servicing what it sells, Yale and its distributors, such as Anglewicz, provide a chain of original parts and custom service. Yale Equipment in Menomonee Falls still services a 1946 Yale lift truck, as well as equipment manufactured by competitors.

"It's a very competitive business in which we have about a 20 percent market share," Anglewicz says. "You have to give customers reason to

THE SHOP SERVICE DEPARTMENT AT YALE EQUIPMENT & SERVICES, INC. HOUSES 10 MECHANICS WHO SERVICE ALL BRANDS.

YALE EQUIPMENT'S PARTS DEPARTMENT HAS A $1 MILLION RETAIL INVENTORY FOR PICKUP OR DELIVERY.

· 366 ·

Milwaukee

YALE EQUIPMENT'S 75 EMPLOYEES ARE COMMITTED TO CUSTOMER SERVICE EXCELLENCE EVERY DAY.

change suppliers, so our job is to provide those reasons."

Anglewicz was presented awards in the Yale Dealer of Excellence program in the years 1995 through 1999 by the parent company, based on meeting certain financial and customer service performance criteria. He is also chairman of the Dealer Advisory Board for Yale, which represents the 46 dealers across the country. Overall, parent company Yale Material Handling Corporation and its distributors are ranked first in industrial sales in the U.S. material handling industry.

Importance of Service

"The largest customers come to us and stay with us because our focus is service," Anglewicz says. "We understand that their equipment has to work all the time because downtime and lost productivity are extremely expensive."

A typical new lift truck costs more than $15,000, so rentals and service are key components of the lift truck business. Yale dealers service other makes of equipment, ranging from welding and painting to complete reconditioning. Sometimes Anglewicz is even called upon to help in the design of warehouses so that material handling can be as efficient as possible.

A key element of effective service and an efficient workforce is providing the necessary tools to do the job. Not only does each employee in Anglewicz's dealership have at least one computer, but also, in 2001, computers will be installed in the company's service vans. Accessing and downloading parts orders will be faster and easier than ever.

"We've heard over and over again that we are the most technically advanced Yale dealership," Anglewicz says. "Typically, the industry is not technologically advanced, so we have an edge with our customers. I came from the automotive business where everything is computer automated. I'm always looking for ways to do things better for less money."

Every employee at Anglewicz's dealership receives weekly or monthly training, and a customized Web site is being developed under the direction of Tracey Clark, Anglewicz's daughter and vice president/general manager. The Web site, with its secured reporting and electronic invoicing, coupled with a unique scanning system, will help streamline the business and move the dealership toward a paperless system.

"We believe that when we retain employees, we retain customers," Anglewicz says. "Not only do we build more effective, lasting relationships, but customers like to see that we're investing in our people and new equipment to remain efficient."

ALL RENTAL EQUIPMENT IS STORED INSIDE YALE EQUIPMENT'S BUILDING TO ENSURE QUICK, CLEAN DELIVERY TO CUSTOMERS.

City by the Waters

TEC

The Executive Committee, better known as TEC, was a revolutionary concept when the organization was founded by Robert Nourse in Milwaukee in 1957. By bringing together high-ranking businesspeople—namely CEOs, business owners, and presidents—to meet on a regular basis, the organization provides insights into companies quite unlike their own.

Many business leaders feel isolated and have little access to unbiased feedback. The peers of their TEC group form an executive roundtable, and provide valuable input by sharing their experiences and perspectives. Enlightened leaders turn to one another to help develop and implement new solutions for both common and uncommon business problems.

The core of TEC is still the small groups of 10 to 14 business leaders who meet regularly to help each other run their businesses more effectively. Group members ask tough questions of each other and share their thoughts and observations, which are helpful in making better and faster decisions. The organization encourages its members to become more accountable in the process toward attaining their goals and identifying priorities. The type of support TEC provides—and the flexibility it breeds—is more important than ever in a dynamic global economy.

TEC chairmen and staff gather for a meeting in Milwaukee.

Harry S. Dennis III is president and owner of TEC in Wisconsin and Michigan.

By Invitation Only

Today, TEC operates worldwide, with more than 7,500 members in some 125 cities. TEC members run companies that total more than $175 billion in annual sales and have nearly 1 million employees. TEC in Wisconsin and Michigan, headed by Harry S. Dennis III, has approximately 50 TEC groups with some 600 members. When Dennis, with a partner, purchased TEC from Nourse in 1977, local membership was about 35 people. As then, membership today is by invitation only.

There are two local TEC programs for CEOs, company presidents, and business owners: leaders of companies with $3 million or more in annual sales and 25 or more employees, and those with sales of $750,000 to $3 million and five to 25 employees. The local TEC organization typically serves leaders of small to midsize companies, along with a few large multinational corporations.

Each TEC group consists of members from noncompeting industries who have no business relationships with each other. But as experienced leaders, members provide insights that transcend industries and corporate cultures.

"In a challenging and highly confidential format, members engage in frank discussions," Dennis says. "These may cover strategic and competitive issues, capital structure and financing, significant management issues, and other business problems, such as anticipating change." Sometimes personal issues or other sensitive topics are aired as well. TEC, in any event, is not a networking group, social club, or political organization.

Members share their experience and expertise, exchange ideas and opinions, and offer objective feedback without fear of recrimination. They have a personal stake in the success of each other's businesses and are steadfastly committed to the long-term success of each company. CEOs need coaching, too, and each group meeting provides up to 14 coaches and consultants for every member. The value to members is not always in positive feedback; sometimes they are encouraged to avoid a bad decision,

or they may receive an early warning signal about a possible problem in the future. In addition, members sometimes find out they are asking the wrong question to begin with.

During some TEC meetings, half of the day is reserved for a resource presentation, conducted by carefully screened national experts who address specific management and leadership issues, chosen with input from the group. This is part of TEC's highly structured member development program.

Individualized and Worldwide

Monthly one-on-one meetings with fierce conversations between each member and the group's paid chairperson play a key role in the professional development of our members," Dennis says. During these sessions, the chair helps explore significant business and personal opportunities, and assists the member in preparing issues for discussion at the group meeting. As coach, confidant, and personal advisor, the chairperson routinely encourages members to implement suggestions raised at previous meetings; members are subsequently held accountable to their TEC peer group.

In addition, each TEC member has protected Internet access to TEC Online, which allows members to contact other members in his or her industry, participate in forum discussions, gather critical information, and share ideas with members around the world. Through its International TEC Network, TEC operates in 12 countries outside the United States. The organization also provides members with access to a confidential TEC roster of participants. Somewhere along the TEC network of CEOs, there is an answer to virtually every business question.

"TEC's primary focus is on results—tangible, measurable results," says Dennis. "The organization is dedicated to increasing the effectiveness and enhancing the lives of CEOs." Dennis points to the return on investment realized by CEOs who join TEC: cutting-edge ideas and information, mistakes avoided, professional and personal growth, and savings in time, money, and energy.

Says Kent Raabe, chairman of the Raabe Corp., echoing the thoughts of many members: "The one-on-one sessions with my TEC chair and the regular meetings have been invaluable because of the way they stretch my creative thinking."

As the demands on business leaders change, it becomes increasingly important for them to expand their problem-solving strategies, creativity, and shared insights. As TEC grows in size and scope, the firm will continue to be a vital training and development tool for its members and their respective companies for generations to come.

TEC will continue to promote itself as an organization that is both high tech and high touch. The company's signature statement will remain its ability to assemble resources at both ends of this business paradigm.

CLOCKWISE FROM TOP LEFT: TIM HOEKSEMA, CHAIRMAN, PRESIDENT, AND CHIEF OPERATING OFFICER OF MIDWEST EXPRESS AIRLINES, IS A TEC MEMBER.

KENT RAABE, CHAIRMAN OF RAABE CORPORATION, IS A TEC MEMBER.

SPEAKER GEORGE R. DANIELS ADDRESSES A TEC MEETING IN MILWAUKEE.

City by the Waters

· 369 ·

KAEREK BUILDERS INC.

WHETHER THEY ARE NEWCOMERS OR NATIVES, WHEN residents of metro Milwaukee are in the market for a new home they often turn to Kaerek Builders Inc. ■ While employed by the U.S. Postal Service, Richard Kaerek worked diligently on pursuing his dream of building homes. In 1961, upon earning his real estate brokers license, Kaerek began developing land and building homes on the south side of Milwaukee where the company's headquarters remain to this day.

With more than 400 home builders in southeastern Wisconsin, Kaerek Builders has met challenges and become a leader in the industry. Kaerek Builders has developed more than 1,500 lots since 1988 and has constructed more than 5,000 homes since Kaerek began. The company currently builds approximately 200 homes per year, and developed some 250 lots during the year 2000 alone.

"The majority of the homes we build are starter homes for first-time home owners and for people moving up to their second home," says Michael Kaerek, president of the firm and son of the company's founder. "We offer a great deal of customization, but we also build larger homes to accommodate growing families." In recent years, Kaerek has seen a rise in empty-nest customers—parents whose children have grown and left the house.

The majority of Kaerek's homes are in the 1,200- to 2,200-square-foot range. About 60 percent of the time, the firm provides home/lot packages. The remaining homes Kaerek builds are on lots the customer purchased separately.

Larger Kaerek homes, often purchased by repeat customers, can be as much as 3,500 square feet. What allows for this repeat business? "Pleasing customers the first time and exceeding their needs," says Kaerek.

The Norwood I is an economical, yet efficient ranch design that includes the charm of a traditional country home. The design includes 1,200 square feet, three bedrooms, one and a half bathrooms, and a two-car garage. "This time-honored three-bedroom floor plan can also serve as a two-bedroom with a study or playroom," Kaerek notes. "The functional interior is packaged in an exterior that's as neat as a pin."

In comparison, the 2,700-square-foot Somersett II is one of Kaerek's high-end models. It features a covered front porch, an oversized great room with fireplace, a private master suite with expansive whirlpool tub and loft, and a large deck off a second-story den. Two and a half bathrooms, a two-car garage, and an optional three- or four-bedroom floor plan complete this abode.

KAEREK BUILDERS INC. IS BUILT UPON THE DREAM OF FOUNDER RICHARD KAEREK. THE BRIDGEPORT IS JUST ONE OF THE HOME DESIGNS OFFERED BY THE FIRM.

Milwaukee

Each home Kaerek builds comes with a guaranteed list of standard features. These include Kohler plumbing fixtures, a Lennox furnace, and a Honeywell air cleaner and setback thermostat, as well as oak veneer cabinets and trim, a garbage disposal, low emissivity vinyl windows, dishwasher hookups, and an eight-inch poured concrete insulated foundation.

Kaerek also brings savings to customers by offering what the company calls the Kaerek Care Package. Through a hosted video presentation, this package explains the values, products, and options available to new Kaerek customers, including tips on preventing common home maintenance problems through scheduled upkeep.

These valuable amenities are the result of Kaerek's unrelenting industry analysis. To keep pace with the ever changing construction market, Kaerek has implemented its own experienced team of qualified architectural designers, engineers, and staff interior designers. These professionals keep the company abreast of fresh industry trends. From engineered lumber, manufactured trusses, vinyl windows, increased insulation values, and the most energy efficient appliances and furnaces available today, the Kaerek team's effort leaves no stone unturned.

"Some of the trends seen in recent years include the open-concept and airy floor plan, maintenance-free exteriors, more windows and skylights, and larger garages," says Michael Kaerek. "Renewed interest in the larger ranch-style single-floor home is also a trend."

Land Developments

Kaerek's building boom is the result of the company's growing involvement in land developments. Kaerek has established itself as a leader with the development of numerous subdivisions throughout the metro Milwaukee area. Such a venture brings with it many responsibilities, including land acquisition, gaining government approvals, financing the venture, developing the land, and providing any contracted improvements, as well as engineering and marketing for sale of the land.

A large percentage of homes are built within Kaerek's subdivisions. Location means everything, and, since young families buy the bulk of Kaerek's homes, the company's developments aim to promote pleasant neighborhoods with family values. One such subdivision, Victory Creek in Franklin, Wisconsin, sports acres of parkland, walking trails, and other distinguishing amenities.

Other Milwaukee-area Kaerek developments include Fox River Prairie Estates in Rochester; Apple Grove Estates in Oconomowoc; and Georgetown Commons West, Ryan Oaks, and Jenna Prairie Estates in Oak Creek. Kaerek's latest development is Rettler Farms, a 152-lot subdivision in Hartford.

Kaerek Builders Inc. prides itself on providing today's consumers with what they need: good quality and value at affordable prices. This formula has worked for more than 40 years, and, with its continued commitment to detail, Kaerek Builders is sure to be a brand name in southeastern Wisconsin home building for years to come.

WHEN CUSTOMERS PURCHASE A KAEREK HOME—SUCH AS THE LANCASTER—THEY ARE PROVIDED WITH THE KAEREK CARE PACKAGE, WHICH EXPLAINS THE VALUES, PRODUCTS, AND OPTIONS AVAILABLE TO NEW CUSTOMERS.

NORTH AMERICAN CLUTCH CORPORATION

AN ENGINE IS USELESS UNLESS ITS POWER CAN BE TRANSferred properly to a drive mechanism. A car's engine, for example, cannot move the vehicle forward until the transmission has been engaged, transferring power to the drive mechanism and turning the wheels. North American Clutch Corporation (NORAM) manufactures power transmission technologies for a variety of applications for the world's engines to be put to good use.

The firm was founded in the early 1960s by William Hargarten in Cedarburg, Wisconsin. Located in an old barn, the company's employment force consisted largely of Hargarten's eight children. "To succeed, we knew we had to be patient and persistent, and develop a vision for the future," Hargarten says. "There were times when things were so tough that I thought we would not make it." The family, and later the employees, of NORAM committed themselves to the hard-working ideals set by Hargarten's entrepreneurial spirit, and the company soared.

Today, NORAM occupies 50,000 square feet of first-class manufacturing space dedicated to producing power transmission solutions for more than 300 original equipment manufacturers (OEMs) worldwide. NORAM now consists of four operating divisions: centrifugal/mechanical clutches, gearboxes, clutch brakes, and contract manufacturing.

Four Product Lines

NORAM's centrifugal and mechanical clutch products are considered the highest quality in the market today. NORAM's clutches act as inexpensive transmissions and are designed to allow for the safe, no-load, quiet starting of power equipment. Once engaged, NORAM clutches help reduce vibration, utilize peak torque for more efficient engine performance, and provide overload protection for operator and equipment safety.

NORAM clutches are designed to fit engines up to 50 horsepower. They are available in standard, off-the-shelf configurations or are designed to fit the specific requirements of each OEM. NORAM clutches

USING STATE-OF-THE-ART COMPUTER NUMERICAL CONTROL EQUIPMENT, NORTH AMERICAN CLUTCH CORPORATION IS ABLE TO MANUFACTURE QUALITY PRODUCTS THAT ARE SECOND TO NONE IN THE INDUSTRIES THE COMPANY SERVES.

WILLIAM HARGARTEN FOUNDED THE FIRM IN THE EARLY 1960S; EMPLOYEES CONSISTED LARGELY OF HIS EIGHT CHILDREN.

· 372 ·

Milwaukee

are used in construction equipment, chipper-shredders, farm machinery, go-carts, lawn and garden equipment, and more. Altogether, the company's line of clutches has been engineered to respond to a wide range of power-demanding industrial applications, as well as on- and off-road vehicles. For industrial applications, the company provides custom engineering to develop one-of-a-kind designs to meet specific power needs.

NORAM's award-winning reduction gearboxes are designed to fit most small- and medium-frame four-cycle engines, and to safely increase engine torque while reducing output revolutions per minute. Their bolt-on design adapts to all makes and models of engines, making NORAM gearboxes remarkably easy to install and operate. Used on the engines of commercial cement mixers, lawn and garden equipment, roofing equipment, and golf course equipment, among others, NORAM's gearboxes are made of rugged aluminum castings and precision machined gears that provide long life and low maintenance.

"Our gearboxes allow the OEM or the end-user flexibility and choices in engine selection," says Jeff Hargarten, William's son and president of the firm. "No need to purchase special engines, which can cost more and take longer to deliver. Simply purchase a standard engine and bolt on a NORAM gearbox."

The company's patented, award-winning clutch brake product line is designed to provide worry-free service throughout the life of a product by eliminating hundreds of springs, bolts, and pulleys associated with traditional belt tensioning and electric engagement set-ups. Features of NORAM's clutch brakes—such as soft starts, smooth and easy engagements, longer belt life, and a positive, fail-safe brake, which exceeds current European and U.S. blade stoppage requirements—make any piece of power equipment safer and more effective. NORAM's clutch brake easily adapts to various OEM configurations, and is rugged, dependable, and easy to maintain.

Where contract manufacturing is concerned, NORAM was one of the pioneers to implement returnable containers, bar coding, electronic data interchange, and failure modes and effects analysis (FMEA). "We have become a certified supplier to a number of major OEMs," Jeff Hargarten says. "Most of our jobs go directly to an equipment manufacturer's production line without needing to be inspected, warehoused, or altered. Our just-in-time service has resulted in a number of quality awards from these OEMs."

NORAM also offers a custom brazing process, or heat treatment, to predetermined engineering specifications for additional strength and durability. NORAM has the ability to provide machined, brazed, and completed assemblies, and the company's engineering support staff provides design assistance.

A Great Ride

William Hargarten remembers how hard it was to get that first customer 40 years ago. Without a proven product and no customers to speak of, NORAM had difficulty attracting new business. "We literally had to lose money before we could make money," he recalls. "After we landed our first OEM, we then established a little more credibility. This went a long way as we approached more OEMs." For the first five years of the company's existence, it had only one product: a chain saw clutch.

"It has been a great ride, and I still enjoy working on developing our future, seeing the bigger picture to come," William Hargarten says. "My greatest accomplishments have been survival in business as well as raising a happy family."

The NORAM Engineering Team provides a wide variety of services, including designing new products, solving client manufacturing problems, troubleshooting unique customer situations, and developing creative solutions to customer problems (left).

President Jeff Hargarten, representing the second generation in the family-owned business, joined NORAM in 1994 and doubled sales by 2000 (right).

City by the Waters

Ultra Tool & Manufacturing, Inc.

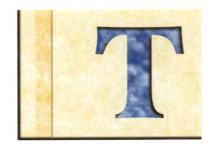

TECHNOLOGY IS EVERYWHERE, AND NOWHERE AS SERIOUSLY as at Ultra Tool & Manufacturing, Inc., a company in a business some might perceive as an old-line manufacturing company. In fact, Ultra has a passionate dedication to technology and defect-free metal stampings. The company, one of Milwaukee's top tooling and metal stamping job shops, occupies a three-year-old, custom-built, 40,000-square-foot building in the Milwaukee suburb of Menomonee Falls.

Ultra produces a wide variety of stamped parts for OEM customers, as well as precision tooling for its own use and for contract and captive stamping operations. Metal stampings account for more than 70 percent of the company's $9 million in sales.

Ultra has seen impressive growth in recent years, and one reason is its ability to respond to its customers' demand for defect-free parts. The company's approach is totally quality driven. "Our customers today expect perfect parts, period," says Terry Hansen, president. "To deliver that, you have to have a total commitment to quality from your people. Then, you give them the best equipment to do the job and let them go."

To meet its customers' expectations, Ultra has even gone so far as implementing automated, single-purpose test equipment to guarantee perfect parts. One such machine recently cost the firm more than $30,000 to design and build, an investment that will pay for itself in 18 months through reduced inspection labor.

Ultra was born in 1969 when Terry's father, Lloyd Hansen—general manager of Tollett Tool and Die—bought the company and changed the name. The firm started as a 10-person tool room, but by the mid-1970s, the move to manufacturing had begun, and Ultra was producing stampings for Harley-Davidson Motor Company. Today, Harley-Davidson remains one of the company's largest customers.

Terry Hansen has developed his knowledge and expertise from the ground up. He has worked in the business in one way or another since his father acquired it, and has held various positions, including punch press operator, journeyman toolmaker, and vice president of

CLOCKWISE FROM TOP:
THIS DIE—USED TO MANUFACTURE A MOUNTING BRACKET FOR A SATELLITE DISH—DEMONSTRATES ULTRA TOOL & MANUFACTURING, INC.'S CONTRACT TOOL MAKING ABILITY.

ULTRA'S 41,000-SQUARE-FOOT HEADQUARTERS, BUILT IN 1998, DOUBLED THE COMPANY'S SPACE.

THIS AUTOMATED IGNITION SWITCH TESTER IS AN EXAMPLE OF ULTRA'S CUSTOM MACHINE BUILDING CAPABILITY.

· 374 ·

Milwaukee

manufacturing. Those experiences have made Hansen particularly sensitive to employee safety and cleanliness. In fact, many people who tour the facility comment on how clean and well organized it is, a fact Hansen is proud to agree with.

Broad Capabilities

During the course of its more than 30 years in business, Ultra has built a strong reputation as an exceptional tool builder, and even today it remains a core strength. Hansen feels the company's toolmakers are unique because of their exposure to the firm's own stamping operation. Ultra's die makers have the advantage of understanding the realities of the press room firsthand and, as a result, produce better-quality tools. Hansen says, "More than one customer has stated that they buy tools from us because our dies work the first time."

Ultra's Stamping Division specializes in precision progressive dies, and is most cost-effective with parts requiring medium- to high-volume production runs involving 50,000 to 1 million or more pieces. The division works with virtually any type of material, but is particularly expert in stainless steel of all kinds. The division also provides customers with completed, ready-to-assemble parts by offering other value-added services like welding, painting, plating, and packaging.

Competitive Advantage: Customer Focus

For a company so focused on quality and customer satisfaction, enduring relationships with customers are common. "Once new customers experience our commitment to producing quality products and our honest, up-front communications, they tend to become long-term customers," says Hansen. An independent customer satisfaction survey gave Ultra high marks, higher than the competition, in the areas most important to customers: delivery as promised, being easy to do business with, and early identification of potential problems with a job.

Scissors manufacturer Fiskars Inc. is one of Ultra's many satisfied customers. Ultra helped solve a production problem for Fiskars several years ago, and was rewarded with many more opportunities to work with the company. Fiskars is now one of Ultra's best customers.

Constant, Continuous Improvement

Ultra's passionate dedication to finding and employing the most advanced technology and the expanded use of electronics in tooling has resulted in many production refinements, all in keeping with the company's goal of 100 percent quality, 100 percent of the time. But it is the constant pursuit of die improvements to correct dimensional discrepancies, along with quality die maintenance, that has the biggest effect on quality. Hansen believes there are no shortcuts in these areas.

Ultra also has an ISO 9000-compliant quality system. Beginning in early 1999, the company began the process of implementing this internationally accepted quality system. The project began with the hiring of a quality specialist to provide a full-time resource to implement the system.

"Milwaukee is a great place to do business," Hansen says. "All of the manufacturing support functions and material suppliers are nearby, which helps us to reduce our lead times and respond faster to customer needs. And the work ethic is terrific." While focusing on quality products and satisfied customers, Ultra Tool & Manufacturing, Inc. has proved its record of success in the Milwaukee area and is well poised for future growth.

CLOCKWISE FROM TOP:
ULTRA FEATURES A BROAD RANGE OF STAMPING CAPABILITY.

ULTRA'S COMMITMENT TO TRAINING IS EVIDENT ON ITS SHOP FLOOR.

ULTRA UTILIZES STATE-OF-THE-ART PRESSES TO MAINTAIN HIGH QUALITY LEVELS.

City by the Waters

Milwaukee Brewers Baseball Club

Only 28 communities in North America are truly major-league cities, and Milwaukee is proud to be among them. Baseball has provided the city with many popular personalities and lasting memories for generations of local fans—Hank Aaron, Eddie Mathews, Warren Spahn, Lew Burdette, Paul Molitor, Robin Yount, and Bob Uecker, not to mention the 1957 World Championship, the 1958 National League pennant, and the 1982 American League pennant.

Beginning in 1953, the Braves called Milwaukee home, but moved to Atlanta in 1966. On April 1, 1970, Allan H. "Bud" Selig, now the commissioner of Major League Baseball, and Edmund Fitzgerald purchased the Seattle Pilots franchise and returned baseball to the city after a four-year absence.

"Over the decades, baseball has been an important part of the fabric of life in Wisconsin," says Laurel Prieb, vice president of corporate affairs for the Milwaukee Brewers Baseball Club and one of 70 employees in the organization's front office. "We are very proud of the memories we provide for people.

Like many baseball fans, Prieb still remembers his first Major League Baseball game. In fact, the ticket from that game on July 31, 1965, still hangs in his office. He was nine years old when he and his family drove more than four hours from their home in South Dakota to see the Minnesota Twins play. He still relishes memories from that day—the smells of the ballpark, the greenness of the perfectly manicured grass, and the excitement of the game.

Today, in Milwaukee, the Brewers provide that same big-league experience every time they take the field.

New Stadium, New Expectations

The Brewers are Wisconsin's team, and the new Miller Park is Wisconsin's ballpark for baseball," Prieb says. "As we enter the 21st century, we are turning a very exciting page. We carry with us the pride and memories of previous seasons going forward into a new, top-echelon baseball stadium."

The Brewers' former home, County Stadium, opened in 1953 and is one of the largest stadiums in professional baseball, with a capacity of about 53,000. In almost 50 years, nearly 65 million people passed through County Stadium's turnstiles for a baseball game. And while many consider the facility a grand baseball stadium, it didn't allow the Brewers organization to offer the total entertainment package that fans have come to expect, particularly as competition for entertainment dollars has made consumers more sophisticated in their expectations.

Miller Park, scheduled to open for the 2001 season, represents a great,

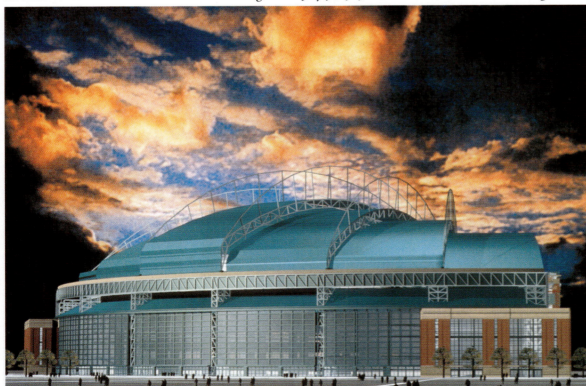

Miller Park—the new home of the Milwaukee Brewers Baseball Club—represents a great new baseball age for Milwaukee and the state of Wisconsin. The park features a natural-grass field, upon which the traditions of America's favorite pastime have been built.

Milwaukee

"The expectations of our fans are high and we expect to exceed them with the help of our new stadium," says Wendy Selig-Prieb, Brewers president and chief executive officer, as well as daughter of Bud Selig, "but our job doesn't end with the completion of Miller Park. Miller Park is really just the beginning."

EVERY TIME THEY TAKE THE FIELD, THE BREWERS PROVIDE A BIG-LEAGUE EXPERIENCE FOR BASEBALL FANS IN MILWAUKEE AND THROUGHOUT THE REGION.

More Than Baseball

Baseball is entertainment, but what the Brewers present is more than the game itself. The franchise not only provides a significant financial impact to the Milwaukee area, but a very strong quality of life and psychological impact as well. "Baseball is good for the soul of a city," says Selig-Prieb. "The game also has the ability to bring direct and indirect fund-raising benefits to so many local charitable organizations. That's another part of our responsibility and influence on the community."

The Brewers organization itself supports many causes in the state, particularly youth and educational groups. It cosponsors the Strive for Excellence Day for local junior high school students, and supports the Child Abuse Prevention Fund and the Hank Aaron Chasing the Dream Foundation, among many others. Recently, the Brewers also announced the birth of Brewers Charities, Inc., designed to assist youth and the underprivileged in Milwaukee and throughout Wisconsin.

Fans of all ages have upheld the baseball tradition in Milwaukee with their ongoing support and enthusiasm. By providing both new entertainment options for fans and benefits for the greater community, the Brewers are playing a major-league role in maintaining Milwaukee's vitality.

new baseball age for Milwaukee and the state of Wisconsin. Seating approximately 43,000, its smaller size and split-bowl seating will further enhance the experience of spectators, bringing more fans even closer to the action.

Miller Park also provides a greater diversity of seating types. There will be 70 suites and four seating levels. Fully one-third of the seats at the new stadium will cost $10 or less and some just $6 per game. Prices may be further discounted with special promotions. "Part of the reason for offering a mix of seating is to allow everyone to experience a baseball game at Miller Park, regardless of his or her personal financial situation," Prieb says.

With a retractable radial roof that opens and closes like a fan, Miller Park will be the only one of its kind in North America. The seven roof panels, weighing a total of 12,000 tons, are linked at a pivot point behind home plate. When opened, four panels nest on the third base side and three nest along the first base side. In addition to providing warmth and comfort, the roof's design more closely mirrors the shape of a baseball field, resulting in a seating configuration that is more intimate than in most ballparks. The entire building conforms to the shape of the field and its unique roof.

Equally important, Miller Park features a natural-grass field, upon which the traditions of America's favorite pastime have been built.

Miller Park is also a unique, compelling destination for any social occasion. There will be diverse entertainment opportunities, such as Stadium Club, an exciting theme restaurant; interactive children's areas; and an enormous novelty store. Many of these facilities will be open year-round.

DeRosa Corporation

Initially, Joseph DeRosa planned to be a bank examiner after college. Instead, he took a position as an assistant manager at a family restaurant. Seven months later, he decided to start his own restaurant, thus giving birth to the Chancery—a name DeRosa picked by opening a thesaurus and randomly placing his finger on a page—and the DeRosa Corporation.

"In 1972 in southeastern Wisconsin, you had basically two types of places to go to dinner: a tavern or a supper club," DeRosa recalls. "I wanted to provide a nice place for families to go out to dinner and have a cocktail if they wanted to, without having to spend a lot of money."

DeRosa also tried to introduce new and interesting tastes to the area. The Chancery brought blackened Cajun food to Milwaukee in the late 1970s and stir-fry in the 1980s. While DeRosa looked to various parts of the country for flavor sensations, he always planned to keep the Chancery chain local. The menu and interior design went a long way toward enhancing the Chancery brand.

There are now two Chancery restaurants located in Milwaukee, two in Racine, and one each in Kenosha, Mequon, Waukesha, and Wauwatosa. All eight Milwaukee-area Chancery restaurants have their own personalities—some use wood-burning stoves and others offer breakfast—but all share a common main menu. The restaurants are legendary for their superb customer service, which makes guests comfortable with the place, people, and product, and keeps customers loyal to the local chain.

"We wanted each Chancery to be unique, rather than having a cookie-cutter approach," DeRosa says. "Often, the site dictated the style and design of the restaurant. Each one was to be fresh and new." The Chancery in Wauwatosa, for example, was originally a bank, and the former vault now serves as a small dining room. In recent years, DeRosa's wife, Pam, an interior designer, has been involved in creating the look and feel of the company's restaurants.

Expanding beyond Chancery

Recently, the DeRosa Corporation began expanding into the fine dining market with Eddie Martini's, a 1940s-style supper club that opened its doors in 1995. Another fine dining experience, Sticks and Stones, opening in the spring of 2001 in Brookfield, will feature regional dishes and truly unique cooking methods.

◄ KEVIN MIYAZAKI, MILWAUKEE MAGAZINE

The walls of Eddie Martini's display witty quotes from celebrities, while its impeccable, retro-style service level features servers in white jackets and ties. One of the city's most sought-after places for dinner reservations, Eddie Martini's also boasts one of Milwaukee's most impressive wine lists.

The DeRosa Corporation was also chosen to be the managing partner of a Harley-Davidson restaurant and other food service facilities at the Harley-Davidson Experience Center, set to open in 2002. The proposed banquet facilities—Milwaukee's second-largest banquet space—will accommodate 700 guests, while providing them with views of the city skyline, a riverbank location near the Milwaukee River, and a connection to the Riverwalk.

Employee Importance

With some 750 employees in eight locations, a strong training and development program is crucial, and is one of the DeRosa Corporation's strongest tools. DeRosa Corporation employees are able to

Joseph DeRosa, founder of the DeRosa Corporation, has the same leadership philosophy after 30 years of service: Do basic things right. This list of basics includes providing legendary service, good food and drink, and clean restaurants.

take charge of just about any situation and are shown, from day one, what is expected of them.

Each DeRosa Corporation employee plays a tremendous role in the organization's overall success. The DeRosa Corporation is 51 percent owned by the DeRosa Corporation Employee Stock Ownership Plan. After a minimum of 1,000 hours worked and one year of service, an employee becomes an owner of the company, receiving an annual allocation of stock based on the value of the company and the employee's yearly compensation.

DeRosa believes in giving back to the industry that helped him make a life for himself and his family, and sits on the board of directors or is a member of many professional organizations. DeRosa's newest interest is Heartlove Place, a neighborhood recreation and family center serving as a safe place for central city youth. The Heartlove founders and board members consider personal responsibility, positive ambition, respect for individuals, and faith in God to be essential values for a healthy society. "It's an important central city initiative that will help people thrive in their lives," DeRosa says of the facility, slated to open in January 2001.

After some 30 years of service, DeRosa's leadership philosophy is still the same: Do basic things right. This list of basics includes providing legendary service, good food and drink, and clean restaurants.

"Looking back, I didn't have the ability to make all of this happen," DeRosa says. "But the Lord brought us to the right place and brought together a great group of people to make it happen. The genuine friendliness of the staff makes it possible to really care about guests in our restaurants."

CLOCKWISE FROM TOP LEFT: EDDIE MARTINI'S, A 1940S-STYLE SUPPER CLUB, OPENED IN MARCH 1995 AND REMAINS ONE OF THE MOST SOUGHT-AFTER RESERVATIONS IN THE MILWAUKEE AREA TODAY.

TWO CHANCERY LOCATIONS SERVE BREAKFAST, AND ALL EIGHT FEATURE LUNCH AND DINNER.

THE CHANCERYS ATTRACT FAMILIES WITH THEIR EXTENSIVE MENU FEATURING BURGERS TO BAYOU SALMON AND EVERYTHING IN BETWEEN. A SPECIAL KIDS' MENU AND CLUB IS AVAILABLE TO PINT-SIZED GUESTS 10 AND UNDER.

City by the Waters

EARTH TECH

ENGINEERING PROBLEM SOLVERS IS ONE WAY TO DESCRIBE Earth Tech. Whether engineering municipal water and wastewater treatment or storm water facilities, or designing bridges and roadways, or addressing environmental concerns of private industry, the company is making the world a better place to live by ensuring that essential infrastructure is sound and functioning.

Today, with revenues approaching $40 million annually and more than 100 employees in Milwaukee and about 370 statewide, the company is the largest engineering firm in Wisconsin, where it has had offices since 1910. Based in Long Beach, California, Earth Tech's world-wide operations of more than 7,000 employees are owned by multinational Tyco International Ltd., whose resources provide a firm financial foundation for the company as well as investment dollars for its clients' design/build/finance/operate projects.

Because of its size, Earth Tech can provide total water management, environmental and remediation, and transportation services to its clients without having to rely on outside subconsultants. These services include drinking water, wastewater, storm water management, and water resources projects. Earth Tech's designs help municipalities and private clients operate water and wastewater plants and facilities efficiently and in regulatory compliance. The firm has specific expertise in the areas of financial/cost of services, water audit/leak detection, water and sewer distribution system studies, and facilities design. Earth Tech's professionals have been involved in transportation projects from rural route designs, sound pavement management, and traffic engineering, to complex corridor studies of urban freeways. Because preventing environmental degradation can increase productivity, Earth Tech's environmental, pollution prevention, ecological, and energy-related services are routinely used to solve clients' day-to-day operation concerns.

Also, because of Earth Tech's size, technical depth, and financial strength, it is able to deliver services in a traditional design/bid/build delivery system or a complete turnkey delivery system including design/build/operate.

The Expertise to Succeed

Perhaps Earth Tech's greatest asset is its team of experienced, devoted employees. "Earth Tech employees each develop an expertise and industry knowledge essential to his or her specialties," says James T. Kunz, senior vice president in the Milwaukee office. "In smaller firms, everyone is a generalist, but our Milwaukee office is large enough to have entire departments dedicated to specific services. This allows us to take on challenging, complex, high-profile projects that have diversified needs." In addition to its large staff of specialists in Milwaukee, the office has access to experts throughout the company.

As established experts in regulations, industry trends, and funding sources, Earth Tech employees develop solutions that are not only functional, but also appropriate in terms of the political realities of gaining approval and being affordable. Using its in-house experts, coupled with advanced computer technology, Earth Tech is able to examine many design alternatives and secondary impacts of a design in terms of the big picture and long-term effects, such as maintenance costs and future environmental regulations.

An Essential Part of Milwaukee's Growth

Earth Tech has provided its services for several high-profile projects throughout the Milwaukee area. For example, the company has worked with the Milwaukee Metropolitan Sewerage District on many projects, including the South Shore Wastewater Treatment Plant and an evaluation of the downtown sewer system, which was constructed at the turn of the century.

When the City of Milwaukee needed to prevent a reoccurrence of the cryptosporidium outbreak that sickened residents in 1993, it turned to Earth Tech. The company acted as the city's technical representative during the design and construction improvements to the Linnwood and Howard Avenue water treatment plants, and the conversion to ozone technology to more effectively ensure

EARTH TECH SERVES AS PROGRAM MANAGER FOR THIS HIGHLY VISIBLE, CHALLENGING REPLACEMENT OF THE SIXTH STREET VIADUCT IN MILWAUKEE. CO-DESIGNED BY EARTH TECH AND KAHLER SLATER AS A CABLE-STAYED STRUCTURE, THE BRIDGE INCLUDES SIDEWALKS AND BIKE LANES CONNECTING TO DOWNTOWN MILWAUKEE FROM THE PROPOSED HENRY AARON RECREATIONAL TRAIL.

that all waterborne diseases are being removed.

Earth Tech is currently managing the reconstruction of the $50 million Sixth Street Viaduct project in downtown Milwaukee. The existing structure was built in 1908, and for years, was restricted to two lanes of traffic due to its structural deterioration.

The viaduct project is an important first for both Earth Tech and the Wisconsin Department of Transportation. Earth Tech worked with the city, county, and state, as well as the Federal Highway Administration, to utilize a design/build delivery system for this project. Although this delivery approach is widely used in private industry, the Sixth Street Viaduct project is the first major transportation project to utilize this approach in the state and one of only a handful in the country. Through this delivery approach, it is estimated the project duration will be shortened by 15 months and realize a 10 to 15 percent reduction in cost. Construction began in 2000, and the viaduct will be completed in 2002.

Because of the company's attention to detail, it's little surprise that the Wisconsin Department of Transportation selected Earth Tech as a district program manager to manage and deliver the Local Roads Program throughout eight counties in southeastern Wisconsin. This program provides state funding to local municipalities for arterial roads and bridges not on the state highway system. More than 75 projects are typically under way at one time. "Our customer focus is based on providing solid technical work in a timely fashion to meet our clients' needs," Kunz says. "More than 90 percent of Earth Tech's business is from repeat clients, many of which have been clients for over 50 years. We are very proud of that fact."

WORKING WITH THE WISCONSIN DEPARTMENT OF NATURAL RESOURCES AND THE TOWN OF DELAVAN, WISCONSIN, EARTH TECH HELPED REVERSE 40 YEARS OF DETERIORATION IN DELAVAN LAKE WITH A SIX-PHASE LAKE REHABILITATION PROGRAM (LEFT).

EARTH TECH HELPED TRANSFORM A 63-ACRE BROWNFIELD SITE IN KENOSHA FROM A HEAVY INDUSTRIAL SITE TO A NEW AND VITAL WATERFRONT RECREATIONAL AND RESIDENTIAL COMMUNITY (RIGHT).

EARTH TECH DESIGNED AND BUILT THE 7TH STREET PLAZA AS PART OF RACINE LAKEFRONT DEVELOPMENT'S MAIN PEDESTRIAN ACCESS, WHICH CONNECTS TWO ARCHITECTURALLY DIVERSE BUILDINGS, THE HISTORIC MEMORIAL HALL AND THE NEW LIBRARY.

City by the Waters

SHORELINE COMPANY INC.

For years, the East Side of Milwaukee has been one of the city's most desirable residential areas, particularly for the city's "old money" families, young professionals, and college students. Today, as baby boomers become empty nesters and as downtown Milwaukee continues its renaissance, the neighborhood is more popular than ever.

The combination of classic apartment and condo dwellings, plus access to an ever growing list of amenities, is attracting suburbanites back to the city, particularly to the historic and fashionable East Side. Leading the way in this revival is the management firm Shoreline Company Inc.

East Side Origins

Shoreline, with the purchase of its first building in the summer of 1973, today owns approximately 50 buildings with about 2,500 units—from studios to penthouses—which means there's something to fit every lifestyle.

During the summer, it's easy to spot a Shoreline holding—bright flowers are planted in front of each building. It's a small thing, but such attention to detail illustrates the care the company takes in regard to each of its buildings and each of its residents.

Most Shoreline properties are located on the East Side and North Shore suburbs bordering Lake Michigan, lending an obvious name to the company. Today, the firm has approximately 150 employees, including on-site building managers, maintenance technicians, and office staff.

Shoreline is headquartered in the Plaza Hotel and Apartments on North Cass Street. This charming art deco building was originally constructed as two buildings in 1925, and included an on-site grocery market, bar, and restaurant. The original owner kept the building until 1984, when he sold it to Shoreline. Nestled in a quiet, tree-lined neighborhood, the Plaza maintains its warm atmosphere, characterized by traditionally furnished hotel suites and unfurnished studio apartments.

Today, the Plaza has about 185 apartment units and hotel suites, a beauty salon, and a café. Fax and copy service as well as a 24-hour switchboard with voice mail service are also available. For more than 30 years, the Plaza has been the home of many performers in the Milwaukee Repertory Theater, the Skylight Opera, and other theater troupes. Residents and visitors—some new arrivals in the city—appreciate the convenience of the concierge services and the Plaza's desirable location near everything lively the city has to offer.

Location, Location

One of the unique aspects of living on the East Side is the variety of residents. The area is a people-watcher's paradise, and one of the few neighborhoods in the Midwest where Italian, German, Polish, Russian, and Yiddish are spoken on a regular basis. From college freshmen

THE LARGEST APARTMENT COMMUNITY IN THE STATE OF WISCONSIN, SHORELINE COMPANY INC.'S JUNEAU VILLAGE TOWERS HAS A HEATED, OLYMPIC-SIZED OUTDOOR SWIMMING POOL.

THE PLAZA HOTEL AND APARTMENTS, ONE OF SHORELINE'S MANY PROPERTIES, IS A CHARMING ART DECO BUILDING CONVENIENTLY LOCATED WITHIN WALKING DISTANCE OF LAKE MICHIGAN AND THE DOWNTOWN BUSINESS DISTRICT.

to Jewish seniors, and from urban families to Italian grocers, variety is definitely the spice of life in the neighborhood.

Key East Side thoroughfares are often home to more than one Shoreline building. The company's properties pepper Prospect Avenue; Lake Drive; and Astor, Cass, Jackson, and North Marshall streets.

Not far from the Plaza is another Shoreline classic, the Astor Hotel, built for Milwaukee hotel tycoon Walter Schroeder and completed in 1920. Originally known as Astor-on-the-Lake, it is a nine-story building housing permanent residents in its apartments and temporary guests in its hotel rooms. The Astor contains 125 apartments, 96 hotel rooms and suites, the Astor Street Restaurant, and full banquet facilities, including a grand ballroom.

Today, as then, the Astor's guest services are a particular focus. If a guest needs something, he or she only has to phone the front desk. There are still bellmen at the Astor, a throwback to the glory days of grand hotels. In 1984, the Astor was added to the National Register of Historic Places.

The other Shoreline properties—typically 20- to 100-unit buildings—offer a sense of community, encouraging a social atmosphere among residents. Shoreline clients enjoy living in older buildings filled with the charm and character of a bygone era, whether it's hardwood floors, plaster moldings, or solid, noise-proof walls. The company offers vintage studio and one-, two-, and three-bedroom apartments, as well as fully furnished corporate apartments.

While Shoreline specializes in the East Side and North Shore locations, the company also has prominent holdings located near the Milwaukee County Regional Medical Complex and downtown. In fact, the largest apartment community in Wisconsin is a Shoreline property located downtown. Built in 1966, Juneau Village Towers consists of three buildings,

CLOCKWISE FROM TOP LEFT: THE ROSALIND COURT APARTMENT BUILDING IS A BEAUTIFUL COURTYARD BUILDING LOCATED ON NORTH LAKE DRIVE.

INBUSCH HOUSE, BUILT IN THE LATE 1800S, IS NOW HOME TO CHARMING APARTMENTS WITH 12-FOOT CEILINGS AND FIREPLACES WITH MARBLE MANTELS.

ASTOR HOTEL IS A CLASSIC VINTAGE MASTERPIECE LISTED ON THE NATIONAL REGISTER OF HISTORIC PLACES.

SHORELINE'S DEVONSHIRE APARTMENTS ARE HOUSED IN AN ENGLISH TUDOR MASTERPIECE SITUATED ON A BLUFF OVERLOOKING LAKE MICHIGAN.

City by the Waters

CLOCKWISE FROM TOP LEFT: SHORELINE'S PARK LANE APARTMENTS IS AN ART DECO JEWEL LOCATED ON NORTH PROSPECT AVENUE.

BUILT IN THE 1920S, SHORELINE'S MARSHALL HALL APARTMENTS HAVE A ROOFTOP SUNDECK OVERLOOKING LAKE MICHIGAN AND THE CITY'S SKYLINE.

JUNEAU VILLAGE TOWERS ALSO BOASTS AWARD-WINNING PLAZA GARDENS AND A FOUNTAIN.

containing about 600 units and nearly 1,000 residents. With dry cleaning services; an outdoor, heated swimming pool; underground, heated parking; a fully equipped fitness center; an automated teller machine; a rooftop club room and sundecks; and even a car wash, it truly is a village unto itself.

Many Juneau Village units have balconies offering spectacular views of the city and Lake Michigan. Directly across the street in the Juneau Village Shopping Center is the new Kohl's Food Emporium with its pharmacy, bank, liquor store, flower shop, and sushi bar. Apartment management here will even water residents' plants and feed their fish while they are away. The average age of today's residents is 35, but it ranges from 20 to 95, including a number of the building's original residents.

Since taking over the Juneau Village property in 1995, Shoreline has undertaken an ambitious, $2 million-plus revitalization project for the entire complex, inside and out. The newly appointed swimming pool, plaza, and courtyard area recently won a landscape design award.

With a decidedly low-key management style, Shoreline continues to let its buildings do the talking. Because of the company's attention to detail, the Shoreline name has a strong reputation for renters on the East Side of Milwaukee and beyond.

· 384 ·

Milwaukee

© DICK BLAU

1975-1984

1975
Big Brothers Big Sisters, Inc.

1980
Froedtert Memorial Lutheran Hospital

1982
ABB Automation Inc.

1982
ABB Flexible Automation

1982
FABCO Equipment Inc.

1982
Heartland Advisors, Inc.

1983
The Business Journal

1983
Human Resource Services Inc.

1983
Time Warner Cable-Milwaukee Division

1984
Lakeland Supply, Inc.

1984
Midwest Express Airlines

1984
TexPar Energy, Inc.

Big Brothers Big Sisters, Inc.

FOR NEARLY A CENTURY, BIG BROTHERS BIG SISTERS, Inc. (BBBS) has provided adult role models to children all over the country, and the impact has been undeniable. Locally, the agency has been in existence in Milwaukee and Waukesha counties for more than 25 years, and started its most prosperous year in 2000. ■ The history of the organization dates back to the early 1900s, with the Big Brothers organization starting in 1904 and Big Sisters following in 1909 in Milwaukee; in 1977, the chapters merged and reorganized. As of the year 2000, BBBS nationwide had 512 chapters providing service to children, including 21 chapters in Wisconsin. The local agency, with its creative and structured staff, has administrative costs of just 13 percent and is recognized by the national organization as one of the most cost-effective in the country.

Thinking Big

BBBS accepts mentors from all walks of life, including married couples. Anyone who wants to make a difference in a child's life, and is willing to spend time with a child three to four times a month, is encouraged to get involved. "Having a little brother or sister is like having a nephew or niece," says Robert R. Dunn, executive director. "It's about spending time together—typical, everyday activities, perhaps with a few special outings on occasion."

In addition to the traditional BBBS match, where a mentor takes a child into the community for fun, educational, and recreational activities, the organization provides a wide variety of other volunteer opportunities. The U.S. Department of Education recognizes BBBS' newest program, Site or School-Based Mentoring, for its positive impact on children in the school setting. This opportunity allows volunteers to mentor a child in familiar surroundings that provide participation in a wide variety of activities.

"Whether in the computer lab or the gymnasium, BBBS provides adult role models to children in a safe, structured, and fun environment," Dunn explains. Volunteers have the option of meeting a child and converting the relationship into a long-term match. The site-based program may be easier for volunteers, and provides outreach to families with problems who wouldn't normally become involved with BBBS. Dunn predicts that identifying the children who need resources and taking this program into the community will account for the organization's biggest growth.

Other successful programs are Sports Buddies, First Friend, and Family/Couple Match. Sports Buddies allows little brothers on the waiting list to interact with a role model, and provides volunteers the opportunity to experience mentoring without the long-term commitment. First Friend matches an adult woman with a boy under the age of 10, and Family/Couple Match allows a husband and wife—and their children—to involve a child in their family activities.

BBBS is a strictly voluntary agreement for the volunteer, child, and family. Many children are

FOR NEARLY A CENTURY, BIG BROTHERS BIG SISTERS, INC. (BBBS) HAS PROVIDED ADULT ROLE MODELS TO CHILDREN ALL OVER THE COUNTRY, AND THE IMPACT HAS BEEN UNDENIABLE (TOP).

FOLLOWING AN ORIENTATION PROCESS, BBBS VOLUNTEERS ARE CAREFULLY MATCHED WITH A CHILD WHO SHARES SIMILAR INTERESTS (BOTTOM).

referred by a school or social service agency. They might display an early indication that they are at risk for future problems, and a big brother or sister can make all the difference in their future.

Focus on Mentoring

With various match options and other volunteer opportunities within our organization, we find a way for any adult who wants to help a child get involved," Dunn says. "The concept of mentoring is growing, and families in our community are seeing the positive results of the BBBS program." Therefore, a critical challenge facing the agency is finding enough volunteers to meet the demands.

BBBS serves children between the ages of seven and 17, while most children accepted are under the age of 14. More boys generally apply for a big brother, while it is easier to recruit women as role models for young girls. The average BBBS relationship lasts for two and a half years, although many participants become lifelong friends.

The organization's staff of social workers perform a thorough background check, and interview friends and family of potential volunteers to find sincere, dedicated big brothers and sisters. Following an orientation process, volunteers are then carefully matched with a child who shares similar interests. Big brothers and sisters can volunteer as little as one hour per week, and the organization encourages a one-year commitment. Every month, BBBS staff members contact the volunteers and family to provide support and assistance.

"You don't need to know kids or child psychology to be an effective big brother or sister," Dunn says. "Being a good listener is the key. We provide support to help our volunteers answer questions and address problems that may arise."

BBBS' advanced screening, matching, and support functions set the organization apart from similar programs. Its standardized approach, including assessing the needs of children and families, serves as a template for other mentoring organizations.

The positive impact mentors have on a child's life is impressive. According to an independent study of BBBS, children in the program are 46 percent less likely to start using drugs, 33 percent less likely to skip school, and 27 percent less likely to start drinking alcohol.

"Our adult volunteers often say it feels good to be a positive influence in a youngster's life, someone who truly cares about the child," Dunn says. "Big Brothers Big Sisters is more than a nice thing. The simple concept of an adult friend has proved not only to be effective, but also to significantly impact the child and, in turn, our community."

ANYONE WHO WANTS TO MAKE A DIFFERENCE IN A CHILD'S LIFE, AND IS WILLING TO SPEND TIME WITH A CHILD THREE TO FOUR TIMES A MONTH, IS ENCOURAGED TO GET INVOLVED IN BBBS. THE AVERAGE BBBS RELATIONSHIP LASTS FOR TWO AND A HALF YEARS, ALTHOUGH MANY PARTICIPANTS BECOME LIFELONG FRIENDS.

City by the Waters

Froedtert Memorial Lutheran Hospital

Froedtert Memorial Lutheran Hospital came into being largely as a result of the foresight and benevolence of Milwaukee businessman Kurtis R. Froedtert. Froedtert's dreams of attending medical school were diverted by his father's death in 1915, which drew him back to Milwaukee to run the family business, the Froedtert Malt Company.

Through the years, Froedtert provided financial support for several area medical facilities, but his ultimate dream was to build a truly unique hospital for Milwaukee.

In 1965, 14 years after Kurtis R. Froedtert's death, the Froedtert Trust moved ahead with plans for a special hospital with a strong medical education affiliation and specialized medical programs. In 1980, Froedtert Memorial Lutheran Hospital opened its doors and began establishing itself as a leading-edge regional tertiary referral center in partnership with the Medical College of Wisconsin.

Today, Froedtert Hospital has approximately 470 beds and a total staff of about 3,500, including nearly 700 Medical College staff physicians and 250 residents and fellows. During any given year, Froedtert Hospital may record 18,000 inpatients totaling 115,000 days of care, plus more than 300,000 outpatient clinic visits.

A Recognized Leader in Community Care

Froedtert Hospital's mission is to be a nationally recognized teaching hospital distinguished by service excellence, regionally and nationally recognized physicians, technology leadership, and efforts to advance community health," says William D. Petasnick, Froedtert's president and CEO. To achieve this goal, Froedtert Hospital has a unique relationship with the Medical College.

Froedtert has been recognized in Wisconsin and across the country as an innovative health care institution. *U.S. News & World Report* has named it one of the best hospitals for digestive disease treatments. Many Froedtert & Medical College Cancer Center physicians have been selected for *Good Housekeeping* magazine's Top Cancer Specialists for Women list. *Milwaukee* magazine has chosen Froedtert as the best emergency department and named 60 physicians at Froedtert as best doctors.

Froedtert performs an important role as a major training center for many of tomorrow's health care professionals. Students from schools throughout the Midwest come to Froedtert to complete studies and prepare for careers in nursing, radiology, surgical technology, respiratory therapy, and pharmacy, among many other fields.

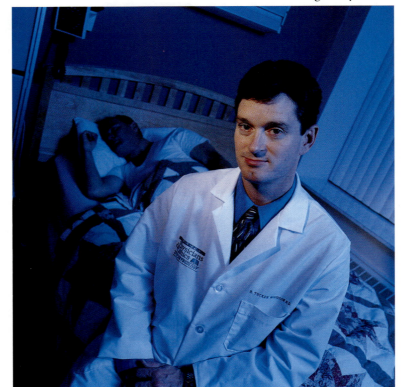

In 1980, Froedtert Memorial Lutheran Hospital opened its doors and began establishing itself as a leading-edge regional tertiary referral center in partnership with the Medical College of Wisconsin.

Froedtert Hospital has approximately 409 beds and a total staff of about 3,500, including nearly 700 Medical College of Wisconsin staff physicians and 250 residents and fellows.

Milwaukee

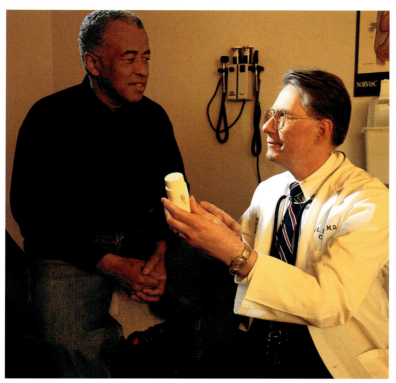 

Froedtert's mission to improve the health status of the communities it serves is reflected in the numerous resources it expends on health education. The Froedtert and Dynacare Community Health Resource Center provides the public with a health library complete with medical books, periodicals, videos, and Internet access. The hospital's Body, Mind, and Spirit health classes run daily, and many health fairs are held throughout the year.

Specialty Programs

At Froedtert Hospital, more than 30 medical specialties work together as multidisciplinary teams providing a close collaboration of wide-ranging medical expertise to diagnose and treat disease and injuries. Froedtert & Medical College have been the site of a long list of medical firsts in the state, including the first epilepsy surgery, the first liver transplant, and the founding of the first spinal cord injury center. The most sophisticated diagnostic and treatment technologies are sometimes introduced at Froedtert & Medical College long before they are available elsewhere in the region.

Froedtert was the first Level I trauma center in the state of Wisconsin to be accredited by the American College of Surgeons. The Froedtert & Medical College Trauma Center is staffed 24 hours a day with trained and certified trauma surgeons and nurses, as well as radiologists, anesthesiologists, and other specialists. Froedtert is also a home base for the Flight for Life helicopters.

The Froedtert & Medical College Transplant Center is a comprehensive, multi-organ transplant program that is recognized as one of the top 15 in the United States. Utilizing state-of-the-art technology, Medical College physicians perform kidney, liver, pancreas, heart, and lung transplants. In all, more than 3,000 organ transplants have been performed with outcomes that consistently meet or exceed national averages.

The Froedtert & Medical College Cancer Center features hematology, radiation, and surgical oncology services under one roof. Breast cancer patients are treated with the advanced technologies and coordinated care of multi-disciplinary treatment teams from the hospital's breast care center. Unique services such as genetic screening for various cancers are also available. The center's bone marrow transplant program is rated as one of the nation's top five centers for unrelated bone marrow transplants.

The Froedtert & Medical College Neurosciences Center, which includes stroke and epilepsy programs, is staffed by specialists in neurology, neuropsychology, neuroradiology, and neurosurgery. The stroke program is Southeastern Wisconsin's clinical leader in stroke diagnosis, treatment, and rehabilitation. The Neurosciences Center also offers leading-edge technology such as the gamma knife, which destroys inoperable brain tumors with precisely focused radiation beams—without open incisions.

The Froedtert & Medical College Birth Center is located within neighboring Children's Hospital of Wisconsin. It offers easy access to a state-of-the-art neonatology intensive care unit and a full range of pediatric medical and surgical care. Physicians provide expertise in areas such as normal and high-risk births, infertility, diabetes in pregnancy, and anticoagulation in pregnancy.

With a high level of specialized care, a nurturing staff, and a commitment to the community, the Froedtert Hospital of today is its namesake's vision come to life. "Everyone at Froedtert Hospital is sensitive to the reality that a stay in our facility is a major event in the life of a family," says Petasnick. "We take this responsibility seriously and are grateful for the opportunity to advance the health of the communities we serve."

AT FROEDTERT HOSPITAL, MORE THAN 30 MEDICAL SPECIALTIES WORK TOGETHER AS MULTIDISCIPLINARY TEAMS PROVIDING A CLOSE COLLABORATION OF WIDE-RANGING MEDICAL EXPERTISE TO DIAGNOSE AND TREAT DISEASE AND INJURIES (LEFT).

UNIQUE SERVICES SUCH AS RESEARCH AT THE FROEDTERT & MEDICAL COLLEGE EYE INSTITUTE BENEFIT PATIENTS THROUGHOUT THE REGION (RIGHT).

ABB Automation Inc.

When employees and managers of ABB Automation Inc.'s Drives & Power Products Group and the company's Pulp & Paper, Printing and Metals Systems Drives Divisions get together to work and play, they think locally and globally at the same time. ■ Locally, the some 425 employees of the New Berlin-based manufacturing and office facility participate as volunteers for Special Olympics events, which ABB sponsors annually on a regional and national level. Hundreds of employees also contribute thousands of dollars to United Way and, with the company providing matching dollars, are a leading source of support for local community programs throughout Waukesha, Milwaukee, and the surrounding counties where ABB employees live.

Challenges also abound for employees to help ABB push the envelope as a worldwide leader in technology. As part of the key automation business segment of Zurich-based ABB Group—one of the world's largest global technology companies—the New Berlin facility is responsible for the product development, applications design, manufacture, and servicing of AC and DC drives, engineered drives and control systems, motors, and high-power conditioning systems.

Utilizing advanced technology, ABB's in-house Research and Development Center has developed the industry's first "smart" electronic bypass series—AC drives with next-generation, microprocessor-based controllers for the commercial HVAC market. ABB engineers also pioneered Direct Torque Control, an open-loop control feature that enables ABB's industrial low-voltage and medium-voltage AC drives to calculate the state (torque and flux) of a motor 40,000 times per second.

Through the addition of a unique factory-within-a-factory at the company's 190,000-square-foot facility in New Berlin, ABB employees are producing further new technologies that enable ABB drives to perform better, be more energy efficient, be smaller in size, and integrate easily with automation systems. Under the direction of Chuck Clark, president of ABB Drives & Power Products Group, this global factory for borderless markets serves North America, and is a mirror image of ABB's automated facilities in Finland and China. The modular assembly facility produces a made-to-order, low-voltage AC drive, featuring a total of 35 parts, every 20 minutes. New ABB DC drives—modular motor controllers that are designed to make wiring and start-up incredibly fast and easy for end users—continue to be developed as well.

ABB New Berlin also is a key supplier of IEC motors to Grainger, the leading North American provider of maintenance, repair, and operating supplies and services. And the market for the company's large, medium-voltage motors continues to double as well. In addition, ABB builds high-power conditioning systems for use in alternative power-generation sources, such as wind turbines and fuel cells.

The company's Pulp & Paper, Printing and Metals Systems Drives Divisions supply engineered drive system solutions for control of paper machines, printing presses, melt shops, and rolling mills. ABB is the worldwide leader in the control of paper machines with the AccuRay quality control systems, as well as a leading supplier to metals producers with the Metals Profile Mill control systems.

Such technological innovation, leadership, and response to local market needs help ABB Automation Inc.'s employees continue to serve customers across a wide range of industrial and commercial applications.

Personal participation and contribution at both a local and global level are encouraged and highly valued at the manufacturing, engineering, sales, and services offices of ABB Automation Inc.'s Drives & Power Products Group and the company's Pulp & Paper, Printing and Metals Systems Drive Divisions in New Berlin (top).

At two assembly stations adjacent to the staging line of ABB Automation Inc.'s global factory in New Berlin, all components required in each of the company's new ACS/ACH 400 drives line are installed. The entire drive includes 35 parts (bottom).

ABB Flexible Automation

Companies continue to look to ABB Flexible Automation to provide their manufacturing operations the strategic advantages that robotic systems offer—quality, reliability, and flexibility. ■ In 1973, ABB introduced the world's first all-electric robot, and the company continues to be an industry pioneer in providing manufacturers with innovative solutions. ABB Flexible Automation is the one of the world's leading manufacturers of industrial robots and industrial robotic systems—worldwide headquarters are located in Zurich and U.S. operations have been headquartered in New Berlin since 1982.

The New Berlin facility houses one of ABB's Flexible Automation Centers (FACs), where robotic systems are assembled using robots that are manufactured in Sweden, Switzerland, and Norway. These centers, located in more than 30 countries, provide ABB's customers with a worldwide organization that has a strong local presence in individual markets. In North America, ABB FACs are located in Auburn Hills, Michigan; Grand Rapids; Denver; Fort Collins; and Toronto. These centers represent a core, world-class technical expertise in design, engineering, process expertise, project management, system capabilities, and service support for robotic systems. They facilitate the transfer of knowledge and expertise among countries and companies, and assure customers the quickest and most cost-effective solutions for their manufacturing system requirements. The New Berlin Center provides robot systems for a wide range of industries that include appliance, automotive, food, beverage, glass, off-road, plastic, textile, mail, and consumer goods.

ABB has more than 21,000 robots installed in U.S. plants and more than 900 U.S. employees. Worldwide, ABB has more than 90,000 robotic systems installed and 5,600 employees.

Automotive applications still dominate the robotic business. The Big Three American automakers are major customers, including General Motors' utility-vehicle plant in Janesville, which utilizes more than 240 robots—most of which are ABB robots. Major automotive component suppliers also rely on ABB Flexible Automation, including Milwaukee's Tower Automotive, as well as other Milwaukee and Wisconsin manufacturers such as Harley-Davidson, Falk, Bemis, Vollrath, and Penda.

Other industries, however, are the fastest-growing customers of ABB Flexible Automation. They have recognized—as automotive manufacturers did long ago—that ABB robotic systems ensure increased efficiency, enhanced productivity, and improved product quality. As time-based competition sweeps industry worldwide, customers are recognizing the benefits that ABB Flexible Automation provides in helping to shorten product-to-market cycles. With their high degree of flexibility, ABB's robotic systems provide ideal solutions for arc and spot welding, palletizing, painting, dispensing, machine tending, deburring, and grinding applications.

Whether ABB Flexible Automation's employees are volunteering for Special Olympics or providing North American industry with robotic systems, the company is committed to providing the best to its community—both locally and globally.

ABB Flexible Automation robots are used in a variety of applications, including automobile manufacturing.

City by the Waters

· 393 ·

FABCO EQUIPMENT INC.

CLOCKWISE FROM TOP:
JERÉ C. FABICK (LEFT), FABCO EQUIPMENT INC. PRESIDENT AND CEO, AND JOSEPH G. FABICK, CHAIRMAN OF THE BOARD, OPEN A NEW FABCO FACILITY.

CATERPILLAR EMERGENCY STANDBY ELECTRIC POWER GENERATION SYSTEMS LIKE THIS INSTALLATION AT MILLER PARK IN MILWAUKEE ARE SUPPLIED BY FABCO ENGINE SYSTEMS.

FABCO rents, sells, and services Caterpillar® and related products in virtually every sector of the economy. From Caterpillar excavators, loaders, and tractors at work in construction, mining, and agriculture, to Cat power generation systems used in emergency standby and load management applications, to Cat diesel engines for powering trucks that deliver products across America, FABCO is a strong partner providing essential support to industry.

Operating out of more than a dozen facilities located throughout Wisconsin and Upper Michigan, FABCO's 70,000-square-mile service area covers one of the largest Caterpillar dealership territories in North America. The diversified economy of the region offers FABCO the unique opportunity to market Caterpillar's complete product line of over 300 models. FABCO employs more than 500 people, with some 125 working out of locations in the Greater Milwaukee area.

A Historic Foundation

We've built our business on a very straightforward philosophy: Treat people with respect, focus on building long-term relationships, and always provide superior value," says Jeré C. Fabick, president and CEO.

Jeré marks the third generation within the Fabick family business. FABCO's experience in the sales and service of equipment and engines dates back to 1917, when John Fabick Sr. founded the first Fabick Company in St. Louis. Originally, the company merchandised Cletrac crawler tractors and John Deere farm implements.

In 1921, John Fabick expanded his business to include tractors manufactured by C.L. Best. Four years later, Best and Holt Manufacturing merged to form what has become the largest and most respected manufacturer of equipment and engines in the world, Caterpillar Inc. The historic tradition turned north in 1982 when Caterpillar consolidated dealer territories in Wisconsin and Upper Michigan, and awarded representation of its products and services to one experienced dealership. The newly formed FABCO Equipment Inc. was founded by Joseph G. Fabick, John's son and then-president of John Fabick Tractor Company in St. Louis. Fabick Company operations continue in Missouri and Illinois, and although there is no common ownership between the two dealerships, family ties remain strong.

Meeting Customer Needs

Under the experienced leadership of Joseph Fabick, a team of the finest employees in the industry has been assembled; facilities continue to be added, service

· 394 ·

Milwaukee

capabilities refined, and the product line expanded. Above all, FABCO demonstrates a commitment to the industries it serves, and has earned the trust of contractors and other business associates throughout Wisconsin and Upper Michigan.

"Our customers depend on their equipment to be successful," says Jeré Fabick. "For contractors, machines are the factories used to produce their product or service. Without dependable equipment, everything stops."

Supplying productive and reliable equipment and providing the highest possible level of product support are responsibilities that FABCO takes very seriously. In addition to the company's facilities, over 100 FABCO service vehicles are in operation throughout the service territory. And because maintaining equipment is so critical, more than 70 percent of FABCO's workforce is dedicated to parts- and service-related operations. Supported by an in-house training center, sophisticated diagnostic test equipment, and specialized tools, FABCO's factory-certified technicians are available for emergency service 24 hours a day, every day of the year.

To make sure customers have the parts they need—where and when they need them—FABCO's interbranch shuttle system logs more than 2,600 miles each day transporting parts among FABCO branches, 50 additional parts drop locations, and Caterpillar parts facilities. "This system allows us to combine the parts inventories of all FABCO locations and Caterpillar's worldwide parts distribution system into one huge supply source," says Jeré Fabick.

FABCO continues to make significant investments in its infrastructure of people, facilities, tooling, and technology. "Some things never change, and helping our customers operate more profitably will always be a critical factor in our success," states Joseph Fabick.

New Opportunities

FABCO's management team has outlined an ambitious plan to diversify operations and advance the company to higher levels. In addition to maintaining FABCO's leadership position in heavy construction and mining equipment, other opportunities for growth have been targeted by the company.

The escalating demand for electric power, a greater necessity for emergency standby installations, and favorable load management partnerships with utility companies all predict a very bright future for FABCO Engine Systems. A complete line of Caterpillar rubber-tracked agricultural tractors, combines, and loaders represents significant new opportunities in this important sector of the local economy. Caterpillar's introduction of small and very versatile equipment, such as skid steer loaders and mini-excavators, is allowing FABCO to reach out to entirely new markets of potential customers. And, responding to industry demand for short-term equipment rentals, a growing network of FABCO RENTS outlets are emerging in major population centers throughout FABCO's service territory.

"My father's goal of creating a premier Caterpillar dealership is being accomplished," says Jeré Fabick. "His vision of building a company that benefits customers, employees, and communities will continue."

CLOCKWISE FROM TOP LEFT: FABCO IS THE LEADING SUPPLIER OF HEAVY CONSTRUCTION EQUIPMENT IN WISCONSIN AND UPPER MICHIGAN.

FABCO SUPPORTS COMMUNITIES WHERE THEY DO BUSINESS. AS A MAJOR SPONSOR OF THE GREAT CIRCUS PARADE IN MILWAUKEE AND DOZER DAY IN SUSSEX, FABCO BRINGS HAPPINESS TO FAMILIES THROUGHOUT SOUTHEASTERN WISCONSIN.

THE INTRODUCTION OF SMALLER CATERPILLAR EQUIPMENT SUCH AS SKID STEER LOADERS AND MINI-EXCAVATORS PROVIDES FABCO WITH THE OPPORTUNITY TO REACH OUT TO ENTIRELY NEW MARKETS.

City by the Waters

· 395 ·

HEARTLAND ADVISORS, INC.

Founded by William Nasgovitz in 1982, Heartland Advisors, Inc. has established itself as America's Value Investor®. Heartland's commitment to the value investment style—focusing on great companies whose stock prices simply do not reflect the firms' true worth—is unwavering. While other investors may be willing to chase after market trends in search of short-term results, Heartland remains committed to its value discipline for the long term.

The firm manages money for individual investors in its mutual funds and separate accounts, and also manages substantial assets for institutional clients. Heartland is 100 percent employee-owned.

Value Investing

Heartland's value approach to investing transcends investment fads and focuses on identifying companies trading at deep discounts to their intrinsic values. Just as a value-oriented shopper hunts down high-quality goods available at a discount to make a purchase, value investors look for companies that have strong fundamental qualities reflecting their financial strength, management, and products, and that have stock prices lower than their peers'.

Heartland finds these companies through exhaustive, painstaking research based on the firm's proprietary, 10-point investment grid.

"The grid is designed to do more than tell us the potential of a stock," Nasgovitz says. "It is also meant to quantify the downside risk." Because it provides a thorough assessment of companies, the grid is quite detailed, centering on three key areas: fundamentals, risk reduction, and catalyst for recognition.

Heartland scrutinizes countless pages of financial data and travels coast to coast to learn more about companies firsthand. This research is time consuming and challenging, but it is at the core of Heartland's passion for value.

Value investing is more than just another investment fad. The first publications laying out the benefits of value investing date back to 1934. Value investing is a time-tested approach—Heartland wouldn't accept anything less as the cornerstone of the company.

About William Nasgovitz

Heartland's devotion to value investing comes directly from founder and president Nasgovitz. Heartland's 10-point investment grid is among the innovations he has developed during his career. In his more than 30 years in the investment field, Nasgovitz has employed his value discipline in a variety of market conditions—from steep recessions to euphoric bull markets.

"Value investing isn't usually a glamorous pursuit," Nasgovitz notes. "But it's the path that makes sense if you're more concerned with long-term results than short-term excitement. That's why I've dedicated my career to it."

Service: Another Value

Along with its devotion to value investing, Heartland has other priorities as well. Chief among them is delivering high-quality service to investors and clients. To this end, Heartland has assembled a team of representatives dedicated to serving the needs of these investors, encompassing everything from simple transactions to long-term planning issues.

Whether communicating in person, through the mail, on the phone, or over the Internet, Heartland's aim is to deliver the same level of value it demands from the companies it invests in.

WILLIAM NASGOVITZ, PRESIDENT OF HEARTLAND ADVISORS, INC.

HUMAN RESOURCE SERVICES, INC.

IN THE HIT-OR-MISS WORLD OF HIRING, PROMOTING, AND retaining capable employees, Human Resource Services, Inc. (HRS), an outsource and research firm in Greenfield, has transformed what was an art into a science. Founded in 1983, the firm assesses candidates using job-specific tools to predict how they will behave once in the job. Besides profiling a candidate's personality, HRS has designed role-playing tools to understand how a candidate's personality traits will manifest themselves under specific circumstances. For these services, client companies often fly in job candidates from all over the country to be assessed by HRS.

Jessica L. Ollenburg, CMC, CPCM, president and CEO of HRS, states, "We optimize financial resources in relation to human resources functions, such as turnover reduction and productivity maximization. We build teams that pull together and buy in." Ollenburg, a founding member of the HRS team, succeeds Phyllis Pinter as CEO. Pinter now serves as a part-time consultant to the HRS Behavioral Assessment Center. Both have earned noteworthy recognition for advancement with assessment validations.

HRS has grown primarily through client referrals, press articles, word of mouth, and, most recently, via Internet promotion through its Web site, www.hrsteam.com.

Better Employees, Bigger Profits

Conducting behavioral assessments, writing accurate and efficient job descriptions, performing training needs analyses, and matching appropriate candidates for jobs only make up part of HRS' activities. The firm also recommends, coordinates, and implements corporate training programs. HRS also acts as a third-party objective source for employee retention ideas, performance management, wage analyses, job transfers, and promotions, as well as providing clients with legal compliance services and a resource library.

The typical HRS client is committed to minimizing turnover and employs between 80 and 500 team

members. HRS also serves small, growing companies that don't yet need full-time human resources staff, as well as Fortune 500 companies who outsource specific HR functions.

Treating Its Own Employees Right

HRS makes sure to practice what it preaches, which results in low turnover of its own employees. With consistently evolving proprietary software and base-lined instruments, more sophisticated than any available in the marketplace, HRS has maximized its own productivity. The firm has attained 300 percent realized growth without an increase in staff and with improvements in quality.

"Each HRS team member enjoys consistent career growth," says Ollenburg. "State-of-the art leadership, incentives, performance management, and training occur here. Our carefully selected internal team members are proud and are participating in the incentives of our increasing successes."

HRS receives significant media attention for its expertise with these concepts. Up-and-coming ideas in workplace retention and motivation tools, such as casual dress days and

on-site child care, found early testing at HRS prior to becoming more commonplace.

In addition to Ollenburg, the key team at HRS is expanding with controlled growth. This team—or multi-rater—approach to evaluation leads to increased consistency in all cases and greater reliability with client services.

CLOCKWISE FROM TOP RIGHT: WITH CONSISTENTLY EVOLVING PROPRIETARY SOFTWARE AND BASE-LINED INSTRUMENTS, MORE SOPHISTICATED THAN ANY AVAILABLE IN THE MARKETPLACE, HUMAN RESOURCE SERVICES, INC. (HRS) HAS MAXIMIZED ITS OWN PRODUCTIVITY. THE FIRM HAS ATTAINED 300 PERCENT REALIZED GROWTH WITHOUT AN INCREASE IN STAFF AND WITH IMPROVEMENTS IN QUALITY.

"WE OPTIMIZE FINANCIAL RESOURCES IN RELATION TO HUMAN RESOURCES FUNCTIONS, SUCH AS TURNOVER REDUCTION AND PRODUCTIVITY MAXIMIZATION," SAYS JESSICA L. OLLENBURG, CMC, CPCM, PRESIDENT AND CEO OF HRS, AN OUTSOURCE AND RESEARCH FIRM IN GREENFIELD.

IN THE HIT-OR-MISS WORLD OF HIRING, PROMOTING, AND RETAINING CAPABLE EMPLOYEES, HRS HAS TRANSFORMED WHAT WAS AN ART INTO A SCIENCE.

City by the Waters

The Business Journal

NOT LONG AGO, BUSINESS NEWS WAS DELIVERED BY DAILY newspapers and a few national publications. But in the early 1980s, business leaders demanded more. They demanded more information, more depth, and more explanation. Because of that demand, *The Business Journal Serving Greater Milwaukee* was born in 1983. ■ It quickly became one of the most successful publications of its type in the country—with a solid circulation and advertiser base. Today, it is the leading source of business news in southeastern Wisconsin, publishing a weekly news section and regular special sections that reach more than 65,000 readers each issue. It also has helped create one of the top business Internet sites in the country and has partnered with television and radio stations to provide even more timely delivery of business news. "*The Business Journal* is truly a publication that was created because the reader demanded it," says Publisher Mark Sabljak.

The real key to the publication's success—whether it is on the printed page, a computer or TV screen—Sabljak says, has been *The Business Journal*'s reporting and editing staff, which has helped make the publication's business news different than any other source. The reporting staff is made up of individuals who have made business news their livelihood. They specialize in a specific industry, such as commercial real estate or health care, and spend years building background and gaining the trust of the top sources within those industries.

Those sources trust the publication's reporters to get their stories right, which is why business leaders will take phone calls from *Business Journal* reporters above all others. And if you're a business leader, you're likely to hear from the publication before you expect. The publication's definition of news is information no one else knows. *Business Journal* reporters don't rely on press releases or press conferences to determine what to write about.

Instead, the publication prides itself on staying a step ahead of the competition in finding news, getting the stories first, and getting the stories right. But breaking news isn't the only information published in *The Business Journal*.

Special Sections

Each week, *The Business Journal* features sections named "Focus," "Small Business Strategies," "For the Record," and "People on the Move," along with comment and opinion pieces by leading experts in business who offer different perspectives on issues.

The publication's "Focus" section targets a specific industry, such as health care, and takes an in-depth look at the people, trends, and developments within the category. The "Small Business Strategies" section is aimed at solving the problems of

NO ONE CAN BE ABSOLUTELY CERTAIN WHAT THE FUTURE WILL BRING TO BUSINESS, BUT BY READING *THE BUSINESS JOURNAL* EACH WEEK, READERS ARE THE FIRST TO KNOW (LEFT).

LEONARDO DA VINCI GREETS GUESTS AT A *BUSINESS JOURNAL* SPECIAL EVENT (RIGHT).

· 398 ·

Milwaukee

the publication's readers by taking issues within small business, and looking at solutions that are working for real-life companies in the area. "For the Record" provides the nuts and bolts of business, such as awards, tax liens, and new incorporations. People on the Move features different promotions and hirings in the area.

At least twice a month, a special section is included, which contains information that can be found in no other place. Among the special sections are the quarterly "Commercial Leasing and Sales Guides," with rental rates and sale prices for commercial, industrial and retail buildings; the "40 Under 40" section, which highlights up-and-comers in the community; and—for new and growing business—the "How to Book and Small Business Resource Guide."

Providing Valuable Resources

The publication annually gathers up its weekly Top 25 lists to publish one of the area's most valuable resources, the *Book of Lists*. It is there that readers will find the top 25 largest employers in the area, the highest-paid executives, and the leaders in other key business categories.

Special events help *The Business Journal* deliver information and provide networking opportunities at the same time. *The Business Journal*'s events fill meeting rooms and banquet halls throughout the year, bringing together the area's most interesting and controversial newsmakers.

At quarterly Power Breakfasts, business leaders whose companies are in the news face a panel of editors and reporters before a live audience. And two new programs in 2000 proved to be instant successes. The Women of Influence publication and awards luncheon highlights top women in business and the Beyond The Paycheck section/event showcases some of the best places to work in southeastern Wisconsin.

The Business Journal has continued to find new ways to provide essential business information. Early in 2001, a *Business Journal* reporter began delivering daily business news on the evening newscast of Fox Channel 6.

No one can be absolutely certain what the future will bring to business, but by reading *The Business Journal* each week, readers are the first to know.

THE BUSINESS JOURNAL PRIDES ITSELF ON STAYING A STEP AHEAD OF THE COMPETITION IN FINDING NEWS, GETTING THE STORIES FIRST, AND GETTING THE STORIES RIGHT.

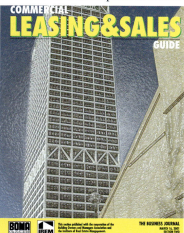

The Business Journal

Vol. 18, No. 17 $2.00 /Published Weekly   **SERVING GREATER MILWAUKEE**   www.bizjournals.com/milwaukee   January 12, 2001

Harnischfeger disputes state's severance claims

By Steven Jagler

Harnischfeger Industries Inc. is asking two federal judges in Delaware to dismiss Wisconsin Attorney General James Doyle's attempt to recover as much as $10 million in severance pay for 335 former workers of the company's Beloit Corp. subsidiary.

Attorneys for Harnischfeger are contending that the state's laws for protecting workers' severance rights are superseded by the federal bankruptcy code and aren't applicable in the case.

Doyle says the verdict in Delaware could have a long-standing effect on the rights of employees in the workplace.

"There's a very crucial legal issue here, which, if it goes against us, would be harmful to the state's employees," Doyle said. "It would be harmful to the people of this state ... This is something we have pursued strongly. You have an agreement, and then you just shut down and don't pay them (the employees). I just think that's morally wrong."

The Wisconsin Department of Justice has filed a proof of claim against Harnischfeger for $10 million in U.S. Bankruptcy Court in Wilmington, Del. The department also filed a proof of claim against Beloit Corp. for $8.4 million with the court.

The state agency is hoping Bankruptcy Court Judge Patrick Walsh will allow one of the claims to be included in Harnischfeger's reorganization settlement, said assistant attorney general Jerry Hancock, who will testify before Walsh in a Feb. 17 hearing.

"We're hopeful that, on Feb. 17, we will have an opportunity to argue the merits of the claim," Hancock said. "This is a unique situation. To my knowledge, this is a case of first impression."

St. Francis-based Harnischfeger, a mining equipment manufacturer, filed for Chapter 11 reorganization on June 7, 1999.

The company sold its Beloit Corp. subsidiary in May 2000 to Valmet Corp., a subsidiary of Metso Corp., Helsinki, Finland, for about $160 million. Valmet has since been renamed Metso Paper Inc.

The Wisconsin Department of Workforce Development (DWD)

Please turn to page 44

Doyle

Big shoes to fill

George W. Bush orders shoes from AllenEdmonds

By Rich Rovito

President-elect George W. Bush won't be wearing cowboy boots with his tuxedo, but the former Texas governor has chosen a pair of shoes manufactured by Allen Edmonds Shoe Corp. that will feature his own personal touch.

An aide to Bush called the Port Washington

Please turn to page 33

Allen Edmonds chief operating officer Ronald Neuman, above, displays two of the shoe models chosen by President-elect George W. Bush for his inauguration. Bush selected a modified version of the Ritz, far left, while his father chose the more traditional Spencer, left, for their inaugurals. Bush asked Allen Edmonds to remove the bows from the Ritz, right.

McCallum lines up key cabinet officers

By Pete Millard

The controversial 2000 presidential election, which sent Gov. Tommy Thompson to Washington, D.C., and pushed Lt. Gov. Scott McCallum into the state's chief executive office, is the second contested election that advanced the political career of McCallum.

McCallum was declared the winner of a recount election in 1976, when he challenged former state Sen. Walter Hollander (R-Rosendale) in a GOP primary. On election night, Hollander was declared the winner by 80 votes, but a recount was demanded.

A bizarre ballot-handling mistake in Hollander's hometown was instrumental in reversing the election. Voting officials in Rosendale had thrown blank ballots into the same bag with counted ballots. During the recount, a state law dictated that, when there are too many ballots in a bag, each candidate takes turns drawing ballots out until the number of ballots equals the number of people who voted.

During the recount, a large number of Hollander ballots remained in the bag, and the recount gave McCallum the victory. McCallum went on to win reelection twice for the state Senate. In 1982, he lost a statewide election to U.S. Sen. William Proxmire (D-Wis.). He was first elected lieutenant governor in 1986.

People underestimated McCallum's political savvy and luck in the beginning of his career, and some may make the same mistake in 2002, a Republican lawmaker says.

McCallum's success over the next 18 months will hinge on who he can convince to join the administration and campaign team, says Bill Smith, president of the Wisconsin branch of the National Federation of Independent Business.

Please turn to page 46

McCallum

NEED HELP?
HireMilwaukee connects employers and job seekers
WWW.BIZJOURNALS.COM/MILWAUKEE

RETENTION PLAN
To motivate workers, firm becomes employee-owned
– PAGE 13

UP THE LADDER
Firms tap state program to train, promote workers
– PAGE 21

Time Warner Cable–Milwaukee Division

Serving 450,000 customers in 131 communities throughout southeastern Wisconsin, Time Warner Cable-Milwaukee Division has provided information and entertainment through its cable TV services since 1983. With high-speed Internet access now available and other information age developments on the horizon, Time Warner is vying to be the area's digital portal to the world.

In 1983, the company offered cable TV service only to residents of the city of Milwaukee. Through constant growth and acquisition—including Viacom, Netravision, Jones Intercable, and Century Cable—Time Warner in Milwaukee has grown from about 100 employees in 1983 to more than 700 current employees. The company has gone from offering about 30 cable channels to providing 200 channels with its new digital cable service. Connecting it all together are about 9,000 miles of cable.

The company's latest innovation, and its debut on the information superhighway, is Road Runner. This high-speed Internet access uses a cable modem that is always on—which means no more waiting to sign on—and is up to 50 times faster than a 56K dial-up telephone modem.

"We consider ourselves to be high-tech, state-of-the-art providers of breakthrough content, whether it be cable TV programming or Internet access," says Bev Greenberg, vice president of community and government relations.

The 2000 merger of America Online (AOL) with Time Warner offers the many advantages of a giant information and entertainment concern. Separately, the two firms were innovators in their fields, and their partnership suggests endless possibilities for meshing traditional media, new media, data, content, and communications. Business units include Warner Bros. music and movies, CNN News Group, Turner Entertainment, HBO, and Time Inc., as well as AOL, the world's largest Internet service.

Community Service

Time Warner Cable-Milwaukee Division is involved in community activities throughout its service area, supporting more than 125 charities with some $2.5 million annually in funding, donations, and special assistance. Children and education have long been areas of emphasis at Time Warner Cable, and the company offers free cable TV and Road Runner service to each of the 1,000 schools in the area, in addition to providing student scholarships and teacher grants.

Time Warner provides workshops to help teachers make the most of cable TV and Road Runner access in the classroom. The company's Cable in the Classroom program offers 540 hours of commercial-free educational programming each month. More than $1 million has been contributed in cash and in-kind donations to develop the program, including TV equipment, cable programming software, computers, and educational materials. The company also provides free Road Runner service to the area's public libraries.

Time Warner has partnered with local organizations such as the Betty Brinn Children's Museum, Boys and Girls Club, Discovery World, Make-A-Wish Foundation, Milwaukee Symphony Orchestra, Milwaukee Zoological Society, Scouting organizations, Urban League, YMCA, and YWCA.

"We are considered a tremendous force in education and child advocacy," Greenberg says. "We have a very sincere president, Tom Sharrard, who is very active in the

(Back row) Bev Greenberg, vice president of community and government relations, Time Warner Cable-Milwaukee Division; U.S. Congressman Tom Barrett; (front row, from left) Milwaukee teachers Sandra Hyden, Lisa Sherman-Colt, and Abby Plummer traveled to Washington, D.C., to accept their Crystal Apple awards (top).

Time Warner Cable-Milwaukee Division President Tom Sharrard shows the public how fast and easy surfing the Internet is when using Road Runner (bottom).

community. We have a strong commitment to making life better wherever we do business."

Time Warner Cable-Milwaukee Division creates nationally recognized educational initiatives such as Time Warner Cable's Kidz Biz and the Cable and Media for Youth Awards, as well as Time Warner Cable's Hang Tough Video Contest. These initiatives, whose focus includes media literacy and drug abuse prevention, have won numerous national, state, and local awards.

Time Warner also pays close attention to the diversity of its employees. Diversity is emphasized at every level of the company, in keeping with the firm's philosophy that the composition of the employee population should reflect that of the community at large. The Milwaukee Division has also made more than $110,000 available to local banks expressly for loans to minority and female entrepreneurs. So far, nearly 40 businesses have been opened with the aid of these funds.

Technology and Service

The company's commitment to technology and customer service is more than lip service. The Milwaukee Division has spent close to $300 million upgrading its cable plant, including such innovations as a fiber-optic network, so that every customer can have access to digital cable TV, Road Runner service, telephone service, and other technologies under development. There are distinct technological advantages to using digital cable TV lines rather than standard telephone lines, for example, for various communication services.

Time Warner has built a customer-focused company largely through general and job-specific training. All customer service employees are trained for a month or more before starting their jobs. Rather than learning on the run, they are equipped to handle any questions they may receive before they answer the phone for the first time. Altogether, the company's customer service representatives handle about 200,000 calls a month. The On-Time Guarantee program averages a success rate of 98 percent.

The company is also upgrading its headquarters. In the second quarter of 2001, Time Warner Cable-Milwaukee Division will relocate to a rehabilitated Commerce Street Power Plant on the Milwaukee River. This long-vacant historical structure will house a day care center, a 24-hour local news channel, and a café. The firm's headquarters building will also serve as one of the northern anchors of the Riverwalk, which has helped lead a renaissance of downtown Milwaukee.

CLOCKWISE FROM TOP LEFT: ASTRONAUT SALLY RIDE (LEFT) SHARES HER EXPERIENCES WITH TIME WARNER CABLE-MILWAUKEE DIVISION'S KIDZ BIZ REPORTER ALLY LAPORTE.

KIDZ BIZ REPORTERS ASHLEY JAMERSON AND HUMBERTO SANCHEZ COVER THE NICKELODEON KIDS CHOICE AWARDS IN LOS ANGELES.

(STANDING, FROM LEFT) MILWAUKEE ALDERMEN FRED GORDON AND TERRENCE HERRON; SCHOLARSHIP RECIPIENTS HUGO CHAIDEZ, BRYAN LATTIMORE, AND STEVEN PICHE; MAYOR JOHN O. NORQUIST; TIME WARNER CABLE-MILWAUKEE DIVISION PRESIDENT TOM SHARRARD; ALDERMEN DONALD RICHARDS, WILLIE HINES, AND JAMES BOHL JR.; AND (SEATED, FROM LEFT) SCHOLARSHIP RECIPIENTS JOSIE LUNAR, AMY COSTELLO, TUYEN NGO, JENNIFER EPPS, AND SALIMAH RASHADA PARTICIPATE IN TIME WARNER'S AWARDS CEREMONY FOR 2000.

BUGS BUNNY JOINS IN FOR A HALLOWEEN CELEBRATION WITH THE BOYS AND GIRLS CLUB.

City by the Waters

Lakeland Supply, Inc.

Founded in 1984 by Larry Schmidt, Lakeland Supply, Inc. began as a husband-and-wife, home-based business selling printed place mats and napkins. Over the next couple of years, new items were added to the product offering, including stretch film, also known as pallet wrap. The stretch film sales quickly grew and became Lakeland's primary distributed product. Along with the wide array of packaging, paper, and janitorial supplies offered by Lakeland, this focus on stretch film and other packaging supplies remains the primary product segment for the company today.

By 1988, the company had grown to a point where it could no longer run as a home-based business. A warehouse was leased, and a full administrative staff, sales force, warehouse crew, and delivery drivers were hired.

Now a thriving wholesale distributor in the Milwaukee area, Lakeland operates out of its newly built, 40,000-square-foot warehouse/office facility in Waukesha. The company's impressive growth and market penetration can be attributed to the type of business environment and leadership created by Schmidt.

Although Schmidt is still involved in the business from an executive level, the day-to-day operations are being handled by his sons: Larry Schmidt II, CPA, general manager, and Vince Schmidt, sales manager. Over the years, the company and its founder have won several awards, including selection to the Metro Milwaukee Future 50 for four consecutive years, winner of the Master Mettle award, and nomination as Entrepreneur of the Year.

God, Family, Lakeland

Along with being a family-run company, Lakeland is a Christian organization. The beliefs and values held by the company's owners play a major role in the firm's day-to-day operations. Each company meeting begins with a prayer and the meeting board reads GOD—FAMILY—LAKELAND, in order to remind everyone not only of the top priorities in life, but also the proper order in which they should be kept.

The Lakeland management team is genuinely concerned with the intellectual, physical, and spiritual well-being of each employee. With the intention of assisting employees to maintain a proper balance in their lives, the team encourages an atmosphere in which fellow employees are treated like family members, and are encouraged to share both their

Lakeland's impressive growth and market penetration can be attributed to the type of business environment and leadership created by founder Larry Schmidt (right).

A thriving wholesale distributor in the Milwaukee area, Lakeland operates out of its newly built, 40,000-square-foot warehouse/office facility in Waukesha (bottom).

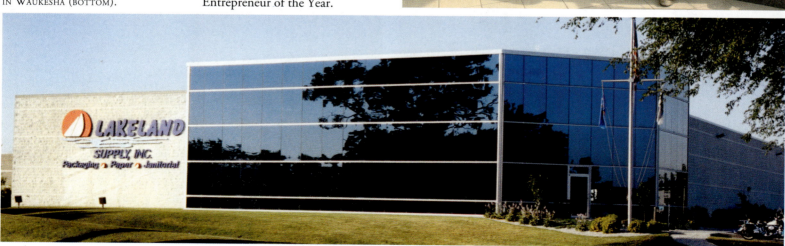

Milwaukee

professional and personal goals.

"In the business world and our personal lives, we have to make important decisions every day," says Larry Schmidt II. "Our values provide us with direction and help us keep our priorities straight."

Work Environment

"The daily atmosphere here is work focused, but it's also fun," Vince Schmidt says. "You hear a lot of laughter with clients and fellow employees during the course of a regular business day. We believe that if you're not enjoying your job, you're missing the boat."

Numerous employee outings help create a collegial environment at Lakeland. Among these activities are Packer and Brewer tailgate parties, company picnics, sponsorship of a baseball and football team, and many other events. At Elkhart Lake racetrack, employees have had an opportunity to test drive the Lakeland-sponsored race car. Also, an iceboat, Miss Lakeland, has been utilized by several daring employees for a midday thrill when the weather conditions cooperate.

"The race car and iceboat allow employees to feel the exhilaration that many people will never experience in their entire lifetime," says Larry Schmidt Sr. "People spend more waking hours at work than they do at home, and we do whatever we can to make their time at Lakeland fun and somewhat spontaneous."

Giving Back

Lakeland is involved in many community service activities, and prides itself on giving back to the community where its people live and work. The company and its employees participate in United Way fund-raising, Relay for Life cancer walk, Spikes for Tykes, Operation Clean Sweep, Ride for the Arts, and sponsorship of needy families at Thanksgiving and Christmas, among other worthwhile activities.

"We have so much to be thankful for," says Larry Schmidt II. "I am very proud of how our people rally behind the many community service events that we do throughout the year, giving of both their time and their resources to help others in need."

The Lakeland Advantage

Being family owned and operated, Lakeland's decision-making process is fast and efficient. Lakeland employees are encouraged to make decisions during their daily activities, in order to meet customers' needs as they arise.

Another advantage of a family owned and operated business versus a large corporation is clear to Lakeland's customers, according to Vince Schmidt. "We bring a family environment through to our customers," he says. "They know we are people of integrity, and that we stand behind our word, our people, and our values."

The meaning behind everything Lakeland does can be seen in its mission statement: "We Believe . . . In maintaining our families and our faith as the top priorities in life; In holding ourselves to the highest of moral and ethical standards; In treating everyone with respect and integrity–we are people of our word; In giving back to the communities in which we live and work; Customer satisfaction is the essence of our success."

CLOCKWISE FROM TOP LEFT: LAKELAND EMPLOYEES ENJOY TEST DRIVING THE COMPANY-SPONSORED RACE CAR AT ELKHART LAKE RACETRACK.

LAKELAND EMPLOYEES SEEKING THRILL RIDES UTILIZE MISS LAKELAND, THE COMPANY'S ICEBOAT, WHEN THE WEATHER PERMITS.

LARRY, VINCE, AND LARRY II KNOW HOW TO WORK AND PLAY HARD TO CREATE A COLLEGIAL ENVIRONMENT FOR THEIR EMPLOYEES.

LAKELAND IS INVOLVED IN MANY COMMUNITY SERVICE ACTIVITIES, AND PRIDES ITSELF ON GIVING BACK TO THE COMMUNITY WHERE ITS PEOPLE LIVE AND WORK.

Midwest Express Airlines

FLYING HIGH ABOVE THE RISKY, HYPERCOMPETITIVE AIRLINE industry is the national success story of Milwaukee's Midwest Express Airlines. While other airlines have reduced services, eliminated meals, and downsized amenities, Midwest Express continues to provide a premium service experience for coach fare. ■ The nation's 17th-largest airline has outperformed the industry for the past decade. In fact, Midwest Express was one of just two U.S. jet carriers to consistently report an annual profit during the 1990s.

Midwest Express began service on June 11, 1984, under K-C Aviation, a subsidiary of Kimberly-Clark Corporation. As early as 1948, Kimberly-Clark was providing corporate air transportation for executives traveling between its headquarters and company mills. Today, Midwest Express Airlines owns Astral Aviation, which operates Skyway Airlines, the Midwest Express Connection.

Going the Extra Mile

Midwest Express believes in going the extra mile for its customers. At its airport gates, employees offer free coffee and newspapers each morning. And on flights, the airline serves full meals with real china, cloth napkins, glass salt and pepper shakers, and complimentary wine or champagne. In fact, Midwest Express typically spends twice the industry average on its in-flight meals, offering specialty products from Wisconsin-based companies such as Alterra Coffee Roasters, Racine Danish Kringles, Miller Brewing Company, and Capital Brewery. Additionally, baked-on-board chocolate chip cookies and hot towel service are offered on select flights.

Midwest Express and Skyway Airlines have more than 50 aircraft ranging from Skyway's 19-passenger, turboprop aircraft to the Midwest Express 116-seat, MD-80 jets used for longer routes. The latest fleet additions include five of the 32-seat, Fairchild Dornier 328 regional jets, for which Skyway Airlines was the world launch customer.

When hiring and training its 3,000 employees, Midwest Express leaves nothing to chance. Often, a prospective employee must go through four or five interviews before a job offer is tendered. Every new employee attends a mandatory, three-day orientation to learn the company's values and customer service focus. Then, each employee is trained in his or her position before working with customers. Flight attendants have a two-month training period before they begin flying, while reservation agents train for six weeks before handling the telephones full-time.

MIDWEST EXPRESS AIRLINES BELIEVES IN GOING THE EXTRA MILE FOR ITS CUSTOMERS BY PROVIDING A PREMIUM SERVICE EXPERIENCE FOR COACH FARE (TOP).

SKYWAY AIRLINES, WHICH IS OWNED BY MIDWEST EXPRESS, WAS THE WORLD LAUNCH CUSTOMER FOR THE FAIRCHILD DORNIER 328JET (BOTTOM).

Carving Its Own Niche

Having carefully defined the market, Midwest Express has custom-tailored its approach to success. Its *Future Success Defined* brochure not only lays out the company's mission, vision, and values, but also introduces the helpful acronym CHIP: customer focus; highly involved employees; information-based decision making; and process improvement. Meanwhile, the Midwest Express balanced business scorecard clearly defines the company's strategic objectives, as well as its emphasis on customer satisfaction.

Through its strategy of controlled growth and commitment to quality customer service, Midwest Express has carved a niche as an award-winning airline favored by business travelers everywhere. Rather than competing head-to-head with the largest airlines, the airline has focused on providing nonstop service to underserved markets. Together, Midwest Express and Skyway Airlines fly to nearly 50 cities. In addition, Midwest Express is attracting more and more leisure travelers, who are discovering that better service and increased comfort don't necessarily mean a higher ticket price.

Awards and Commitment

"Although our product is already recognized as superior," says Tim Hoeksema, chairman, president, and CEO, "we need to constantly look for ways to make it even better, staying a step ahead of what our customers will want in the future." Hoeksema was selected as one of 12 national master entrepreneurs of 1999 by Ernst & Young.

This intense customer focus has earned the company a long list of honors, including the highest ranking for customer satisfaction in a 1999 *Consumer Report* airline survey; five consecutive number-one ratings for a U.S. airline in a *Condé Nast Traveler* reader's choice poll; two number-one ratings for a domestic airline in Zagat surveys; and two *Travel & Leisure* best domestic airline awards. Other awards have come from *Air Transport World*, *Aviation Week & Space Technology*, and the Federal Aviation Administration.

More important, however, is the airline's commitment to its hometown, which is evident in the new convention center that graces downtown Milwaukee. The $170 million Midwest Express Center is a shining example of function meeting form and utility meeting aesthetics. The airline also contributed to the construction of a pavilion bearing its name at Pére Marquette Park on Milwaukee's Riverwalk.

Of even greater importance is the litany of causes Midwest Express supports to help build a world-class community. These include YWCA, United Cerebral Palsy, Cystic Fibrosis Foundation, Make-A-Wish Foundation, Milwaukee Art Museum, Milwaukee Symphony Orchestra, Rainbow Summer, Milwaukee Repertory Theater, ethnic festivals, the Great Circus Parade, and many others.

"One of our guiding principles has always been to give back to the communities we serve," Hoeksema says. "The airline's contributions are considered more than simply charity. They are an investment in the city."

Midwest Express flight attendants are dedicated to providing the best customer service possible (left).

The airline serves full meals with real china, cloth napkins, glass salt and pepper shakers, and complimentary wine or champagne (right).

City by the Waters

· 405 ·

TexPar Energy, Inc.

What began in 1984 as a residual fuel supplier for the Upper Midwest has become a significant source for petroleum-related products and technologies for a wide variety of industries throughout North America. With more than $100 million in sales annually, TexPar Energy, inc.'s customer base includes such Fortune 500 companies as 3M, Kraft Foods, Ford, AT&T, International Paper, Georgia Pacific, and Oscar Mayer.

Founders Richard Byhre and Robert Rivas previously worked for another oil company in Milwaukee and were able to draw on their 60 years of collective experience to help manage their rapidly growing firm. Through their leadership, TexPar has become a benchmark of reliability, known for holding high ethical standards while quickly and creatively responding to the needs of its customers.

Employee Longevity

Along with the two owners, TexPar has approximately 100 long-term employees, including 35 in the Milwaukee area and 25 in Georgia. This unusual longevity in today's corporate environment can be attributed to the company's mission statement, which promises, "TexPar will equip its employees to realize their full potential, so that TexPar can, in turn, realize its full potential. To do this, TexPar must provide its employees with competitive wages and benefits, training, opportunities in both hiring and advancement, and a quality work environment." TexPar's staff is one of the company's greatest strengths. They are drawn from a wide variety of related industries including oil, utilities, and transportation. This hands-on experience allows them to meet the difficult challenges of supply and demand.

Diversity of Products and Resources

Diversity is another key factor contributing to TexPar's success. Currently, the company's offering of products and services covers residual fuel oils, carbon black feedstocks, EcoTex® emulsified fuel, Butaphalt® polymer modified asphalt, diesel fuel, roofing asphalts, propane, and logistics and materials handling services.

The Residual Fuels and Carbon Black groups source product from more than 40 major and independent oil refineries. The diversity in its supply base allows TexPar to provide consistent-quality products, maintain a consistent supply, and proactively manage the price fluctuations common in the oil market. From this base, TexPar supplies residual oils that can be used as boiler fuel or as a carbon black feedstock. Because TexPar prides itself on being able to deliver the required

Clockwise from top:
TexPar Energy, inc. developed the patented Butaphalt® system that reduces highway costs and enhances the performance of polymer modified asphalt.

TexPar's Terminal-On-Wheels is a self-contained materials-handling system that allows petroleum products to be safely pumped out of railcars and into tanker trucks.

A fleet of more than 1,000 railcars delivers TexPar's petroleum products throughout North America.

Milwaukee

amount to any customer when and where they need it, the company has its own strategically located inventory storage sites and a fleet of more than 1,000 railcars. By using the inland waterways, the railroad system, and the interstate highway system, TexPar is able to supply its customers anywhere on the continent. According to Secretary/Treasurer James Bahr, who has been with the company for more than 15 years, "Industry experts might consider our operation more typical of a gulf coast location. To our credit, we are small enough to be flexible, yet large enough to satisfy the heavy demands that typically would only be available from large suppliers."

Responsive to Customers' Needs

For customers who have no rail facilities, TexPar has developed Terminal-On-Wheels, a self-contained materials handling system that allows the product to be safely pumped out of railcars and into tanker trucks. This system allows TexPar's customers to take advantage of the lower cost that rail offers. TexPar's Web site customers can view their delivery schedules, railcar activity, histories, and account information on a 24-hour basis. Large, nationally known corporations such as Goodyear, Owens Corning, and Lucent Technologies, along with numerous utilities, universities, and manufacturers, use residual fuels from TexPar to provide heat and process fuels for their facilities.

Out of concern for the environment, as well as for Environmental Protection Agency burning requirements, TexPar has developed its own EcoTex technology to create an emulsified fuel—an oil and water mix—that burns more efficiently and reduces volatile organic compounds (VOCs) and particulate matter released to the atmosphere.

With its carbon black feedstocks, TexPar continues to be a key supplier to the carbon black industry. Carbon black is used in the manufacture of tires, cable, rubber goods, printing inks, paints, and plastics. Most of the major U.S. carbon black manufacturers use feedstocks supplied by TexPar.

Innovative

TexPar has also gained recognition as a technology leader in the development of advanced products and services for the paving industry. Claremore, Oklahoma, is the site of the firm's state-of-the-art laboratory, overseen by TexPar's Asphalt Technology Division. Here, chemists and chemical engineers design custom asphalt products to meet a wide variety of climate and traffic conditions. The patented Butaphalt process was developed at Claremore. It significantly reduces highway costs and enhances the performance of polymer-modified asphalt by reducing the occurrence of rutting and cracking, as well as by reducing the effects of extreme temperature fluctuations, traffic loads, and high speeds. Butaphalt meets or exceeds Department of Transportation specifications. Along with the Butaphalt technology, TexPar offers propriety process technology packages for licensing.

"TexPar is largely in the petroleum services and solutions business," says President Craig Witte. "We provide our customers with the product that is needed, when and where they need it."

TexPar is affiliated with Minnesota-based OSI Environmental, Inc., an upper midwestern full-service environmental remediation and recycling firm that has facilities in Butler, Wisconsin, and on Jones Island in Milwaukee, along with a number of other facilities within the Great Lakes region. OSI's ability to manage petroleum-based clean-up and removal, and its knowledge of waste stream management and compliance, assures a business that its needs will be handled in the most efficient and cost-effective manner possible.

BY STRATEGICALLY LOCATING ITS INVENTORY STORAGE SITES, TEXPAR ASSURES DELIVERY OF THE REQUIRED AMOUNT OF PRODUCT.

TEXPAR'S OSI ENVIRONMENTAL, INC. AFFILIATE HAS FACILITIES THROUGHOUT THE GREAT LAKES REGION.

City by the Waters

© DICK BLAU

1985-1995

1985
The Bradley Foundation

1986
Milwaukee Radio Group

1986
Stratagem, Inc.

1987
Coventry Homes Ltd.

1989
Heritage Relocation Services

1991
Potawatomi Bingo Casino

1993
Multi Media Catalog Corporation

1994
Verizon Wireless

1995
CDI Information Technology Services, Inc.

The Bradley Foundation

When the Allen-Bradley Company was sold to Rockwell International in 1985, a charitable trust the company had administered was transformed—by independence and the inheritance of about $290 million—into the Bradley Foundation, the largest private grant-making institution in Wisconsin. The Foundation is dedicated to continuing the legacy of the company's founders, brothers Lynde and Harry Bradley, by preserving and extending the guiding principles and philosophy with which the Bradleys built their enterprise and participated in community and national affairs as active citizens.

Today, in faith with the Bradley legacy, the Foundation is dedicated to "strengthening American democratic capitalism and the institutions, principles, and values which sustain and nurture it." Believing that a good society was a free society, the Bradleys were committed to preserving and defending the tradition of free representative government and private enterprise that enabled the nation—and essentially the Western world—to flourish both intellectually and economically.

In public policy, the Bradley legacy upholds the ideal of a limited, competent government that admires and encourages the authority and responsibility of the institutions of civil society—family, neighborhood, church, and community. Recognizing that responsible self-government depends on enlightened citizens and informed public opinion, the Foundation supports scholarly studies and academic achievement within a dynamic marketplace for economic, intellectual, and cultural activity, as well as a vigorous defense both

HARRY BRADLEY (SEATED AT RIGHT), COFOUNDER OF THE ALLEN-BRADLEY COMPANY, CONFERS WITH PLANT MANAGERS IN 1917.

THE BRADLEY FOUNDATION IS DEDICATED TO CONTINUING THE LEGACY OF THE ALLEN-BRADLEY COMPANY'S FOUNDERS, BROTHERS LYNDE AND HARRY BRADLEY. HERE, LYNDE BRADLEY, IN SHOP CAP, OVERLOOKS A DRAWING IN 1910.

Milwaukee

at home and abroad of American ideas and institutions.

Foundation Grants

Meeting quarterly to review grant proposals, the Foundation's board of directors seeks to encourage projects that focus on cultivating a renewed, healthier, and more vigorous sense of citizenship among Americans and people of other nations. In applying for Foundation grants, prospective grantees must first submit a brief letter of inquiry describing their organization and its intended activities. The Foundation will then request applicants whose objectives are in line with its program interests to submit a formal proposal, as outlined in program guidelines that are made available to all prospective grantees. Final authority for grant awards lies with the board of directors, which acts on all requests after proposals have been comprehensively reviewed by the Foundation's staff.

Within its first 15 years, the Bradley Foundation's cumulative grant awards exceeded the total endowment with which the institution was established by more than 34 percent. With more than $390 million awarded from 1985 to 2000, the Foundation has given an average of $26 million per year, with about 40 percent of all awards being made to state and local institutions.

Additional information on Foundation grants and other aspects of the Foundation can be found on the Foundation's Web site, www.bradleyfdn.org.

Architectural Treasures

The Foundation conducts its business from a headquarters that includes two of Milwaukee's architectural treasures, the Lion House and the Hawley House—adjoining properties on the city's east side that are today connected by an aesthetically integrated passageway.

Considered by the Historic American Buildings Survey as "the finest surviving pre-Civil War home in Milwaukee," the Lion House—named for the carved lions crouched upon its portico—was purchased by the Bradley Foundation in June 1995, 140 years after it was built by one of Milwaukee's many German immigrants, who modeled it on a villa he had seen as a youth in Europe. Expansion to the next-door Hawley House was completed in 2000. Renovation of that century-old, former residence included restoration of a distinctive oriel window that had been removed by a former proprietor.

"The move affirms the purpose as well as the place of the Bradley legacy, for restoration is an act in which respect for the past and faith in the future are equally implied," says Michael Joyce, Foundation president, reflecting on the decision to take on stewardship of two historic and architecturally important city buildings.

Describing the Foundation's institutional perspective, Joyce adds: "As grateful heirs of a magnificent heritage—from the Bradley family, from Milwaukee, from Wisconsin, from America—we are committed to culling history as it unfolds for successes to preserve, failures to discard, and new ideas to study. One of those successes, which we will maintain in and from Milwaukee throughout the new millennium, is the Bradley legacy."

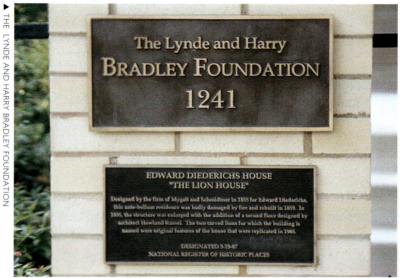

Considered by the Historic American Buildings Survey as "the finest surviving pre-Civil War home in Milwaukee," the Lion House—now part of the Bradley Foundation headquarters—anchors the city's historic First Ward Triangle (top).

The Hawley House, restored in 2000, is one of two buildings that make up the Bradley Foundation headquarters in a Milwaukee neighborhood where the Bradley family once lived (bottom).

MILWAUKEE RADIO GROUP

EACH WEEK, MORE THAN 500,000 Milwaukee-area listeners tune into the radio stations that comprise the Milwaukee Radio Group (MRG): WKLH 96.5 FM, WLZR 102.9 FM, WJMR 106.9 FM, WFMR 98.3 FM, and WJYI 1340 AM. MRG offers not only the two top-rated morning shows, but also a variety of programming that includes classic rock, active rock, jammin' hits, classical music, and contemporary Christian.

WKLH and WLZR: Market Leaders

MRG, also known as Lakefront Communications, got its start in 1986 with WKLH, which plays hits from such legendary artists as the Rolling Stones, the Who, Eric Clapton, Elton John, the Beatles, Fleetwood Mac, and the Eagles. WKLH has kept the same popular format since its inception, as well as many of its on-air personalities.

Weekdays at WKLH are anchored by the morning show team of Dave Luczak and Carole Caine, a fixture in Milwaukee for more than 15 years. They have been the city's number-one coed morning team for more than a decade. The show often features local and national comics, as well as special guests from the sports world, including members of the Green Bay Packers and the Milwaukee Brewers.

Deejays Patti Genko, Jeff Bell, and "Downstairs" Dan have also been with WKLH for many years. Genko hosts the most popular midday show in Milwaukee, while Bell's afternoon drive-time show features 96 minutes of continuous hits and *The KLH Time Tunnel*. "Downstairs" Dan is on the air from 7 p.m. until midnight, Monday through Friday, and hosts *'70s at Seven* and *The Ultimate Album Side*.

Complementing WKLH's classic rock format, WLZR, which was purchased by MRG in 1993, features the best active rock of today mixed with the best album rock, including Pearl Jam, Metallica, Nirvana, Led Zeppelin, Foo Fighters, Creed, and Pink Floyd. Popular on-air personalities include Marilynn Mee and Craig Kilpatrick, who are both well-respected industry veterans.

For years, WKLH's morning show went head-to-head with WLZR's team of Bob Madden and Brian Nelson, the top-rated morning show in almost every demographic. Both Milwaukee-area natives, Madden and Nelson have performed together since high school. Today, located under one roof, the two morning shows still compete each day, ranking first and second in the Milwaukee market.

EACH WEEK, MORE THAN 500,000 MILWAUKEE-AREA LISTENERS TUNE INTO THE RADIO STATIONS THAT COMPRISE THE MILWAUKEE RADIO GROUP (MRG), INCLUDING WLZR 102.9 FM, FEATURING AN ALBUM ROCK FORMAT; WJMR 106.9 FM, WHICH PLAYS JAMMIN' HITS; AND WKLH 96.5 FM, MRG'S ORIGINAL STATION.

With its Pure Rock slogan, WLZR features the best active rock of today mixed with the best album rock, including Pearl Jam, Metallica, Nirvana, Led Zeppelin, Foo Fighters, Creed, and Pink Floyd, and sponsors many music events in Milwaukee each year. Popular on-air personalities include Marilynn Mee and Craig Kilpatrick, who are both well-respected industry veterans.

"Bob, Brian, Dave, and Carole not only display unequaled morning talent, but are also superb humanitarians," says Tom Joerres, MRG president and general manager. "They're good parents and good spouses. There has always been mutual respect between the two morning teams. They all share a passion to win in the ratings, but not at the expense of the corporation."

The friendly competition between the two stations has been very profitable for MRG. During all daytime hours, WKLH and WLZR are usually ranked first and second, respectively, and WKLH ranks as the number-one classic hits station in the nation. In addition, in a national survey of program directors, WKLH Program Director Bob Bellini was ranked number four and WLZR Programming Director Keith Masters was ranked number six in their respective formats.

WJMR, WFMR, and WJYI

Playing the hits of the '60s, '70s, and '80s, WJMR strikes a responsive chord with the area's affluent, baby boomer professionals. The station features hits by the Commodores; the Chi-Lites; Earth, Wind & Fire; and Marvin Gaye, capturing the spirit of this generation.

WFMR (Fine Music Radio) was established in Milwaukee in 1955 and was purchased by MRG in 1997. In addition to the masterpieces of Beethoven, Bach, and Brahms, WFMR plays a broad range of orchestrated music. The station's core audience, the 35-to-64 age group, is extremely loyal and has the market's highest average income per household.

WJYI's slogan is "We play the music that can change your day—and it could change your life." Artists on this Christian Contemporary station include Amy Grant, Jars of Clay, Michael W. Smith, 4 Him, and Out of Eden. This format only makes up about 5 percent of all stations in the country, so its listeners tend to be very loyal. On occasion, WJYI also broadcasts live local sporting events.

Community Influence

Altogether, MRG has about 125 employees. Its prominence in the community provides the company many opportunities to render helpful services.

For more than a decade, the WKLH morning team has sponsored Christmas for Kids, a special event for 5,000 disadvantaged youngsters. The duo's *Best Of* CD has raised more than $250,000 for the event, and their annual radiothon for the Children's Miracle Network has raised more than $1 million for Children's Hospital of Wisconsin, which named a hospital wing for WKLH.

Madden and Nelson's favorite charities include the Hunger Task Force and the Leukemia Society. Proceeds from their *Best Of* CD, totaling about $300,000, benefit the Hunger Task Force. Their radio marathon at State Fair Park has also raised a total of 150 tons of food for the organization. And each year, the team raises about $100,000 for the Leukemia Society during a 28-hour radiothon. Smaller fundraisers for other local groups are supported throughout the year by personalities at each of the stations.

"Every quarter, we carefully assess the needs of the community to ascertain where our public service efforts may do the most good," says Ed Christian, chief executive officer. "We always want to put in more to the community than we take out."

City by the Waters

Stratagem, Inc.

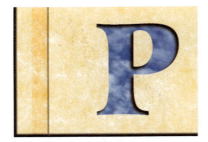

PROVIDING PRIVATE- AND PUBLIC-SECTOR CLIENTS THROUGHout Milwaukee and southeastern Wisconsin with the highest-quality information technology (IT) consulting services available has been half of Stratagem, Inc.'s winning equation since 1986, when it opened its doors for business in downtown Milwaukee. The other half has been equally important for the company—building mutually rewarding, long-term relationships with its workforce of IT professionals, who provide Stratagem's consulting services to those clients.

Stratagem's consultants help develop and support the enterprise software applications, design and implement the network infrastructures, and deliver the project-based, leading-edge IT solutions that keep clients' businesses competitive. Those businesses span a wide range of commercial and industrial sectors, from insurance and financial services to manufacturing, health care, retail, government, software, and utilities.

A diverse team, including more than 350 professional employees, works to provide Stratagem's consulting services—in a professional staffing capacity; through project-based solutions or entire strategic solutions; or in a combination of those service delivery methods. Team members draw their expertise from a variety of disciplines: e-business, technology design architecture, project management, process engineering, development, knowledge transfer, networking, and database analysis.

A Plan for Local Growth

From the beginning, a small, dedicated team of professionals worked diligently to build Stratagem's local reputation, providing high-level, business-to-business staffing expertise. By 1990, the firm had established offices in Madison and Appleton. The company is now a regional organization, with an office in Minneapolis/St. Paul.

Consultants who live and work in those communities serve local clients; out-of-town travel is kept to a minimum. By following that model of local service and by providing high-quality consulting services, Stratagem has enjoyed client relationships based on confidence and trust. Clients typically return to Stratagem for repeat business. Quite often, those relationships span many years and hundreds of projects.

Project-Based Solutions

In 1992, Stratagem began offering clients its project-managed services. This decision gave the firm's clients access to a greater level of strategic IT services, which today include e-business, application outsourcing, and knowledge transfer. Stratagem now draws from its full complement of services to form customized project solutions and professional staffing services.

"In the early days, we concentrated on professional staffing, but we began to recognize that customers needed wider-ranging IT service delivery solutions," says Gary L. Krieger, president and CEO. "We made a commitment to address those needs, adding value and strength to our existing clients' business relationships. Our project approach ensures that a more comprehensive project-based business solution is available to them."

The move enabled Stratagem to respond to a growing appetite for broader-based IT consulting services. The company also provided its consultants with a wider array of opportunities for achieving greater professional and career growth and for assuming increased responsibilities.

Stratagem is now Wisconsin's largest private locally owned provider of IT consulting services. A partial list of clients includes such prominent Milwaukee-area employers as the American Society for Quality, CNH Global (formerly Case Corp.), Miller Brewing Company, Milwaukee County, Northwestern Mutual, ProVantage, Rockwell Automation, Tenneco Automotive, and United Wisconsin Services. In 1999 and

GLOBAL CONSULTING FIRM ARTHUR ANDERSEN HAS NAMED STRATAGEM, INC. TO ITS 1999 AND 2000 FAST TRACK WISCONSIN LISTS. ANDERSEN GIVES THIS AWARD TO WISCONSIN-BASED PRIVATE COMPANIES THAT HAVE DEMONSTRATED THE ABILITY TO GENERATE SIGNIFICANT GROWTH OVER A PERIOD OF SEVERAL YEARS.

IN LATE 1999, STRATAGEM'S CORPORATE AND MILWAUKEE OFFICES RELOCATED INTO MORE SPACIOUS QUARTERS AT WOODLAND PRIME, A NEW OFFICE PARK DEVELOPMENT IN SUBURBAN MENOMONEE FALLS.

2000, Arthur Andersen recognized Stratagem as one of the state's top privately held firms by naming the company to its Fast Track Wisconsin list.

Relationships a Key

Stratagem's consulting staff is well equipped to employ a myriad of methods, tools, and programming languages in today's workplace. Yet, according to Krieger, the firm realized early on that the consulting business is at its core a people business.

"Over the last 14 years, we have seen our market expand from a predominantly mainframe base to a wide range of computing platforms and new technologies, and the number just keeps growing," says Krieger. "But our success hinges today—as it always has—on our ability to do two things well: to listen to our clients so that we understand their needs and concerns, and to provide our consultants with the opportunities to grow and develop professionally. When we stick to that formula, everybody wins."

Adhering to that basic principle, Stratagem rejects a tendency within the IT consulting industry to emphasize prepackaged, one-size-fits-all responses to clients' requests for assistance. By listening to its clients and learning about their needs, Stratagem crafts tailored service solutions that create client satisfaction and lead to longer-term business relationships.

Community Service

Stratagem supports its employees in their public service and community interests. Employees have been involved in such activities as the Briggs & Stratton annual run/walk to support Children's Hospital of Wisconsin and the Special Olympics. In partnership with Goodwill Industries of Southeastern Wisconsin, Stratagem sponsors the Abil*ITy* Connection, which recruits and mentors individuals with disabilities to help them train for and pursue IT careers. Stratagem also supports the YMCA, Milwaukee's United Performing Arts Fund, participates in the annual Muscular Dystrophy Association telethons, and maintains outreach involvement with a public elementary school on Milwaukee's northwest side.

Looking Ahead

Stratagem has remained an independent, focused, and flexible company since its first day of business. The firm's plan for future growth continues to build around the interests and needs of its clients and consultants. By 2000, Stratagem's corporate and Milwaukee offices had outgrown their facilities in Milwaukee, and moved to Woodland Prime, an office development in suburban Menomonee Falls.

As the IT consulting services landscape has changed, Stratagem has changed with it, expanding services into such areas as e-business; health care and Health Insurance Portability and Accountability Act (HIPAA) administrative simplification; software selection and implementation; and application outsourcing. But, by maintaining its commitment to local service and strong relationships with its clients and consultants, Stratagem has positioned itself for future growth and leadership in Wisconsin's IT consulting services marketplace.

Stratagem consultants stop for a quick schedule check in the atrium of Northwestern Mutual. Known as the Quiet Company, Milwaukee-based Northwestern Mutual is one of Stratagem's major clients.

Rick Laatsch (second from left), Miller Brewing's director of business systems development, and Joan Schultz, Miller's Manager-Information Systems Strategy and Planning, talk over the day's activities with Jerry LaBonte (left) and John Schauble (right) of Stratagem. Miller has been a mainstay of the Milwaukee economy for more than 140 years.

City by the Waters

· 415 ·

Coventry Homes, Ltd.

Established in 1987 by Richard A. Schneider, company president, Coventry Homes, Ltd. focuses on constructing and customizing a small range of homes that suit customers' individual tastes and needs. Coventry Homes' customers find a firm that is refreshingly different, with a philosophy that revolves around perfecting the design of a new home before construction begins. The company's customers, most of whom are in the 30- to 50-year-old age range, are looking for details and customization, as well as larger homes when making the step up from their existing homes.

When designing a new home or customizing an existing plan, Coventry's design team brings together individuals of diverse backgrounds and experiences. Together, they work out such details as traffic flow and room size. They also discuss potential problems and search for ways to make customers' preferences affordable.

As one of the first local home builders to offer an in-house interior design studio that helps customers select various materials, Coventry prides itself on being better by design, and the company leaves nothing to chance. Coventry employs a unique expediting system that manages the details from start to finish, and there is a specialized expediter for each phase of every project. An expediter is there from preliminary engineering of surveys and permits, to foundation excavation and initial framing, to roughing in drywall and exterior masonry, to finishing—which includes floor coverings, cabinetry, plumbing, electrical, and decorative features. Instead of having one expediter cover the entire process, each of Coventry's expediters operates in a specific area of expertise, providing increased quality assurance.

Home Features and Design

Common to Coventry homes are such details as elliptical archways, columns, integrated fireplaces and entertainment centers, and gourmet kitchens featuring double ovens, built-in appliances, granite or Corian™ countertops, and customized range tops.

By carefully studying home-building trends in other areas of the country, such as the West Coast and the resort areas of Florida and Arizona, Coventry is truly able to offer leading-edge design. This includes new interior features, landscaping, and new construction and decorating materials that are equal to or superior to current industry standards. Coventry's design style, incorporating the casual contemporary influences of Florida, California, and the Mediterranean, is less traditional than those of other local builders.

Coventry offers home buyers a choice of nine basic styles: Grand La Salle, Presidio, Garden Court, Hawthorne, Prestique, Sierra, Summitview, Windsong, and Windsong Petite. The Grand La Salle and Presidio are the company's most popular styles.

The exterior of the Grand La Salle home design welcomes buyers home with detailed European styling achieved with a blend of stonework, cedar, handcrafted millwork, majestic rooflines, and picturesque window designs. In every detail that goes into this style, the Grand La Salle is notable for its excellent function and design.

The Presidio home design offers a brick and cedar exterior combined with steeply pitched hip roofs; graceful, elliptical archways between rooms on the first floor; and a unique double

Coventry Homes, Ltd. offers home buyers a choice of nine basic styles, including one of its more popular designs, the Presidio (top).

By carefully studying home-building trends in other areas of the country, Coventry is truly able to offer leading-edge design (bottom).

· 416 ·

Milwaukee

stair arrangement that provides quick second-floor access from the kitchen. A unique second-floor children's wing uses French doors to separate three bedrooms from the master bedroom, and includes bookshelves, a two-person learning station, and indirect lighting.

Getting Started

Upon making the decision to build a new Coventry home, each customer is supplied with guides about the construction process, as well as construction schedule guides. Both documents enable the customer to gain a clearer understanding of the process before it begins.

The *Getting Started Guide* welcomes home buyers to Coventry. This guide shows customers who will be working with them, as well as informing clients about Coventry's philosophy that customers are part of the team while their homes are being constructed. In order for everyone involved to be able to communicate effectively, several meetings are scheduled—each discussing a different part of the process—including the color selection meeting, electrical layout and coordination meeting, final walk-through, and closing meeting.

Also part of the *Getting Started Guide* is an outline of the process of obtaining a building permit. This process does not begin until the company has the necessary information and confirmations that are gathered during the customer orientation meeting. The section on understanding the building process gives customers tips about avoiding the emotional roller coaster, maintaining a relationship of trust and confidence with the builder, and managing the busy schedule.

The *Construction Schedule Guide* helps buyers understand the process of constructing a new home. Each phase of the process—the foundation stage, rough-in stage, exterior finish and drywall stage, trim carpentry stage, and final finishes stage—is covered in this guide. Customers are given schedules for each stage, as well as lists of possible reasons for delays, important notes, and customer responsibilities.

With the company's unique style and ability to work well with customers, it is no wonder that Coventry Homes, Ltd. was listed 13th among the largest Milwaukee-area single-family home builders in August 2000. The company's attention to detail and commitment to creating exceptional features are sure to move it farther up the list in years to come.

CLOCKWISE FROM TOP LEFT: INTEGRATED FIREPLACES AND ENTERTAINMENT CENTERS ARE COMMON IN COVENTRY HOMES.

THE GARDEN COURTYARD ATRIUM IS PART OF COVENTRY'S UNIQUE STYLE.

THE ELLIPTICAL ARCHWAY FEATURE IS A TYPICAL DESIGN FOUND IN COVENTRY HOMES.

City by the Waters

Heritage Relocation Services, Inc.

Founded in 1989 by Neil J. Coakley Jr., Heritage Relocation Services, Inc. is a moving company that serves the needs of corporate businesses not only in Milwaukee, but also around the world. ■ With an impressive roster of services, Heritage can handle the relocation of its clients' employees' furnishings and belongings anywhere.

"We're more than just a good moving company," says Neil J. Coakley Jr. (right), founder of Heritage Relocation Services, Inc. "We're a complete relocation service for our corporate accounts."

In addition, it can coordinate Realtor selection, house-hunting trips, temporary housing, and mortgage assistance. "We're more than just a good moving company," Coakley says. "We're a complete relocation service for our corporate accounts."

As a direct result of this complete service, Heritage has developed corporate accounts outside the Milwaukee area. "We relocate employees for companies in California, Michigan, and Illinois, because we are one of the few moving companies that provide all of these services," Coakley says.

A Strategic Partnership

Since its beginning, Heritage has maintained a strategic partnership with Indianapolis-based Wheaton World Wide Moving, which has a solid reputation among consumers and industry experts. Consumer Reports has repeatedly rated Wheaton as a premier carrier, and it has also earned Good Housekeeping's seal of approval every year since 1964.

"It's the only service company that still has the seal of approval," Coakley notes. "Anybody can move furniture," he adds, "but it's how you take care of your customers that really matters."

More Than a Normal Moving Company

Heritage relocates companies' employees and facilities. In the past, the firm has moved complete corporate offices, manufacturing plants, and medical facilities. To prepare its employees for handling challenging moves, Heritage has an extensive training program that covers everything from packing china and carrying various types of furniture to loading trucks and providing effective customer service.

In recent years, Heritage has taken on an increasing number of projects for the medical community, which means even tighter schedules and more sensitive equipment. The skill and care required in moving sensitive medical equipment in a working hospital with tight time schedules is unique and demanding. According to Coakley, there are very few moving companies that could even attempt some of these projects.

Heritage can relocate different departments within hospitals during renovations, or move entire hospitals from one facility to another. In addition, Heritage provides a complete consulting and planning service for hospital relocations. "Our people work directly with the hospital administration to develop a plan for the relocation with all of the hospital departments," says Coakley. "The hospital must stay functional throughout the move process."

Ultimately, Heritage's focus on top-quality service and client satisfaction has made it a success not only in Milwaukee, but also throughout the world. Says Coakley, "We're not your normal moving company."

Heritage has extensive experience with many different types of moves involving many different types of equipment, including pianos in residential moves.

Milwaukee

Verizon Wireless

When Bell Atlantic Mobile, AirTouch Cellular, GTE Wireless, PrimeCo Personal Communications, and AirTouch Paging joined forces in 2000 to create the country's largest wireless company with a coast-to-coast digital network, Verizon Wireless was formed. Today, Verizon Wireless has coverage in 96 of the nation's 100 largest markets. Of the country's some 118 million wireless users, more than 27.5 million are Verizon Wireless customers.

Verizon Wireless offers innovative, competitively priced voice and data products and services of the highest quality, along with best-in-class customer service. As technology evolves and consumer preferences change, Verizon Wireless pledges to continue to provide innovative product offerings and competitive service plans, offering solutions for every individual.

"With Verizon Wireless' national scale and scope, we're able to offer customers more coverage, more choice, and better prices," says Jim Breitzman, area director for Verizon Wireless' Wisconsin operations.

The company launched wireless phone service in Milwaukee in 1996 as PrimeCo Personal Communications. In doing so, it offered the state's first digital PCS (personal communications service) network. The company helped make wireless technology affordable to practically everyone, from soccer moms to college students.

Today, Verizon Wireless has about 165 employees in Wisconsin, some 120 of whom are in Milwaukee. "In Wisconsin, we have some of the best skilled employees in the industry," says Breitzman. "They are a team committed to excellence."

Verizon Wireless is the official wireless provider for the Milwaukee Bucks and the Bradley Center in Milwaukee. The company is also the official wireless provider for the Green Bay Packers.

Verizon Wireless offers a variety of calling plans to meet different usage patterns and budgets. There are local, regional, and national plans that come with a number of included extras, such as voice mail, call waiting, and call forwarding. The company also gives its customers increased convenience and accessibility to wireless products and services with nine Verizon Wireless stores and kiosks in the Milwaukee metropolitan area.

VERIZON WIRELESS' WISCONSIN HEADQUARTERS IS LOCATED IN MILWAUKEE'S HISTORIC TANNERY OFFICE PARK AT 700 W. VIRGINIA ST.

A Commitment to Community

Verizon Wireless in Milwaukee has a unique approach to community service. The company promotes Contagious Acts of Kindness through such spontaneous actions as giving away free bus passes to Milwaukee County transit riders, distributing free flowers on downtown streets on Secretary's Day, or giving out PayDay candy bars to people mailing their taxes on April 15. On one occasion, the company presented some 3,000 pounds of pet food to the Wisconsin Humane Society.

The primary focus of Verizon Wireless' community commitment is on putting wireless products and services to work to combat domestic violence. The company has secured hundreds of phones for shelters in the Milwaukee area to help provide safety and independence to domestic violence victims. In addition to domestic violence, the company's philanthropic activities extend to assisting in public safety campaigns, disaster relief, and numerous nonprofit causes, including the Make-A-Wish Foundation of Wisconsin.

Verizon Wireless' combination of versatility, strong customer support, and commitment to community all contribute to this company's well-earned success. The company's development and implementation of the latest technology ensure that this success will continue unabated.

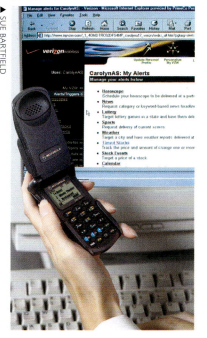

VERIZON WIRELESS OFFERS CUSTOMERS INNOVATIVE SERVICES SUCH AS MOBILE WEB, WHICH COMBINES THE MOBILITY OF WIRELESS COMMUNICATIONS WITH ACCESS TO WORLD WIDE WEB-BASED INFORMATION.

City by the Waters

Potawatomi Bingo Casino

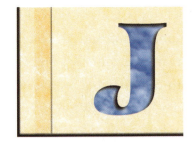

JUST A FEW MINUTES FROM DOWNTOWN MILWAUKEE lies Potawatomi Bingo Casino, one of the top 15 Indian gaming properties in the country. The casino opened in March 1991, just three years after the signing of the Indian Gaming Regulations Act. Fall 2000 marked the completion of an expanded gaming and entertainment property, incorporating the storied history and rich culture of the Potawatomi tribe into a facility five times the size of the original.

With the addition of five world-class dining facilities and two concert venues, Potawatomi Bingo Casino is spearheading the area's development as an entertainment destination. The economic and cultural impacts of the facility are being felt throughout the Menomonee Valley.

A Long History and an Important Legacy

The story of the Potawatomi tribe is one of struggle, self-sufficiency, honor, and remembrance. The tribe traces its legacy back to centuries ago, when roughly 10,000 members controlled about 30 million acres around Lakes Huron and Superior. The Potawatomi allied with the Ottawa and Chippewa tribes, each taking on a particular responsibility in the pact. The Potawatomi were charged with tending and guarding the sacred fire, thus earning the name Keeper of the Fire.

During the 1600s, the Potawatomi had their first encounter with Europeans, when French explorer Jean Nicolet traveled through their lands. This meeting led to a profitable, century-long trading alliance with the French.

When the United States was established as a sovereign nation, the government forcibly removed the Potawatomi from their land. In 1833, the tribe traveled to reservations in the West via the Trail of Death, named for the many tribal members who did not survive the arduous trek. By 1913, the Potawatomi had gained official recognition from the U.S. government, and reservation lands were set aside in northern Wisconsin's Forest County.

Today, the Forest County reservation, along with other Potawatomi sites throughout the state, teems with tribal pride. With more than 1,000 enrolled members, the tribe is able to keep its culture strong—honoring family and the environment, and emphasizing collective tradition and individual moral worth.

CLOCKWISE FROM TOP LEFT: OLD-STYLE MOCCASINS WITH FLORAL, BEADED DESIGN ARE CHARACTERISTIC OF WOODLAND CULTURES.

CHIEF'S DRUM IS USED IN CHIEF'S DANCE AND NAMING CEREMONIES.

LOCATED ON CANAL STREET, THE CASINO HAS THE LOOK OF AN ENTERTAINMENT DESTINATION WHILE MAINTAINING A NATURAL THEME THAT IS UNDENIABLY NATIVE AMERICAN.

FIREWORKS LIT THE NIGHT SKY AT POTAWATOMI BINGO CASINO'S GRAND OPENING IN THE FALL OF 2000. THE OCCASION INCLUDED A CEREMONIAL LIGHTING OF THE FLAME ATOP THE BUILDING.

Expanding Entertainment and Cultural Presence

In its quest to become the Midwest's premier entertainment destination, Potawatomi Bingo Casino has incorporated the tribe's culture and spirit into the facility's decor. The casino recently underwent a $120 million renovation and expansion, growing five times in size to become not only a strong entertainment presence in the area, but also an important cultural institution.

In 1998, the casino began construction as part of a plan to grow the property from 45,000 square feet to more than 256,000, thus allowing for more gaming space and new entertainment facilities. Potawatomi Bingo Casino features the breathtaking Grand Lobby, which houses the popular 120-foot flame tower, a shining beacon recognizable to all Milwaukeeans.

The first floor of the casino contains the 75,000-square-foot gaming area for players 21 and older. Here, guests will find exciting reel and video slot machines, including numerous Jeopardy!®, MoneyTime®, Wheel of Fortune®, and Elvis® progressives, just to name a few. Blackjack is also offered on the gaming floor. The Chi Sho nya (Big Money Games) area has increased limits for high rollers.

Central to the area is the Circle of Life, a one-hour simulation that features thunder, lightning, rainfall, birds chirping, and even an appearance of the sun that causes rocks to steam. These natural events occur in timed intervals that mirror the changing of the seasons, based on the Potawatomi reverence for all living things. The Circle of Life is divided into four arcs, each marked by a different color that represents a direction and season. Facing east is the red arc, representing spring, the beginning of life and the rising of the sun. Yellow faces south, symbolizing summer; the west side of the circle is blue, which denotes fall and the setting of the sun; and to the north is white, which signifies winter and dormancy. The gaming floor is arranged by the Circle of Life and divided into four seasons, each featuring a unique decorating scheme. Completing the nature theme are touches of birch bark, floral designs, woodland patterns, and other Potawatomi symbols adorning the walls, columns, and tables.

CLOCKWISE FROM TOP LEFT: POTAWATOMI BINGO CASINO HAS INCORPORATED THE TRIBE'S CULTURE AND SPIRIT INTO ITS DECOR.

THE CASINO'S GRAND LOBBY IS CENTERED AROUND A BREATHTAKING, 120-FOOT FLAME TOWER.

POTAWATOMI BINGO CASINO'S MAIN GAMING FLOOR CONTAINS REEL AND VIDEO SLOT MACHINES AND BLACKJACK TABLES SET IN DECORATIVE NATURE THEMES.

City by the Waters

THE CIRCLE OF LIFE, THE CENTERPIECE OF POTAWATOMI BINGO CASINO'S MAIN GAMING FLOOR, FEATURES THUNDER, LIGHTNING, RAINFALL, BIRDS CHIRPING, AND EVEN AN APPEARANCE OF THE SUN THAT CAUSES ROCKS TO STEAM. THESE NATURAL EVENTS OCCUR IN TIMED INTERVALS THAT MIRROR THE CHANGING OF THE SEASONS, BASED ON THE POTAWATOMI TRIBE'S REVERENCE FOR ALL LIVING THINGS.

GUESTS CAN VISIT BYA WI SE NEK (EVERYBODY COME AND EAT) FOR A VAST SELECTION OF ETHNIC AND AMERICAN CUISINE. THE BUFFET RESTAURANT IS OPEN DAILY FOR BREAKFAST, LUNCH, AND DINNER.

Also on the first floor is the Fire Pit Sports Bar & Grill, a casual dining facility that features plasma screen TVs broadcasting the latest sporting events from around the world. On the second floor of the casino is Bya wi se nek (everybody come and eat), a 300-seat buffet restaurant serving a variety of American and ethnic cuisine. Level two also houses Dream Dance, a fine dining restaurant serving steaks and seafood. To ensure that every meal served at Potawatomi Bingo Casino is first-class, all dining operations are managed by Milwaukee's famed Bartolotta Restaurant Group.

Potawatomi Bingo Casino has two concert venues—an intimate, cabaret-style theater and a large showroom—that both host big-name entertainment. The 550-seat Northern Lights Theater features table-side service, and has already hosted such luminaries as the Isley Brothers, blues legend B.B. King, and comedian George Carlin. The Nest of Life Concert Hall, with 1,800 seats, was inaugurated by Tony Bennett at the casino's grand opening. Since then, acts such as Chubby Checker, Sinbad, and Jay Leno have graced the stage.

Bringing Big Bingo Magic to Milwaukee

When Potawatomi Bingo Casino opened in 1991, it focused primarily on bingo, and the new property has improved and expanded bingo operations tremendously. The Nest of Life Bingo Hall has some 2,000 seats where smoking is allowed, as well as 500 additional seats in a nonsmoking area. The two rooms are separated by a glass partition, and a state-of-the-art ventilation system continually refreshes the air throughout the building. Three private bingo suites are available for parties and corporate outings.

The bingo hall has also expanded the variety of games offered. Now available are Hot Ball, Bonanza, Pot-of-Gold, All Star Special, Pick 8 Special, Speed Ball, Money Machine, and many more. In addition, guests can play electronically on Power Bingo™ and Rocket Bingo™ machines. A team of bingo ambassadors is available to assist novice players and those with special needs.

Providing Excellent Guest Service

Potawatomi Bingo Casino realizes that beautiful facilities and extensive amenities alone will not draw repeat visitors, so it has assembled a diverse team of highly skilled employees to provide attentive guest service.

The casino maintains a staff of some 1,500 people, making it one of the largest employers in the

Menomonee Valley. Employees receive competitive compensation and full benefits, and are extremely well trained. Before they start their jobs, employees attend an intensive orientation. Throughout their tenure at the casino, they participate in ongoing training sessions with peers, supervisors, and management. This type of employee development is consistent with Potawatomi Bingo Casino's mission to provide the highest-quality service to everyone who passes through its doors.

In addition, the casino has two publications that reach out to loyal and first-time guests alike. The monthly *Potawatomi Times* newspaper outlines casino events and promotions, provides a full entertainment lineup, and shares strategies and tips. Likewise, the quarterly *Parlay* magazine contains articles of interest on a variety of gaming topics.

As part of its guest-oriented philosophy, Potawatomi Bingo Casino offers numerous incentives to its players. The Fire Keeper's Club, for instance, allows members to accumulate points that can be applied toward an extensive catalog of prizes. With an accumulation of 250 to 500 points, winners can choose from items such as hotel discount vouchers, Hertz car rental certificates, or $100 gift certificates to Spiegel or the Sharper Image. With even more points, members can race high-speed automobiles in the Richard Petty Driving Experience, or fly state-of-the-art jets as part of the Fighter Pilot for a Day program.

Sharing with the Community

Along with its dedication to tribal culture and commitment to high-quality guest service, Potawatomi Bingo Casino is a major player in the area's economic arena. Through membership in the Menomonee Valley Business Association and support of the Menomonee Valley Business Improvement District—both of which strive to create a comprehensive growth strategy for the area—the casino drives continued development. On a yearly basis, the casino gives nearly $13 million to state and local governments, and attracts visitors that bring in at least $40 million to Milwaukee's food, lodging, service, and entertainment industries.

Perhaps most important, however, are the tribe's donations to charitable causes. In one year, the Forest County Potawatomi Community Foundation, together with Potawatomi Bingo Casino, distributed a total of $4.2 million to more than 200 charitable and cultural organizations in the community.

By building upon the strong Potawatomi legacy, the casino has made a difference not only within the tribe, but also throughout the state. Its success comes from honoring the past while looking toward the future, as well as from incorporating tribal traditions into an active business strategy. Such dedication to cultural and economic achievement will ensure greater triumphs in the years to come.

CLOCKWISE FROM TOP LEFT: THE NORTHERN LIGHTS THEATER, WHICH PROVIDES AN INTIMATE CONCERT SETTING, FEATURES A LAYOUT THAT WAS DIGITALLY DESIGNED TO ENSURE EXCELLENT VISIBILITY FROM EVERY SEAT IN THE HOUSE. PERFORMERS WHO HAVE GRACED THE STAGE INCLUDE GLADYS KNIGHT, MARTINA MCBRIDE, AND GEORGE CARLIN.

BINGO ENTHUSIASTS FROM ALL OVER THE COUNTRY VISIT THE NEST OF LIFE, WHICH SEATS MORE THAN 2,000 PEOPLE AND OFFERS THE NATION'S LARGEST PAYOUTS. THE HALL, ALSO USED FOR CONCERTS, HAS THREE SUITES FOR PRIVATE PARTIES AND A NONSMOKING SECTION.

POTAWATOMI BINGO CASINO ACTIVELY SUPPORTS THE REVITALIZATION OF THE MENOMONEE VALLEY.

City by the Waters

Multi Media Catalog Corporation

In 1993, RR Systems, Inc. and Technology Consulting Corp. (TCC), two high-tech companies based in Waukesha, worked together to form Multi Media Catalog Corporation as a strategic alliance to provide solutions to retailers that depend on catalogs. RR Systems was the primary developer of the software, called Catalog Composer, while TCC provided certified consultants and important people services, including training, system integration, installation, and maintenance. Continuing that effort, TCC helps clients establish ownership of product data and images that may be currently maintained off-site by unrelated marketing firms. TCC also provides staff augmentation and recruitment services to fulfill specific project needs at Multi Media Catalog Corporation and RR Systems.

Ronald M. Rudolph, president and CEO of Multi Media Catalog Corporation and RR Systems, describes the alliance's mission: "We supply the latest and greatest development talent and Microsoft technology to provide a Web-enabled electronic commerce solution tailored to each client's specific needs."

Catalog Composer

Whether it's the traditional paper catalog or the latest on-line, real-time networked catalog, Internet catalog, or digital CD-ROM, Multi Media Catalog Corporation's primary product, Catalog Composer, can perform a number of design tasks to create a variety of products.

More than simply a design tool, however, Catalog Composer acts as a powerful database. It can take product information from various sources, servers, and locations, and bring it all together in a cohesive, manageable whole. Whether information comes from the engineering department, sales, marketing, manufacturing, or administration, it is unified in the Catalog Composer database. What's more, the department supplying the information maintains ownership of its data for maximum accountability. And with a click of a button, the catalog can be translated into different languages for the global marketplace.

Catalog Composer is not intended for retailers with only a few items, but is ideal for manufacturers or distributors with many products and constantly changing sales data or specifications. For these firms, a paper catalog is unwieldy and instantly out of date—not to mention expensive to reproduce. Therefore, most Catalog Composer clients are Fortune 5000 companies.

"The nature of the Catalog Composer tool helps retain freshness of product information," says John Marksworth, a principal in Multi Media Catalog Corporation and president of TCC. "It's a digital revolution in how sales catalogs are developed and presented to buyers."

RR Systems

Founded in 1987, RR Systems is highly skilled at rapid application development. Instead of taking six to eight months to merely analyze a challenge, RR Systems quickly determines what a client needs, develops the software product, and delivers it to market as soon as possible. Additional improvements can be made while the software is performing its primary function and enabling the client to be more competitive in today's marketplace.

RR Systems continually tests beta software—software that is still under development and has not been released yet for use by the general

Multi Media Catalog Corporation resulted from a strategic alliance between RR Systems Group, Inc. and Technology Consulting Corp. (TCC), two high-tech companies based in Waukesha. TCC's team of consultants averages more than 10 years of experience and crosses multiple technical environments, which encompass AS/400, Windows, Unix, Windows NT, Novell, client/server, and mainframe platforms.

Milwaukee

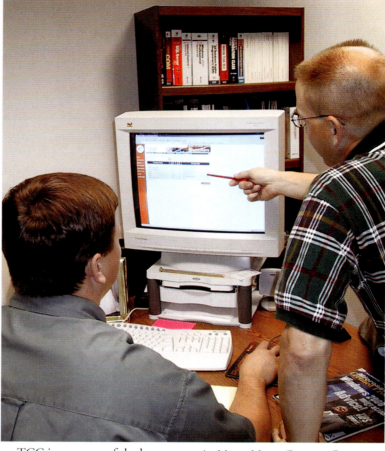

public. Beta testing software usually has significant advantages over software currently being used by most companies, and gives RR Systems—and its clients—a jump on the competition.

In fact, RR Systems has such strong relationships with today's leading software developers that the company has been the first in the world to use a new product in a mission-critical public application. As a Microsoft Certified Solution Provider and Solution Developer, RR Systems receives a great deal of support from developers in its efforts.

RR Systems' own development strengths include high-end data-driven software applications and Web sites, such as industry exchange sites, that utilize emerging technologies in the PC industry. RR Systems has won more Windows Wide Open awards than any other company in the world—tangible evidence of its success in meeting its clients' challenges.

Technology Consulting Corp.

Established in 1978, TCC's specialties include application development, hardware and software solutions, systems integration, data management, communications, LAN/WAN engineering, help desk administration, and Web development. TCC's team of consultants averages more than 10 years of experience and crosses multiple technical environments, which encompass AS/400, Windows, Unix, Windows NT, Novell, client/server, and mainframe platforms.

Business partnerships with leading international hardware and software manufacturers, such as IBM and Microsoft, give TCC greater visibility and a sharper technical edge. The company is both an IBM Premier Business Partner and a Microsoft Certified Solutions Provider, and has partnership relationships with DataMirror, Dell Computers, Hewlett-Packard, Compaq, and Lotus Corporation.

TCC is now one of the largest full-service cross-platform information systems support organizations in the Midwest. Of its approximately 200 employees, about 60 percent are permanent staff, while the remainder are contractors brought in to address specific client needs.

With offices in Milwaukee, Chicago, Green Bay, and Madison, TCC works with all types of clients, including financial, communications, manufacturing, distribution, municipal, health care, insurance, and data services organizations. Most clients fall in the $2 million to Fortune 100 range. TCC focuses on a balanced partnership between client and consultant to meet the challenges of today's information technologies industry.

Balance, flexibility, and direction are all points of pride for TCC, RR Systems, and Multi Media Catalog Corporation. Together, these three companies will make multimedia cataloging easier for their clients, finding innovative ways to keep information up to the minute in an ever changing technological environment.

AT MULTI MEDIA CATALOG CORPORATION, EMPLOYEES STRIVE TO MAKE MULTIMEDIA CATALOGING EASIER FOR CLIENTS AND TO FIND INNOVATIVE WAYS TO KEEP INFORMATION UP TO THE MINUTE IN AN EVER CHANGING TECHNOLOGICAL ENVIRONMENT (RIGHT).

MULTI MEDIA CATALOG CORPORATION'S PRIMARY PRODUCT, CATALOG COMPOSER, CAN PERFORM A NUMBER OF DESIGN TASKS TO CREATE A VARIETY OF PRODUCTS. MORE THAN SIMPLY A DESIGN TOOL, HOWEVER, IT ACTS AS A POWERFUL DATABASE, TAKING PRODUCT INFORMATION FROM VARIOUS SOURCES, SERVERS, AND LOCATIONS, AND BRINGING IT ALL TOGETHER IN A COHESIVE, MANAGEABLE WHOLE TO DELIVER THREE MEDIA: PAPER, CD, AND THE INTERNET (LEFT).

City by the Waters

CDI Information Technology Services, Inc.

For two years in a row, *Fortune* magazine has termed Philadelphia-based CDI Information Technology Services, Inc. "the biggest company you've never heard of." In some cities, it's mentioned in the same breath as Ford and Microsoft. A publicly owned, $1.6 billion company with some 35,000 employees worldwide, CDI has been making a name for itself in the Milwaukee business arena.

As a full-service staffing organization, CDI supplies consultants in information technology (IT) positions, engineering, automation, and management/administration. In particular, CDI has forged strategic partnerships to recruit highly skilled, hard-to-find talent for the IT field, including help-desk services, personal computer support, system architecture, software development, network administration, and database administration. A strong recruiting staff seeks top-notch talent who are not necessarily looking for a job. Over time, CDI builds relationships with individuals employed elsewhere to eventually find them the perfect opportunity with a CDI client company. This method ensures that CDI always has the best talent available.

In addition, CDI has the world's largest management search and recruitment organization in its subsidiary, Management Recruitment International, Inc. CDI's Todays Staffing, Inc. subsidiary is a leading provider of temporary legal, financial, administrative, and clerical staff.

CDI's Information Technology Services division, which employs approximately 100 people, has been providing staffing solutions to prominent corporations across the United States for decades; the division opened its Milwaukee office in 1995. John F. D'Agostino, a Detroit native and CDI veteran, moved to the city to open the Milwaukee office; he is branch manager of both the Milwaukee and Chicago CDI offices, and also oversees a Madison branch. "From Harley-Davidson to Miller Brewing, Milwaukee has a number of large and growing companies that can benefit from our services," D'Agostino says. "We saw Milwaukee as a largely untapped market and decided it was time to open an office here."

Retention and Growth

At CDI, employee retention is an essential part of the company's success. The minimum contract for a CDI employee at a client company is six months and many last up to three years. While serving in positions at client companies, all CDI consultants remain full-time, permanent CDI employees. After the term of the contract, the client may hire the consultant or the consultant will be kept on staff at CDI for another temporary employment opportunity. As a result, turnover of CDI IT employees is less than 4 percent annually, a very low rate in this field.

In a time of low unemployment, finding the right employee is more difficult than ever, and CDI's corporatewide recruiting database of some 65,000 résumés is a definite asset. By developing close relationships with its client companies, CDI knows exactly which skill sets and personality traits will provide a custom fit for the client and the employee.

This dedication to its clients and its employees has resulted in steady growth for CDI. "In a short period of time, we have grown to a $10 million business in Milwaukee," D'Agostino says. "Our reputation is spreading, and local companies are beginning to recognize that we have the capability to enhance their success."

As a full-service staffing organization, CDI Information Technology Services, Inc. supplies consultants in information technology positions, engineering, automation, and management/administration.

Milwaukee

© JOHN J. BACIK III

1996-2001

1996
High Gear, Inc.

1996
The Revere Group

1998
Milwaukee Neurological Institute

1999
Rockwell Automation

High Gear, Inc.

High Gear, Inc., an information technology firm based in Brookfield, has been instrumental in successfully leading a broad spectrum of companies—ranging from dot-com start-ups to Fortune 500® companies across many industries—into the e-business era. Founded by Ron Cox in 1996, High Gear has experienced significant growth through its focused strategy of applying emerging technologies as a strategic business asset for its clients. In 2000, High Gear was selected as a Future 50 company for the second conse-cutive year—an annual recognition of fast-growing companies in the Milwaukee area.

E-Business Initiatives

Mission-critical information, which not long ago required days or weeks to process and disseminate, is now available to multiple users on a real-time basis, anywhere in the world. High Gear is at the forefront of helping companies develop mission-critical e-business solutions, extend mission-critical information to their mobile workers, and create customer-centric Web-based marketing strategies.

High Gear's expertise in emerging technologies such as Java, Internet, and Object-Oriented programming, enables custom development of highly effective distributed computing systems. The company's highly skilled information technology consultants fill such roles as project manager, technical and/or application architect, systems analyst, object designer, and programmer/analyst. The company has developed systems for a wide range of clients to help them create competitive advantages, improve workflow efficiencies, introduce new products, optimize marketing and pricing strategies, and launch new lines of business.

High Gear also develops mobile computing solutions, integrating handheld computing devices such as Palm with enterprise systems. Mobile computing holds the promise of fundamentally changing the way people work by increasing their teamwork and communication, speeding their decision making, and generally improving their ability to get the job done. High Gear's focus on distributed systems means that its employees have a high degree of expertise in the skills required to build the custom middleware that integrates mobile devices into the enterprise, independent of the chosen handheld device.

In addition, High Gear employs a marketing and Web integration process for Web site development and hosting. The turnkey process helps businesses link their marketing programs, selling processes, and e-business initiatives. This customer-focused process model results in a powerful yet affordable, closed-loop

High Gear, Inc.'s offices reflect a warm, colorful mixture of form and function.

High Gear's unique software development area creates an environment for creativity and collaboration.

Milwaukee

e-business strategy and operating system for clients. High Gear's goal: to bring e-business to small business.

"Our expanding team of professionals uses an advanced business model that delivers quality results," says Cox, company president and CEO. "We enjoy numerous long-term client relationships—a strong indicator that our entire team is focusing on clients' needs."

High Standards

High Gear utilizes rigorous standards to select the software development tools it uses. Rather than following the fickle indicator of market popularity, the company tests and selects the best-of-breed tools it believes in. High Gear partners with software tool developers and is considered an early adopter of such technology as well.

The same high standards are applied when High Gear recruits employees: applicants are ranked on a scale of one to five, and every attempt is made to hire only level-five employees. In an industry where about 50 percent of job offers are accepted, almost all of the offers High Gear has made to potential employees have been accepted.

"We have a very thorough recruiting process with a minimum of three interviews, plus a technical interview and on-line testing," Cox says. "Hiring employees is a very serious matter with us. We do not rush into decisions. It is not uncommon for us to spend weeks talking with prospective employees before making a decision that's in the best interests of the firm and the employee."

High Gear, which offers interesting work using leading-edge technologies, is dedicated to working both hard and fast. Although technology is the focus, the entrepreneurial environment gives employees additional opportunities. For example, employees who develop new sales leads receive generous bonuses. In addition, they earn the option of more money or more time off when they work additional client hours. Employee training is integral to the company philosophy, and employees receive bonuses for obtaining certifications. About 70 percent of the company's technical staff are Sun Microsystems-certified Java programmers, and 20 percent are Sun-certified Java architects.

Furthermore, the High Gear business model emphasizes long-term thinking. The company was an early adopter of Java and eschewed year 2000 compliance projects because of the short-term emphasis. High Gear uses Rapid Application Development techniques, coupled with the Rational Unified Process. The latter unifies best practices from many disciplines into a consistent, full life cycle process that allows development teams to decrease time to market while increasing the predictability of the software they produce. The process allows high-quality software to be developed with clear, repeatable processes.

"One of the keys to High Gear's success is the highly professional, energetic environment that we've created," says Jean Cox, vice president. High Gear's new facility includes specialized breakout areas for project research, technology team areas designed for optimum software development, and a sophisticated conference room incorporating the latest technology and ergonomics.

"There are a lot of factors in building a successful business," Ron Cox says. "But this is the finest group of people I've ever had the pleasure to work with. With a team like this, building a successful company was inevitable."

HIGH GEAR ASSOCIATES DISCUSS HOW EMERGING TECHNOLOGIES CAN SOLVE BUSINESS PROBLEMS FOR THE COMPANY'S CURRENT AND PROSPECTIVE CLIENTS (LEFT).

JEAN AND RON COX SET THE STRATEGIC VISION AND CREATE THE ENVIRONMENT FOR HIGH GEAR'S ACCELERATING GROWTH (RIGHT).

AN OPEN-AIR MEETING SPACE—COMPLETE WITH NETWORK CONNECTIONS, WHITEBOARDS, AND AN EXTENSIVE LIBRARY—ENCOURAGES KNOWLEDGE SHARING AMONG HIGH GEAR EMPLOYEES.

City by the Waters

The Revere Group

As the first satellite office of The Revere Group's Deerfield, Illinois, headquarters, the Milwaukee office was founded in 1996. The Revere Group's target market for potential clients comprises middle-market corporations, with roughly $200 million to $2 billion in assets. With the firm's solid mix of medium-sized companies in a variety of industries—from manufacturing and health care to insurance and professional services—Milwaukee seemed a perfect fit. The company has since expanded to Boston; Charlotte; Cleveland, Ohio; and Denver.

The Revere Group offers a comprehensive strategy for digital solutions, including digital processes, technologies, and management. The company's expertise is local and character-driven, where integrity ranks as high as technical and management ability. One of the ways The Revere Group distinguishes itself from competitors is that clients have access to the knowledge and experience of the firm's principals and senior staffers at all times. The company is based on a solid business model emphasizing predictable, repeatable, and profitable growth, which makes it a strong partner for client companies.

Focus on Strategy

The Revere Group focuses on companies that are not served by other major consulting firms, and specializes in e-formation and e-transformation. The former refers to emerging dot-com companies, and the latter to old-economy enterprises that need to transform from brick and mortar to "click and mortar" in the way of digital business.

"We bring experience and expertise to our clients, and we do it from a local office," says Bob Gleason, managing director of the Milwaukee branch. "We are located in the communities we serve. We understand the local business environment and involve local employees whenever possible." The Revere Group has more than 500 employees, including more than 50 in Milwaukee.

"As we enter the e-business age, companies are less likely to throw money at the Internet," Gleason says. "It's important that they make sure their e-business is linked properly to the rest of their business strategy. E-business should support and enhance the company's overall business strategy. Strategy is critically important and you get the highest payback for digital investment—if it's done right. We design, develop, and deploy high-impact digital technologies through an integrated suite of solutions."

More Than E-Commerce

Typically, e-commerce is thought of as relationships with retail customers or trade partners using Internet technology. The Revere Group's approach to e-business is much more than that; the firm uses technology to make the flow of all types of information to and from the client company more efficient.

A manufacturer, for example, may have internal information technology systems and digital Internet capabilities that have been cobbled together through the years from various vendors using a variety of applications that have grown in inefficiency as well as in scope. The Revere Group acts as a consultant to determine if such a system should be replaced or better integrated, and

The Revere Group's Milwaukee office is located in the 100 East Wisconsin building in the heart of the city's downtown area.

At The Revere Group, people make the difference, including the company's project team at Robert W. Baird.

Milwaukee

then provides all the pieces to make that happen. As a consulting firm, The Revere Group's expertise goes beyond e-business to a broad understanding of business strategy and managing organizational change.

"We are not a rent-a-programmer, temporary assignment firm," says Gleason. "We offer specialized expertise to solve business problems. We leverage technology to get business results." In fact, about 45 percent of The Revere Group's staff members are experts in various areas of business, including human resources, financing, or manufacturing, for example. The remainder of the firm's staff focuses on providing technology solutions.

"We hire really smart people who work well together," Gleason says. In an industry where average employee retention is about 65 percent, The Revere Group averages 83 percent across the company and closer to 90 percent in its Milwaukee office. Company employees frequently have left significant opportunities at other firms for the chance to build something special. It helps that The Revere Group's core founding values nurture knowledge, talent, and a balanced life.

Growing Expertise

An example of The Revere Group's expertise is its work with a large professional services firm whose office systems were no longer supporting the company's rapid growth, including district offices around the country. The Revere Group began by examining the client's basic electronic accounting systems—general ledger, accounts payable and receivable, and project estimating. The Revere Group developed a plan to replace the financial system processes without holding the company back. It then developed 17 priority initiatives regarding technology and business processes. The Revere Group's consultants are not only integrators of technology, but also trusted advisers.

Another client, a privately held manufacturer, came to The Revere Group to upgrade its financial computing systems to make the company year 2000 compliant. When the client company realized the value The Revere Group brings, the firm gladly agreed to a joint venture to develop and market a manufacturing management system.

Milwaukee's Revere Group accounted for about $8 million of the corporation's $75 million in revenue in 2000. The Milwaukee office has experience and expertise in professional services, health care, manufacturing, financial services, and insurance. Companywide, The Revere Group's goal is 30 percent annual growth in revenue. The Milwaukee office has experienced 35 percent annual growth, and expects that rate to continue.

With strategic focus on quality and client satisfaction, The Revere Group has made its mark in both Milwaukee and in the industry.

THE REVERE GROUP'S PROJECT TEAM AT ROBERT W. BAIRD REVIEWS FINANCIAL REPORTS DURING A PEOPLE SOFT SOFTWARE IMPLEMENTATION (LEFT).

WHETHER IT'S INCREASING SUPPLY CHAIN EFFICIENCY, DEVELOPING AN E-BUSINESS STRATEGY, OR COORDINATING A WEB-ENABLED SOLUTION, THE REVERE GROUP'S CONSULTANTS WORK SIDE BY SIDE WITH THE COMPANY'S CLIENTS TO HELP THEM REACH THEIR GOALS (RIGHT).

REVERE GROUP CONSULTANTS, USING RAPIDLY DEVELOPING TECHNOLOGY, WORK TO INCREASE THE EFFICIENCY OF A CLIENT'S INFRASTRUCTURE.

City by the Waters

ROCKWELL AUTOMATION

THE HISTORY OF ROCKWELL AUTOMATION SPANS ALMOST an entire century, weaving together a unique record of world-class product innovation across multiple industries. Rockwell Automation (formerly Rockwell International Corporation) is a $4.5 billion company based in Milwaukee. It traces its roots back to the early 20th century when Lynde Bradley and Dr. Stanton Allen joined together in 1903 and formed the Compression Rheostat Company—renamed Allen-Bradley in 1909—with an initial investment of just $1,000. The company was an early developer of industrial controls, such as electrical relays, switches, and programmable logic controls, bringing major efficiencies to factory operations.

A couple years later, and across town, Willard Rockwell bought a small axle plant called Wisconsin Parts Company to produce, based on his own designs, a new and improved axle. That was 1919. The two neighbors would one day join together to form one of the most powerful factory automation and communications companies in the world.

Today, Rockwell Automation creates the automation solutions that give customers the competitive edge they need to be successful in a rapidly changing world. The company produces more than 500,000 products carrying brand names that have been providing automation solutions for nearly a century. Brands like Allen-Bradley, Reliance Electric, Dodge, and Rockwell Software and brands known for their leading-edge technology and responsiveness to customers' needs.

Today, under the leadership of Chairman of the Board and CEO Don H. Davis Jr., Rockwell Automation has some 20,000 employees working at more than 200 facilities in 80 countries, and is well known for its dedication to quality, service, and technological innovation.

The products are used in virtually every industry and market segment. Allen-Bradley programmable logic controls carefully control the batch mixture of major ice cream manufacturers. Reliance Electric motors power conveyors and generate power at the largest mines in the world. Software products integrate systems within a plant, like conveyors and sensors, allowing managers to carefully control and monitor output.

Electronic Commerce and Research

The company is primarily an automation controls company, following the spin-off of Rockwell Collins. But, Rockwell Automation also owns a successful call center business, based in Wood Dale, Illinois. Rockwell Electronic Commerce is a leading supplier of customer call center systems. It works aggressively with technology providers to increase its systems' functionality and efficiency. Rockwell Electronic Commerce also flourishes with technological advancements. In 1999, it introduced the first Windows NT-based call center in the world. On its list of products are the Galaxy, Spectrum, Transcend, 3CS, and Call Center Studio brands.

Rockwell Automation also manages an interest in the research-

ROCKWELL AUTOMATION PRODUCTS PROVIDE PRECISE AND RELIABLE CONTROL OF CRITICAL EQUIPMENT THROUGHOUT A FACTORY (LEFT).

CONSUMER PRODUCT MANUFACTURERS, LIKE THIS MAJOR CLOTHING COMPANY, USE ROCKWELL AUTOMATION PRODUCTS AND SERVICES TO ADD EFFICIENCY TO ITS FULFILLMENT PROCESS (RIGHT).

oriented Rockwell Science Center in Thousand Oaks, California. The facility lists as clients the U.S. Government, Boeing, Meritor, and Coxenant.

The Future of Manufacturing

Against this history of innovation, Rockwell Automation will continue to develop progressive technology and programs that adapt to the rapidly changing manufacturing landscape. Manufacturing is currently evolving into a "build-on-demand" state of operating—a concept typically called e-manufacturing. Rockwell Automation is once again at the forefront in driving this advancement.

E-manufacturing has the potential to radically reshape the way companies use information to conduct their business. Simply put, e-manufacturing will tightly integrate valuable shop floor information with top floor business systems, and ultimately connect the information across the entire supply chain, producing a host of benefits.

Plant floor information hasn't always played a critical role in a company's business operation. However, the factory of the future will tap into valuable plant floor information to better manage manufacturing assets—the people, machines, and raw materials. Under an e-manufacturing scenario, connectivity via the Internet will allow a machine to schedule maintenance and order supplies almost automatically, reducing transaction and procurement costs. Such a system will also be able to provide the front office with a complete, up-to-the-minute view of critical plant-floor assets from anywhere in the world, giving managers greater agility to quickly adapt to changing customer needs.

The real benefit of e-manufacturing will be in achieving the next level of manufacturing productivity gains through tightly synchronized communication–from the top floor to the shop floor and across the entire supply chain.

Manufacturing has come a long way from those early days of Rockwell and Allen-Bradley back in the early 1900s. Rockwell has been there every step of the way. And, with a dedicated focus on helping customers succeed, Rockwell Automation has created the platform for a bright future.

VIRTUALLY EVERY INDUSTRY USES ROCKWELL AUTOMATION INDUSTRIAL AUTOMATION CONTROL PRODUCTS. CONTROLLOGIX™ BRINGS ADDED FLEXIBILITY TO USABILITY TO CUSTOMERS AROUND THE WORLD.

City by the Waters

• 435 •

Milwaukee Neurological Institute, SC

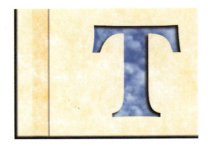

The Milwaukee Neurological Institute, SC (MNI) is an independent group of physicians and professionals whose careers have been dedicated to helping people with diseases and injuries to the brain, neck, and spine. From thorough evaluation and precise diagnosis to progressive use of sophisticated technology and treatment, MNI's staff offers hope and healing in a friendly, patient-centered environment.

MNI works collaboratively with neurologists, oncologists, radiologists, physiatrists, and pain management specialists, in order to deliver a continuum of care. In treating patients' complex disorders with compassionate care, MNI's chief goal is to restore function and quality of life.

Conservative, Compassionate Treatment

The Milwaukee Neurological Institute's physicians treat head trauma, tumors, and back and neck problems such as ruptured disks or pinched nerves. Many patients presenting at the institute are anxious over perceived, serious health threats or are in pain. The manner in which they are treated serves as a point of differentiation and distinction.

At Milwaukee Neurological Institute, patient comfort and care take precedence. First, thorough and thoughtful diagnosis is emphasized. Physicians and staff work meticulously to precisely pinpoint the problem and to properly determine the most effective treatment available.

Throughout this process, patients, family members, and primary care doctors are involved. Staff members take time to observe, listen, answer questions, calm fears, review results, and discuss treatment options. They believe that to care for a patient, they must first care about the patient, and so every effort is made to get to know the people they are treating. Ultimately, this facilitates not only healing, but hope as well.

This conservative, compassionate approach extends to treatment as well. Appropriate diagnostic information is first acquired, with a goal of minimizing the number and invasive nature of tests. Exploring alternative treatment options can also mean reducing or eliminating the need for surgery. This approach demands ongoing discussions with patients to ensure they have proper information, enabling them to share responsibility for their treatment and outcome. In many cases, a successful outcome can be achieved through physical therapy, medication, pain management, or a simple change in lifestyle.

To date, the Milwaukee Neurological Institute has experienced great success thanks to its philosophy. The institute's patients echo fairly common themes: perseverance in finding solutions to complex medical problems; a thorough and thoughtful approach in exploring all options; insistence on answering every question; prudent guidance in enabling patients to regain control; and compassionate treatment.

A Strong Foundation

Spencer J. Block, M.D., an accomplished neurosurgeon, created the Milwaukee Neurological Institute in 1998, the year he was recruited to Milwaukee to organize and implement his vision of an innovative, comprehensive neuroscience center.

Block has received lifetime certification from the American Board of Neurological Surgery, secured fellowship within the American College of Surgeons, and holds active memberships in several neurosurgery and spinal surgery societies. He also holds a clinical faculty appointment at the Medical College of Wisconsin, and serves on advisory boards for the commercial development of new diagnostic modalities and surgical instrumentation.

Relying on traditional and evolving approaches in neurosurgery, the Milwaukee Neurological Institute's commitment to integrating sophisticated technology with personalized patient care has helped it become a leader in the area. Undoubtedly, these same qualities will help the group excel in the future.

Clockwise from top:
Gamma Knife and X-Knife radiosurgery are part of the advanced technology at the Milwaukee Neurological Institute, SC.

A view of Spencer J. Block, M.D., an accomplished neurosurgeon who created MNI in 1998, and the microsurgical team at work.

Clinical staff making use of patient scans and anatomical models are common parts of the educational experience of an office visit at the institute.

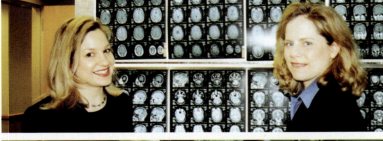

TOWERY PUBLISHING, INC.

Beginning as a small publisher of local newspapers in the 1930s, Towery Publishing, Inc. today produces a wide range of community-oriented materials, including books (Urban Tapestry Series), business directories, magazines, and Internet publications. Building on its long heritage of excellence, the company has become global in scope, with cities from San Diego to Sydney represented by Towery products. In all its endeavors, this Memphis-based company strives to be synonymous with service, utility, and quality.

A Diversity of Community-Based Products

Over the years, Towery has become the largest producer of published materials for North American chambers of commerce. From membership directories that enhance business-to-business communication to visitor and relocation guides tailored to reflect the unique qualities of the communities they cover, the company's chamber-oriented materials offer comprehensive information on dozens of topics, including housing, education, leisure activities, health care, and local government.

In 1998, the company acquired Cincinnati-based Target Marketing, an established provider of detailed city street maps to more than 200 chambers of commerce throughout the United States and Canada. Now a division of Towery, Target offers full-color maps that include local landmarks and points of interest, such as recreational parks, shopping centers, golf courses, schools, industrial parks, city and county limits, subdivision names, public buildings, and even block numbers on most streets.

In 1990, Towery launched the Urban Tapestry Series, an award-winning collection of oversized, hardbound photojournals detailing the people, history, culture, environment, and commerce of various metropolitan areas. These coffee-table books highlight a community through three basic elements: an introductory essay by a noted local individual, an exquisite collection of four-color photographs, and profiles of the companies and organizations that animate the area's business life.

To date, more than 80 Urban Tapestry Series editions have been published in cities around the world, from New York to Vancouver to Sydney. Authors of the books' introductory essays include former U.S. President Gerald Ford (Grand Rapids), former Alberta Premier Peter Lougheed (Calgary), CBS anchor Dan Rather (Austin), ABC anchor Hugh Downs (Phoenix), best-selling mystery author Robert B. Parker (Boston), American Movie Classics host Nick Clooney (Cincinnati), Senator Richard Lugar (Indianapolis), and Challenger Center founder June Scobee Rodgers (Chattanooga).

To maintain hands-on quality in all of its periodicals and books, Towery has long used the latest production methods available. The company was the first production environment in the United States to combine desktop publishing with color separations and image scanning to produce finished film suitable for burning plates for four-color printing. Today, Towery relies on state-of-the-art digital prepress services to produce more than 8,000 pages each year, containing well over 30,000 high-quality color images.

An Internet Pioneer

By combining its long-standing expertise in community-oriented published materials with advanced production capabilities, a global sales

Towery Publishing President and CEO J. Robert Towery has expanded the business his parents started in the 1930s to include a growing array of traditional and electronic published materials, as well as Internet and multimedia services, that are marketed locally, nationally, and internationally.

· 438 ·

Milwaukee

force, and extensive data management capabilities, Towery has emerged as a significant provider of Internet-based city information. In keeping with its overall focus on community resources, the company's Internet efforts represent a natural step in the evolution of the business.

The primary product lines within the Internet division are the introCity™ sites. Towery's introCity sites introduce newcomers, visitors, and longtime residents to every facet of a particular community, while simultaneously placing the local chamber of commerce at the forefront of the city's Internet activity. The sites include newcomer information, calendars, photos, citywide business listings with everything from nightlife to shopping to family fun, and on-line maps pinpointing the exact location of businesses, schools, attractions, and much more.

Decades of Publishing Expertise

In 1972, current President and CEO J. Robert Towery succeeded his parents in managing the printing and publishing business they had founded nearly four decades earlier. Soon thereafter, he expanded the scope of the company's published materials to include *Memphis* magazine and other successful regional and national publications. In 1985, after selling its locally focused assets, Towery began the trajectory on which it continues today, creating community-oriented materials that are often produced in conjunction with chambers of commerce and other business organizations.

Despite the decades of change, Towery himself follows a long-standing family philosophy of unmatched service and unflinching quality. That approach extends throughout the entire organization to include more than 120 employees at the Memphis headquarters, another 80 located in Northern Kentucky outside Cincinnati, and more than 40 sales, marketing, and editorial staff traveling to and working in a growing list of client cities. All of its products, and more information about the company, are featured on the Internet at www.towery.com.

In summing up his company's steady growth, Towery restates the essential formula that has driven the business since its first pages were published: "The creative energies of our staff drive us toward innovation and invention. Our people make the highest possible demands on themselves, so I know that our future is secure if the ingredients for success remain a focus on service and quality."

TOWERY PUBLISHING WAS THE FIRST PRODUCTION ENVIRONMENT IN THE UNITED STATES TO COMBINE DESKTOP PUBLISHING WITH COLOR SEPARATIONS AND IMAGE SCANNING TO PRODUCE FINISHED FILM SUITABLE FOR BURNING PLATES FOR FOUR-COLOR PRINTING. TODAY, THE COMPANY'S STATE-OF-THE-ART NETWORK OF MACINTOSH AND WINDOWS WORKSTATIONS ALLOWS IT TO PRODUCE MORE THAN 8,000 PAGES EACH YEAR, CONTAINING MORE THAN 30,000 HIGH-QUALITY COLOR IMAGES (LEFT).

THE TOWERY FAMILY'S PUBLISHING ROOTS CAN BE TRACED TO 1935, WHEN R.W. TOWERY (FAR LEFT) BEGAN PRODUCING A SERIES OF COMMUNITY HISTORIES IN TENNESSEE, MISSISSIPPI, AND TEXAS. THROUGHOUT THE COMPANY'S HISTORY, THE FOUNDING FAMILY HAS CONSISTENTLY EXHIBITED A COMMITMENT TO CLARITY, PRECISION, INNOVATION, AND VISION (BOTTOM).

City by the Waters

· 439 ·

Library of Congress Cataloging-in-Publication Data

Milwaukee : city by the waters / introduction by Bob Uecker ; art direction by Bob Kimball.
    p. cm. — (Urban tapestry series)
  Includes index.
  ISBN 1-881096-87-4 (alk. paper)
   1. Milwaukee (Wis.)—Civilization. 2. Milwaukee (Wis.)—Pictorial works. 3. Milwaukee (Wis.)—Economic conditions. 4. Business enterprises—Wisconsin—Milwaukee. I. Uecker, Bob. II. Kimball, Bob. III. Series.

F589.M65 M55 2001
977.5'95—dc21

                              00-069079

Printed in Korea

Copyright © 2001 by Towery Publishing, Inc.

All rights reserved. No part of this work may be reproduced or copied in any form or by any means, except for brief excerpts in conjunction with book reviews, without prior written permission of the publisher.

Towery Publishing, Inc., The Towery Building, 1835 Union Avenue, Memphis, TN 38104

www.towery.com

Publisher: J. Robert Towery **Executive Publisher:** Jenny McDowell **National Sales Manager:** Stephen Hung **Marketing Director:** Carol Culpepper **Project Directors:** James Pieper, Paul Withington, Kay Ziegler **Executive Editor:** David B. Dawson **Managing Editor:** Lynn Conlee **Senior Editors:** Carlisle Hacker, Brian L. Johnston **Editors:** Jay Adkins, Rebecca E. Farabough, Danna M. Greenfield, Ginny Reeves **Editor/Caption Writer:** Stephen M. Deusner **Editor/Profile Manager:** Sabrina Schroeder **Profile Writer:** Scott Weinberger **Creative Director:** Brian Groppe **Photography Editor:** Jonathan Postal **Photographic Consultant:** Leslie Bellavance **Profile Designers:** Rebekah Barnhardt, Laurie Beck, Glen Marshall **Production Manager:** Brenda Pattat **Photography Coordinator:** Robin Lankford **Production Assistants:** Robert Barnett, Loretta Lane, Robert Parrish **Digital Color Supervisor:** Darin Ipema **Digital Color Technicians:** Eric Friedl, Brent Salazar, Mark Svetz **Digital Scanning Technicians:** Zac Ives, Brad Long **Production Resources Manager:** Dave Dunlap Jr. **Print Coordinator:** Beverly Timmons

PHOTOGRAPHERS

© ALAN MAGAYNE-ROSHAK

Originally headquartered in London, **Allsport** has expanded to include offices in New York and Los Angeles. Its pictures have appeared in every major publication in the world, and the best of its portfolio has been displayed at elite photographic exhibitions at the Royal Photographic Society and the Olympic Museum in Lausanne.

A self-taught photographer originally from Connecticut, **Howard Ande** has photographs in many national publications, trade journals, books, and international advertisements, and specializes in photography dealing with railroads, industry, and agriculture. He resides in Bartlett, Illinois, with his wife and two children.

Born in Milwaukee, **John J. Bacik III** specializes in computer-aided design and multimedia photography. He currently works for Reimers Photographics and enjoys photographing street scenes and inanimate objects.

Beginning with Highlight Photography while attending Indiana University, **Steve Baker** has contributed to more than 200 publications. His corporate clients include Eastman Kodak, Mobil Oil, the U.S. Olympic Committee, and Budweiser, and he owns a library of more than 50,000 marketable images from his travels across the country. As the grandson of the late Byron Baker of Oconomowoc, Wisconsin, Steve Baker enjoys a rich heritage from the Wisconsin area.

Originally from Wisconsin, **Rebecca** holds a bachelor of fine arts degree from University of Wisconsin-Milwaukee. continues to live in the Milwaukee are

Darryl R. Beers moved to the Milwa area in 1983. As a self-taught photogra and native of Michigan's Upper Pe sula, he specializes in landscape imag the Great Lakes region. Beers' work been published in *Midwest Living*, *Ma Stewart Living*, *Men's Journal*, and sev calendars such as Audubon and Br Trout. He also produced a solo pre

· 444 ·

Milwaukee

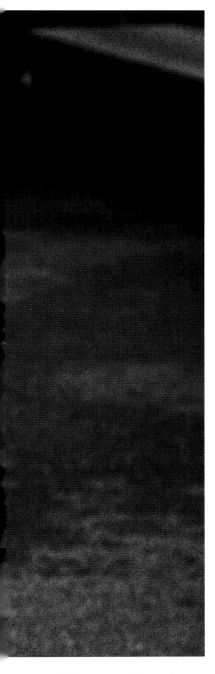

entitled *The Spirit of Door County*, which was published in 1999 by Trails Media Group.

With a bachelor of arts degree from Harvard University in 1965 and a Ph.D. from Yale University in 1973, **Dick Blau** now holds the chair of the Department of Film at the University of Wisconsin-Milwaukee. His photographs have appeared in numerous publications, including *The Daughter's Seduction, Thinking Through the Body, Dreamworks,* and *Changing Chicago*. Blau's work has also been featured in exhibitions at the Houston International FotoFest, Field Museum of Chicago, Milwaukee Art Museum, and PhotoSynkeria/Thessaloniki.

Specializing in NFL, MLB, and NCAA football photography, **Scott Boehm** started his own freelance photo/design business in 1994. His images have been published in various magazines and books, and his clients include advertising agencies and corporations.

A Milwaukee native, **Samuel Castro** specialized in journalism and digital imaging photography while he attended the University of Wisconsin-Milwaukee. He has won awards for his news/features photography and is a member of the University Photographers Association of America.

Troy Leo Freund specializes in black-and-white documentary photography with emphases on weddings and human interest. His work has appeared in the *Milwaukee Community Journal*, Children's Outing Association calendar project, and *Wisconsin Woman Magazine*. A manager with Helix Photoart, Freund also teaches continuing education classes in photography at his alma mater, Cardinal Stritch University.

As a native of Chicago and a photographer with some 30 years of experience, **Ray F. Hillstrom Jr.** specializes in architecture, gardens, historical sites, mountain ranges, and coastlines. His work has been published in several travel magazines, calendars, annual reports, and tourism office literature.

An award-winning amateur photographer, **John Jeutsch** lives in Grimes, Iowa, and specializes in city, people, and travel photography. His most recently completed assignments have taken him from the Indian Sand Caves in northeastern Iowa to the Badlands of South Dakota.

Frederick A. Kilbey works for Risser Digital Imaging and Photographic, and is a photographer for the Milwaukee Wave soccer team. He has combined his love of photography with his interest in photographic equipment and quality production.

Originally from Milwaukee, **Suzanne C. Krull** specializes in fashion photography. As a student at Milwaukee Area Technical College, she won the Best of Student Photography awards for 1998-1999 and 1999-2000, and placed second in the 2000 Milwaukee Historic Society Photo Contest.

John Shimon and **Julie Lindemann** have photographed collaboratively since the mid-1980s. Since then, their photographs have been published in *Metropolis, Milwaukee Magazine, Hope, Money, New York, The New York Times Magazine, Road King,* and *View Camera*. They have mounted thematic solo exhibitions at many Wisconsin museums and galleries, including the Madison Art Center and the Wisconsin Academy Gallery. Both now live in Manitowoc and operate a studio near the shores of Lake Michigan.

Alan Magayne-Roshak, senior photographer for Photo Services at the University of Wisconsin-Milwaukee, specializes in publicity photos, period architecture, and humorous candid shots. He has received 75 awards from various organizations, including the University Photographic Association of America and Wisconsin News Photographers Association.

Specializing in nature and travel photography, **Patrick Manning** has lived in the Milwaukee area for almost 10 years. Now working for Strong Investments, Inc., he has traveled to South Asia to photograph various festivals.

Peggy Morsch came to the Milwaukee area in 1984 after growing up in New York. She is employed by Cedar Creek Images, and specializes in nature, agriculture, and animal photography.

Specializing in travel photography, **Laurie Mullen** has photographed the boundary waters of Minnesota, Costa Rica, and Nice, France.

James and **Nicholas Peterson** are a father-and-son photography team. James Peterson is the chief company photographer for Northwestern Mutual and a past president of Wisconsin Industrial Photographers. His son Nicholas is a student at the University of Minnesota and works as a photographer's assistant.

Listed in *American Artists of Renown*, **Curtis B. Stahr** has photographed life across the United States, and has walked with his camera across Canada from ocean to ocean. He has exhibited in 32 juried/invitational art shows, as well as in 16 one-man shows.

A professional photographer for nearly 20 years, **Mary Jo Walicki** is currently working as a photojournalist for the *Milwaukee Journal Sentinel*. As a 10-year veteran staff photographer for the daily newspaper, she has covered all aspects of news photography and now specializes in nature photography.

Other photographic contributors include the Milwaukee Police Department. For further information about the photographers appearing in *Milwaukee: City by the Waters*, please contact Towery Publishing, Inc.

Index of Profiles

A.N. Ansay & Associates, Inc.	360
ABB Automation Inc.	392
ABB Flexible Automation	393
Andrus, Sceales, Starke & Sawall, LLP	344
The Archdiocese of Milwaukee	284
Big Brothers Big Sisters, Inc.	388
The Bradley Foundation	410
Brady Corporation	323
The Business Journal	398
Catholic Family Life Insurance	304
CDI Information Technology Services, Inc.	426
Children's Hospital of Wisconsin	310
Columbia-St. Mary's, Inc.	288
Corrigan Properties, Inc./Bayshore Mall	361
Coventry Homes, Ltd.	416
Danfoss Graham	342
DeRosa Corporation	378
Earth Tech	380
Emmpak Foods, Inc.	308
The F. Dohmen Co.	297
FABCO Equipment Inc.	394
Fortis Health	316
Froedtert Memorial Lutheran Hospital	390
GE Medical Systems	354
Grede Foundries, Inc.	326
Grubb & Ellis	Boerke Company	332
Heartland Advisors, Inc.	396
Helwig Carbon Products Inc.	346
Heritage Relocation Services	418
High Gear, Inc.	430
Human Resource Services, Inc.	397
HUSCO International, Inc.	362
Kaerek Builders Inc.	370
Kalmbach Publishing Co.	338
Klement Sausage Co., Inc.	336
Lakeland Supply, Inc.	402
Lincoln State Bank	328
Manpower Inc.	356
Midwest Express Airlines	404
Miller Brewing Company	290
Milwaukee Brewers Baseball Club	376
Milwaukee Journal Sentinel	278
Milwaukee Neurological Institute	436
Milwaukee Radio Group	412
Milwaukee School of Engineering	320
Multi Media Catalog Corporation	424
New England Financial/The Marris Group	286
North American Clutch Corporation	372
P&H Mining Equipment	306
Pereles Brothers, Inc.	334
Plunkett Raysich Architects	340
Potawatomi Bingo Casino	420
The Revere Group	432
Rockwell Automation	434
Shoreline Company, Inc.	382
Stratagem, Inc.	414
STS Consultants, Ltd.	358
TEC	368
TexPar Energy, Inc.	406
Thomas A. Mason Co., Inc.	324
Time Warner Cable-Milwaukee Division	400
Towery Publishing, Inc.	438
Ultra Tool & Manufacturing, Inc.	374
Verizon Wireless	419
Vilter Manufacturing Corporation	302
Voss Jorgensen Schueler Co., Inc.	352
Waukesha Engine	318
Western Industries, Inc.	350
Western States Envelope Company	322
Wisconsin Energy Corporation	312
WTMJ-TV	280
WTMJ and WKTI Radio	282
Yale Equipment & Services, Inc.	366
YMCA of Metropolitan Milwaukee	300

© RAY F. HILLSTROM